GREATEST COMEDIES OF
SHAKESPEARE

CLASSICS

Reprint 2023
FiNGERPRINT! CLASSICS
An imprint of Prakash Books India Pvt. Ltd

113/A, Darya Ganj,
New Delhi-110 002
Email: info@prakashbooks.com/sales@prakashbooks.com

facebook www.facebook.com/fingerprintpublishing
twitter www.twitter.com/FingerprintP
www.fingerprintpublishing.com

ISBN: 978 81 9489 883 2

Processed & printed in India

"Sigh no more, ladies, sigh no more,
Men were deceivers ever,
One foot in sea and one on shore,
To one thing constant never."

William Shakespeare was baptized on April 26, 1564. His father John engaged in various trades, and his mother Mary was the daughter of an affluent landowning farmer. John and Mary had eight children, of whom William was the third. It is believed that Shakespeare was educated at King's New School. This was a free school chartered in 1553, and was near to Shakespeare's home. This grammar school, like the others of its kind, had Latin text in its curriculum.

At the age of eighteen, William Shakespeare married Anne Hathaway and they had three children—Susanna, and twins Hamnet and Judith.

Shakespeare began his career as an actor, writer, and part owner of a playing company called the Lord Chamberlain's Men during the reign of Queen Elizabeth I, later known as King's Men when King James I took the throne and became their patron, in London. Most of his known works have been produced between 1589 and 1613. His early plays were mainly comedies and histories which are regarded as some of the best works produced in these genres. In Shakespeare's time, the plays were mainly performed at two places—the Globe, an open-roofed theatre, and Blackfriars Theatre, an indoor theatre built by James Burbage.

Shakespeare's plays are difficult to date. His early classical and Italianate comedies contain tight double plots and precise comic sequences giving way to the romantic atmosphere of his most acclaimed comedies in the mid-1590s. Playwright Ben Jonson, Shakespeare's contemporary, had believed that Shakespeare had no rival when it came to comedy. And in 1598, writer Frances Meres declared him the greatest English writer of comedy and tragedy. *A Midsummer Night's Dream*—a witty mixture of romance, fairy magic, and comic low-life scenes—is one of his most delightful creations, shortly before he turned to *Romeo and Juliet*. Set in the kingdom of Athens and the woods nearby, revolving around the wedding preparations of Theseus and Hippolyta, *A Midsummer Night's Dream* has four interconnected plots, detailing the adventures of four young lovers—Demetrius, Lysander, Hermia, and Helena.

Romeo and Juliet is his most famous romantic tragedy of sexually charged adolescence, love, and death. It marks a departure from his earlier works and from others of the English Renaissance. Shakespeare's plays demonstrate the expansiveness of his imagination and the extent of his learning. Even so, such plays were not well-received by some of the critics. In the seventeenth century, John Dryden, in his essay 'Of Dramatic Poesie', expressed that Shakespeare may excel in imagination but he lacked judgement. He believed this was so because Shakespeare had written his plays for a poorly educated audience. It is a fact that Shakespeare had written plays keeping in mind that they were to be performed, not to be published or circulated among readers. In 1592, Robert Greene's animosity towards the Bard was apparent when he called Shakespeare 'an upstart Crow, beautified with our feathers'. Apart from some such critics, Shakespeare's work had impressed and entertained his audience and other notable writers.

His sequence of great comedies continues with *The Merchant of Venice, Much Ado About Nothing, As You Like It,* and *Twelfth Night.* One of his best-loved comedies, *Twelfth Night* is a romantic drama of confusions, comic sequences, and mistaken identities. With a perfect combination of romance and reality and excellently crafted characters, it has been amusing its audiences for more than four centuries now.

Shakespeare introduced prose comedy in the histories of the late 1590s—*Henry IV, Part I* and *Henry IV, Part II,* and *Henry V*— after the lyrical *Richard II. Julius Caesar* introduced a new kind of drama. Shakespeare wrote the so-called 'problem plays' in the early seventeenth century, *Measure for Measure, Troilus and Cressida,* and *All's Well that Ends Well* being a few of them. Until about 1608, he mainly wrote tragedies including *Hamlet, Othello, King Lear,* and *Macbeth.* The story of a brave Scottish general named Macbeth, the eponymous drama illustrates how the lust for power dooms the fate of a noble person.

Antony and Cleopatra and *Coriolanus*—his last major tragedies, contain some of his finest poetry. Shakespeare wrote tragicomedies, also known as romances, in his last phase. These include *Cymbeline, The Winter's Tale,* and *The Tempest,* as well as the collaboration *Pericles, Prince of Tyre.*

There is no writer, living or dead, whose reputation matches that of the beloved English bard, William Shakespeare—a man who possessed exceptional imagination and intellect, and wrote thirty-eight plays, one hundred and fifty-four sonnets, two long narrative poems, and several other verses. His works have been extensively read, analysed, and performed in many countries and translated in almost all major languages. All his works centre around human nature, which is why these works written more than four hundred years ago have withstood the test of time—because human nature never changes. Speaking of his brilliant contemporary, Ben Jonson's words were, "[Shakespeare] was not of an age but for all time." A true genius, also known as the English national poet, William Shakespeare is considered the greatest dramatist of all time.

About this Edition

This edition encapsulates the best of the world of Shakespearean comedy—a world that is rife with hilarious misconceptions, misunderstandings, and deception, with men and women disguised to switch their sexual identities, and where accidents and errors mysteriously lead to comical and ultimately happy consequences.

Collected in this edition are five of Shakespeare's finest comedies. They were first published in *First Folio* in 1623.

Contents

A Midsummer Night's Dream

"And yet, to say the truth, reason and
love keep little company together nowadays."

A Midsummer Night's Dream

Characters of the Play

HERMIA
LYSANDER
HELENA
DEMETRIUS

} *four lovers*

THESEUS, duke of Athens
HIPPOLYTA, queen of the Amazons
EGEUS, father to Hermia
PHILOSTRATE, master of the revels to Theseus

NICK BOTTOM, weaver
PETER QUINCE, carpenter
FRANCIS FLUTE, bellows-mender
TOM SNOUT, tinker
SNUG, joiner
ROBIN STARVELING, tailor
OBERON, king of the Fairies
TITANIA, queen of the Fairies
ROBIN GOODFELLOW, a "puck," or hobgoblin, in Oberon's service
A FAIRY, in the service of Titania
PEASEBLOSSOM
COBWEB
MOTE
MUSTARDSEED

} *fairies attending upon Titania*

Lords and Attendants on Theseus and Hippolyta
Other Fairies in the trains of Titania and Oberon

Characters of the Play

ACT

I

SCENE I.
ATHENS. THE PALACE OF THESEUS.

Enter THESEUS, HIPPOLYTA, PHILOSTRATE, *and Attendants*

THESEUS

    Now, fair Hippolyta, our nuptial hour
    Draws on apace; four happy days bring in
    Another moon: but, O, methinks, how slow
    This old moon wanes! she lingers my desires,
    Like to a step-dame or a dowager
    Long withering out a young man's revenue.

HIPPOLYTA

    Four days will quickly steep themselves in night;
    Four nights will quickly dream away the time;
    And then the moon, like to a silver bow
    New-bent in heaven, shall behold the night
    Of our solemnities.

THESEUS

    Go, Philostrate,
    Stir up the Athenian youth to merriments;
    Awake the pert and nimble spirit of mirth;
    Turn melancholy forth to funerals;

The pale companion is not for our pomp.

Exit PHILOSTRATE

Hippolyta, I woo'd thee with my sword,
And won thy love, doing thee injuries;
But I will wed thee in another key,
With pomp, with triumph and with revelling.

Enter EGEUS, HERMIA, LYSANDER, *and* DEMETRIUS

EGEUS

Happy be Theseus, our renowned duke!

THESEUS

Thanks, good Egeus: what's the news with thee?

EGEUS

Full of vexation come I, with complaint
Against my child, my daughter Hermia.
Stand forth, Demetrius. My noble lord,
This man hath my consent to marry her.
Stand forth, Lysander: and my gracious duke,
This man hath bewitch'd the bosom of my child;
Thou, thou, Lysander, thou hast given her rhymes,
And interchanged love-tokens with my child:
Thou hast by moonlight at her window sung,
With feigning voice verses of feigning love,
And stolen the impression of her fantasy
With bracelets of thy hair, rings, gawds, conceits,
Knacks, trifles, nosegays, sweetmeats, messengers
Of strong prevailment in unharden'd youth:
With cunning hast thou filch'd my daughter's heart,
Turn'd her obedience, which is due to me,
To stubborn harshness: and, my gracious duke,
Be it so she; will not here before your grace
Consent to marry with Demetrius,
I beg the ancient privilege of Athens,
As she is mine, I may dispose of her:
Which shall be either to this gentleman
Or to her death, according to our law
Immediately provided in that case.

• 18 •

THESEUS

> What say you, Hermia? be advised fair maid:
> To you your father should be as a god;
> One that composed your beauties, yea, and one
> To whom you are but as a form in wax
> By him imprinted and within his power
> To leave the figure or disfigure it.
> Demetrius is a worthy gentleman.

HERMIA

> So is Lysander.

THESEUS

> In himself he is;
> But in this kind, wanting your father's voice,
> The other must be held the worthier.

HERMIA

> I would my father look'd but with my eyes.

THESEUS

> Rather your eyes must with his judgment look.

HERMIA

> I do entreat your grace to pardon me.
> I know not by what power I am made bold,
> Nor how it may concern my modesty,
> In such a presence here to plead my thoughts;
> But I beseech your grace that I may know
> The worst that may befall me in this case,
> If I refuse to wed Demetrius.

THESEUS

> Either to die the death or to abjure
> For ever the society of men.
> Therefore, fair Hermia, question your desires;
> Know of your youth, examine well your blood,
> Whether, if you yield not to your father's choice,
> You can endure the livery of a nun,
> For aye to be in shady cloister mew'd,
> To live a barren sister all your life,
> Chanting faint hymns to the cold fruitless moon.

Thrice-blessèd they that master so their blood,
To undergo such maiden pilgrimage;
But earthlier happy is the rose distill'd,
Than that which withering on the virgin thorn
Grows, lives and dies in single blessedness.

HERMIA

So will I grow, so live, so die, my lord,
Ere I will my virgin patent up
Unto his lordship, whose unwishéd yoke
My soul consents not to give sovereignty.

THESEUS

Take time to pause; and, by the next new moon—
The sealing-day betwixt my love and me,
For everlasting bond of fellowship—
Upon that day either prepare to die
For disobedience to your father's will,
Or else to wed Demetrius, as he would;
Or on Diana's altar to protest
For aye austerity and single life.

DEMETRIUS

Relent, sweet Hermia: and, Lysander, yield
Thy crazèd title to my certain right.

LYSANDER

You have her father's love, Demetrius;
Let me have Hermia's: do you marry him.

EGEUS

Scornful Lysander! true, he hath my love,
And what is mine my love shall render him.
And she is mine, and all my right of her
I do estate unto Demetrius.

LYSANDER

I am, my lord, as well derived as he,
As well possess'd; my love is more than his;
My fortunes every way as fairly rank'd,
If not with vantage, as Demetrius';
And, which is more than all these boasts can be,
I am beloved of beauteous Hermia:

Why should not I then prosecute my right?
Demetrius, I'll avouch it to his head,
Made love to Nedar's daughter, Helena,
And won her soul; and she, sweet lady, dotes,
Devoutly dotes, dotes in idolatry,
Upon this spotted and inconstant man.

THESEUS

I must confess that I have heard so much,
And with Demetrius thought to have spoke thereof;
But, being over-full of self-affairs,
My mind did lose it. But, Demetrius, come;
And come, Egeus; you shall go with me,
I have some private schooling for you both.
For you, fair Hermia, look you arm yourself
To fit your fancies to your father's will;
Or else the law of Athens yields you up—
Which by no means we may extenuate—
To death, or to a vow of single life.
Come, my Hippolyta: what cheer, my love?
Demetrius and Egeus, go along:
I must employ you in some business
Against our nuptial and confer with you
Of something nearly that concerns yourselves.

Egeus

With duty and desire we follow you.

Exeunt all but LYSANDER *and* HERMIA

LYSANDER

How now, my love! why is your cheek so pale?
How chance the roses there do fade so fast?

HERMIA

Belike for want of rain, which I could well
Beteem them from the tempest of my eyes.

LYSANDER

Ay me! for aught that I could ever read,
Could ever hear by tale or history,
The course of true love never did run smooth;
But, either it was different in blood,—

HERMIA

O cross! too high to be enthrall'd to low.

LYSANDER

Or else misgraffèd in respect of years,—

HERMIA

O spite! too old to be engaged to young.

LYSANDER

Or else it stood upon the choice of friends,—

HERMIA

O hell! to choose love by another's eyes.

LYSANDER

Or, if there were a sympathy in choice,
War, death, or sickness did lay siege to it,
Making it momentany as a sound,
Swift as a shadow, short as any dream;
Brief as the lightning in the collied night,
That, in a spleen, unfolds both heaven and earth,
And ere a man hath power to say 'Behold!'
The jaws of darkness do devour it up:
So quick bright things come to confusion.

HERMIA

If then true lovers have been ever cross'd,
It stands as an edict in destiny:
Then let us teach our trial patience,
Because it is a customary cross,
As due to love as thoughts and dreams and sighs,
Wishes and tears, poor fancy's followers.

LYSANDER

A good persuasion: therefore, hear me, Hermia.
I have a widow aunt, a dowager
Of great revenue, and she hath no child:
From Athens is her house remote seven leagues;
And she respects me as her only son.
There, gentle Hermia, may I marry thee;
And to that place the sharp Athenian law
Cannot pursue us. If thou lovest me then,
Steal forth thy father's house to-morrow night;

And in the wood, a league without the town,
Where I did meet thee once with Helena,
To do observance to a morn of May,
There will I stay for thee.

HERMIA

My good Lysander!
I swear to thee, by Cupid's strongest bow,
By his best arrow with the golden head,
By the simplicity of Venus' doves,
By that which knitteth souls and prospers loves,
And by that fire which burn'd the Carthage queen,
When the false Troyan under sail was seen,
By all the vows that ever men have broke,
In number more than ever women spoke,
In that same place thou hast appointed me,
To-morrow truly will I meet with thee.

Lysander

Keep promise, love. Look, here comes Helena.

Enter HELENA

HERMIA

God speed fair Helena! whither away?

HELENA

Call you me fair? that fair again unsay.
Demetrius loves your fair: O happy fair!
Your eyes are lode-stars; and your tongue's sweet air
More tuneable than lark to shepherd's ear,
When wheat is green, when hawthorn buds appear.
Sickness is catching: O, were favour so,
Yours would I catch, fair Hermia, ere I go;
My ear should catch your voice, my eye your eye,
My tongue should catch your tongue's sweet melody.
Were the world mine, Demetrius being bated,
The rest I'd give to be to you translated.
O, teach me how you look, and with what art
You sway the motion of Demetrius' heart.

HERMIA

I frown upon him, yet he loves me still.

HELENA

O that your frowns would teach my smiles such skill!

HERMIA

I give him curses, yet he gives me love.

HELENA

O that my prayers could such affection move!

HERMIA

The more I hate, the more he follows me.

HELENA

The more I love, the more he hateth me.

HERMIA

His folly, Helena, is no fault of mine.

HELENA

None, but your beauty: would that fault were mine!

HERMIA

Take comfort: he no more shall see my face;
Lysander and myself will fly this place.
Before the time I did Lysander see,
Seem'd Athens as a paradise to me:
O, then, what graces in my love do dwell,
That he hath turn'd a heaven unto a hell!

LYSANDER

Helen, to you our minds we will unfold:
To-morrow night, when Phoebe doth behold
Her silver visage in the watery glass,
Decking with liquid pearl the bladed grass,
A time that lovers' flights doth still conceal,
Through Athens' gates have we devised to steal.

HERMIA

And in the wood, where often you and I
Upon faint primrose-beds were wont to lie,
Emptying our bosoms of their counsel sweet,
There my Lysander and myself shall meet;
And thence from Athens turn away our eyes,
To seek new friends and stranger companies.
Farewell, sweet playfellow: pray thou for us;
And good luck grant thee thy Demetrius!

Keep word, Lysander: we must starve our sight
From lovers' food till morrow deep midnight.

LYSANDER

I will, my Hermia.

Exit HERMIA

Helena, adieu:
As you on him, Demetrius dote on you!

Exit

HELENA

How happy some o'er other some can be!
Through Athens I am thought as fair as she.
But what of that? Demetrius thinks not so;
He will not know what all but he do know:
And as he errs, doting on Hermia's eyes,
So I, admiring of his qualities:
Things base and vile, folding no quantity,
Love can transpose to form and dignity:
Love looks not with the eyes, but with the mind;
And therefore is wing'd Cupid painted blind:
Nor hath Love's mind of any judgement taste;
Wings and no eyes figure unheedy haste:
And therefore is Love said to be a child,
Because in choice he is so oft beguiled.
As waggish boys in game themselves forswear,
So the boy Love is perjured every where:
For ere Demetrius look'd on Hermia's eyne,
He hail'd down oaths that he was only mine;
And when this hail some heat from Hermia felt,
So he dissolved, and showers of oaths did melt.
I will go tell him of fair Hermia's flight:
Then to the wood will he to-morrow night
Pursue her; and for this intelligence
If I have thanks, it is a dear expense:
But herein mean I to enrich my pain,
To have his sight thither and back again.

Exit

SCENE II.
ATHENS. QUINCE'S HOUSE.

Enter QUINCE, SNUG, BOTTOM,
FLUTE, SNOUT, *and* STARVELING

QUINCE

Is all our company here?

BOTTOM

You were best to call them generally, man by man, according to the scrip.

QUINCE

Here is the scroll of every man's name, which is thought fit, through all Athens, to play in our interlude before the duke and the duchess, on his wedding-day at night.

BOTTOM

First, good Peter Quince, say what the play treats on, then read the names of the actors, and so grow to a point.

QUINCE

Marry, our play is, *The most lamentable comedy, and most cruel death of Pyramus and Thisbe.*

BOTTOM

A very good piece of work, I assure you, and a merry. Now, good Peter Quince, call forth your actors by the scroll. Masters, spread yourselves.

QUINCE

Answer as I call you. Nick Bottom, the weaver.

BOTTOM

Ready. Name what part I am for, and proceed.

QUINCE

You, Nick Bottom, are set down for Pyramus.

BOTTOM

What is Pyramus?—a lover, or a tyrant?

QUINCE

A lover, that kills himself most gallant for love.

BOTTOM

That will ask some tears in the true performing of it: if I do it, let the audience look to their eyes; I will move storms, I will condole in some measure. To the rest: yet my chief humour is for a tyrant: I could play Ercles rarely, or a part to tear a cat in, to make all split.

> The raging rocks
> And shivering shocks
> Shall break the locks
> Of prison gates;
> And Phibbus' car
> Shall shine from far
> And make and mar
> The foolish Fates.

This was lofty! Now name the rest of the players. This is Ercles' vein, a tyrant's vein; a lover is more condoling.

QUINCE
Francis Flute, the bellows-mender.

FLUTE
Here, Peter Quince.

QUINCE
Flute, you must take Thisbe on you.

FLUTE
What is Thisbe?—a wandering knight?

QUINCE
It is the lady that Pyramus must love.

FLUTE
Nay, faith, let me not play a woman; I have a beard coming.

QUINCE
That's all one: you shall play it in a mask, and you may speak as small as you will.

BOTTOM
An I may hide my face, let me play Thisbe too, I'll speak in a monstrous little voice. 'Thisne, Thisne;' 'Ah, Pyramus, lover dear! thy Thisbe dear, and lady dear!'

QUINCE
No, no; you must play Pyramus: and, Flute, you Thisbe.

BOTTOM

Well, proceed.

QUINCE

Robin Starveling, the tailor.

STARVELING

Here, Peter Quince.

QUINCE

Robin Starveling, you must play Thisbe's mother. Tom Snout, the tinker.

SNOUT

Here, Peter Quince.

QUINCE

You, Pyramus' father: myself, Thisbe's father: Snug, the joiner; you, the lion's part: and, I hope, here is a play fitted.

SNUG

Have you the lion's part written? pray you, if it be, give it me, for I am slow of study.

QUINCE

You may do it extempore, for it is nothing but roaring.

BOTTOM

Let me play the lion too: I will roar, that I will do any man's heart good to hear me; I will roar, that I will make the duke say 'Let him roar again, let him roar again.'

QUINCE

An you should do it too terribly, you would fright the duchess and the ladies, that they would shriek; and that were enough to hang us all.

ALL

That would hang us, every mother's son.

BOTTOM

I grant you, friends, if that you should fright the ladies out of their wits, they would have no more discretion but to hang us: but I will aggravate my voice so that I will roar you as gently as any sucking dove; I will roar you an 'twere any nightingale.

QUINCE

You can play no part but Pyramus; for Pyramus is a sweet-faced man; a proper man, as one shall see in a summer's day; a most lovely gentleman-like man: therefore you must needs play Pyramus.

BOTTOM

Well, I will undertake it. What beard were I best to play it in?

QUINCE

Why, what you will.

BOTTOM

I will discharge it in either your straw-colour beard, your orange-tawny beard, your purple-in-grain beard, or your French-crown-colour beard, your perfect yellow.

QUINCE

Some of your French crowns have no hair at all, and then you will play bare-faced. But, masters, here are your parts: and I am to entreat you, request you and desire you, to con them by to-morrow night; and meet me in the palace wood, a mile without the town, by moonlight; there will we rehearse, for if we meet in the city, we shall be dogged with company, and our devices known. In the meantime I will draw a bill of properties, such as our play wants. I pray you, fail me not.

BOTTOM

We will meet; and there we may rehearse most obscenely and courageously. Take pains; be perfect: adieu.

QUINCE

At the duke's oak we meet.

BOTTOM

Enough; hold or cut bow-strings.

Exeunt

ACT

II

SCENE I.
A WOOD NEAR ATHENS.

Enter, from opposite sides, a FAIRY, *and* PUCK

PUCK

    How now, spirit! whither wander you?

FAIRY

      Over hill, over dale,

        Thorough bush, thorough brier,

      Over park, over pale,

        Thorough flood, thorough fire,

    I do wander everywhere,

    Swifter than the moon's sphere;

    And I serve the fairy queen,

    To dew her orbs upon the green.

    The cowslips tall her pensioners be:

    In their gold coats spots you see;

      Those be rubies, fairy favours,

      In those freckles live their savours:

    I must go seek some dewdrops here

    And hang a pearl in every cowslip's ear.

Farewell, thou lob of spirits; I'll be gone:
Our queen and all our elves come here anon.

PUCK

The king doth keep his revels here to-night:
Take heed the queen come not within his sight;
For Oberon is passing fell and wrath,
Because that she as her attendant hath
A lovely boy, stolen from an Indian king;
She never had so sweet a changeling;
And jealous Oberon would have the child
Knight of his train, to trace the forests wild;
But she perforce withholds the lovèd boy,
Crowns him with flowers and makes him all her joy:
And now they never meet in grove or green,
By fountain clear, or spangled starlight sheen,
But, they do square, that all their elves for fear
Creep into acorn-cups and hide them there.

FAIRY

Either I mistake your shape and making quite,
Or else you are that shrewd and knavish sprite
Call'd Robin Goodfellow: are not you he
That frights the maidens of the villagery;
Skim milk, and sometimes labour in the quern
And bootless make the breathless housewife churn;
And sometime make the drink to bear no barm;
Mislead night-wanderers, laughing at their harm?
Those that Hobgoblin call you and sweet Puck,
You do their work, and they shall have good luck:
Are not you he?

PUCK

Thou speak'st aright;
I am that merry wanderer of the night.
I jest to Oberon and make him smile
When I a fat and bean-fed horse beguile,
Neighing in likeness of a filly foal:
And sometime lurk I in a gossip's bowl,

In very likeness of a roasted crab,
And when she drinks, against her lips I bob
And on her wither'd dewlap pour the ale.
The wisest aunt, telling the saddest tale,
Sometime for three-foot stool mistaketh me;
Then slip I from her bum, down topples she,
And 'Tailor' cries, and falls into a cough;
And then the whole quire hold their hips and laugh,
And waxen in their mirth and neeze and swear
A merrier hour was never wasted there.
But, room, fairy! here comes Oberon.

FAIRY

And here my mistress. Would that he were gone!

Enter, from one side, OBERON,
with his train; from the other, TITANIA, *with hers*

OBERON

Ill met by moonlight, proud Titania.

TITANIA

What, jealous Oberon! Fairies, skip hence:
I have forsworn his bed and company.

OBERON

Tarry, rash wanton: am not I thy lord?

TITANIA

Then I must be thy lady: but I know
When thou hast stolen away from Fairyland,
And in the shape of Corin sat all day,
Playing on pipes of corn and versing love
To amorous Phillida. Why art thou here,
Come from the farthest Steppe of India?
But that, forsooth, the bouncing Amazon,
Your buskin'd mistress and your warrior love,
To Theseus must be wedded, and you come
To give their bed joy and prosperity.

OBERON

How canst thou thus for shame, Titania,
Glance at my credit with Hippolyta,
Knowing I know thy love to Theseus?

Didst thou not lead him through the glimmering night
From Perigenia, whom he ravishèd?
And make him with fair Aegle break his faith,
With Ariadne and Antiopa?

TITANIA
These are the forgeries of jealousy:
And never, since the middle summer's spring,
Met we on hill, in dale, forest or mead,
By pavèd fountain or by rushy brook,
Or in the beachèd margent of the sea,
To dance our ringlets to the whistling wind,
But with thy brawls thou hast disturb'd our sport.
Therefore the winds, piping to us in vain,
As in revenge, have suck'd up from the sea
Contagious fogs; which falling in the land
Have every pelting river made so proud
That they have overborne their continents:
The ox hath therefore stretch'd his yoke in vain,
The ploughman lost his sweat, and the green corn
Hath rotted ere his youth attain'd a beard;
The fold stands empty in the drownèd field,
And crows are fatted with the murrion flock;
The nine men's morris is fill'd up with mud,
And the quaint mazes in the wanton green
For lack of tread are undistinguishable:
The human mortals want their winter here;
No night is now with hymn or carol blest:
Therefore the moon, the governess of floods,
Pale in her anger, washes all the air,
That rheumatic diseases do abound:
And thorough this distemperature we see
The seasons alter: hoary-headed frosts
Far in the fresh lap of the crimson rose,
And on old Hiems' thin and icy crown
An odorous chaplet of sweet summer buds
Is, as in mockery, set: the spring, the summer,
The childing autumn, angry winter, change

Their wonted liveries, and the mazèd world,
By their increase, now knows not which is which:
And this same progeny of evils comes
From our debate, from our dissension;
We are their parents and original.

OBERON

Do you amend it then; it lies in you:
Why should Titania cross her Oberon?
I do but beg a little changeling boy,
To be my henchman.

TITANIA

Set your heart at rest:
The fairy land buys not the child of me.
His mother was a votaress of my order:
And, in the spicèd Indian air, by night,
Full often hath she gossip'd by my side,
And sat with me on Neptune's yellow sands,
Marking the embarkèd traders on the flood,
When we have laugh'd to see the sails conceive
And grow big-bellied with the wanton wind;
Which she, with pretty and with swimming gait
Following,—her womb then rich with my young squire,—
Would imitate, and sail upon the land,
To fetch me trifles, and return again,
As from a voyage, rich with merchandise.
But she, being mortal, of that boy did die;
And for her sake do I rear up her boy,
And for her sake I will not part with him.

OBERON

How long within this wood intend you stay?

TITANIA

Perchance till after Theseus' wedding-day.
If you will patiently dance in our round
And see our moonlight revels, go with us;
If not, shun me, and I will spare your haunts.

OBERON

Give me that boy, and I will go with thee.

TITANIA

>Not for thy fairy kingdom. Fairies, away!
>We shall chide downright, if I longer stay.

Exit TITANIA *with her train*

OBERON

>Well, go thy way: thou shalt not from this grove
>Till I torment thee for this injury.
>My gentle Puck, come hither. Thou rememberest
>Since once I sat upon a promontory,
>And heard a mermaid on a dolphin's back
>Uttering such dulcet and harmonious breath
>That the rude sea grew civil at her song
>And certain stars shot madly from their spheres,
>To hear the sea-maid's music.

PUCK

>I remember.

OBERON

>That very time I saw, but thou couldst not,
>Flying between the cold moon and the earth,
>Cupid all arm'd: a certain aim he took
>At a fair vestal thronèd by the west,
>And loosed his love-shaft smartly from his bow,
>As it should pierce a hundred thousand hearts;
>But I might see young Cupid's fiery shaft
>Quench'd in the chaste beams of the watery moon,
>And the imperial votaress passed on,
>In maiden meditation, fancy-free.
>Yet mark'd I where the bolt of Cupid fell:
>It fell upon a little western flower,
>Before milk-white, now purple with love's wound,
>And maidens call it love-in-idleness.
>Fetch me that flower; the herb I shew'd thee once:
>The juice of it on sleeping eye-lids laid
>Will make or man or woman madly dote
>Upon the next live creature that it sees.
>Fetch me this herb; and be thou here again
>Ere the leviathan can swim a league.

PUCK

> I'll put a girdle round about the earth
> In forty minutes.

Exit

OBERON

> Having once this juice,
> I'll watch Titania when she is asleep,
> And drop the liquor of it in her eyes.
> The next thing then she waking looks upon,
> Be it on lion, bear, or wolf, or bull,
> On meddling monkey, or on busy ape,
> She shall pursue it with the soul of love:
> And ere I take this charm from off her sight,
> As I can take it with another herb,
> I'll make her render up her page to me.
> But who comes here? I am invisible;
> And I will overhear their conference.

> *Enter* DEMETRIUS,
> HELENA, *following him*

DEMETRIUS

> I love thee not, therefore pursue me not.
> Where is Lysander and fair Hermia?
> The one I'll slay, the other slayeth me.
> Thou told'st me they were stolen unto this wood;
> And here am I, and wode within this wood,
> Because I cannot meet my Hermia.
> Hence, get thee gone, and follow me no more.

HELENA

> You draw me, you hard-hearted adamant;
> But yet you draw not iron, for my heart
> Is true as steel: leave you your power to draw,
> And I shall have no power to follow you.

DEMETRIUS

> Do I entice you? do I speak you fair?
> Or, rather, do I not in plainest truth
> Tell you, I do not, nor I cannot love you?

HELENA

    And even for that do I love you the more.
    I am your spaniel; and, Demetrius,
    The more you beat me, I will fawn on you:
    Use me but as your spaniel, spurn me, strike me,
    Neglect me, lose me; only give me leave,
    Unworthy as I am, to follow you.
    What worser place can I beg in your love,—
    And yet a place of high respect with me,—
    Than to be usèd as you use your dog?

DEMETRIUS

    Tempt not too much the hatred of my spirit;
    For I am sick when I do look on thee.

HELENA

    And I am sick when I look not on you.

DEMETRIUS

    You do impeach your modesty too much,
    To leave the city and commit yourself
    Into the hands of one that loves you not;
    To trust the opportunity of night
    And the ill counsel of a desert place
    With the rich worth of your virginity.

HELENA

    Your virtue is my privilege: for that
    It is not night when I do see your face,
    Therefore I think I am not in the night;
    Nor doth this wood lack worlds of company,
    For you in my respect are all the world:
    Then how can it be said I am alone,
    When all the world is here to look on me?

DEMETRIUS

    I'll run from thee and hide me in the brakes,
    And leave thee to the mercy of wild beasts.

HELENA

    The wildest hath not such a heart as you.
    Run when you will, the story shall be changed:
    Apollo flies, and Daphne holds the chase;

The dove pursues the griffin; the mild hind
Makes speed to catch the tiger; bootless speed,
When cowardice pursues and valour flies.

DEMETRIUS

I will not stay thy questions; let me go:
Or, if thou follow me, do not believe
But I shall do thee mischief in the wood.

HELENA

Ay, in the temple, in the town, the field,
You do me mischief. Fie, Demetrius!
Your wrongs do set a scandal on my sex:
We cannot fight for love, as men may do;
We should be wood and were not made to woo.

Exit DEMETRIUS

I'll follow thee and make a heaven of hell,
To die upon the hand I love so well.

Exit

OBERON

Fare thee well, nymph: ere he do leave this grove,
Thou shalt fly him and he shall seek thy love.

Re-enter PUCK

Hast thou the flower there? Welcome, wanderer.

PUCK

Ay, there it is.

OBERON

I pray thee, give it me.
I know a bank where the wild thyme blows,
Where oxlips and the nodding violet grows,
Quite over-canopied with luscious woodbine,
With sweet musk-roses and with eglantine:
There sleeps Titania sometime of the night,
Lull'd in these flowers with dances and delight;
And there the snake throws her enamell'd skin,
Weed wide enough to wrap a fairy in:
And with the juice of this I'll streak her eyes,
And make her full of hateful fantasies.
Take thou some of it, and seek through this grove:

A sweet Athenian lady is in love
With a disdainful youth: anoint his eyes;
But do it when the next thing he espies
May be the lady: thou shalt know the man
By the Athenian garments he hath on.
Effect it with some care, that he may prove
More fond on her than she upon her love:
And look thou meet me ere the first cock crow.

PUCK
Fear not, my lord, your servant shall do so.

Exeunt

SCENE II.
ANOTHER PART OF THE WOOD.

Enter TITANIA, *with her train*

TITANIA
Come, now a roundel and a fairy song;
Then, for the third part of a minute, hence;
Some to kill cankers in the musk-rose buds,
Some war with rere-mice for their leathern wings,
To make my small elves coats, and some keep back
The clamorous owl that nightly hoots and wonders
At our quaint spirits. Sing me now asleep;
Then to your offices and let me rest.

The Fairies sing

FIRST FAIRY
You spotted snakes with double tongue,
  Thorny hedgehogs, be not seen;
Newts and blind-worms, do no wrong,
  Come not near our fairy queen.

CHORUS
    Philomel, with melody
    Sing in our sweet lullaby;
Lulla, lulla, lullaby, lulla, lulla, lullaby:
    Never harm,
    Nor spell nor charm,

Come our lovely lady nigh;
So, good night, with lullaby.

FIRST FAIRY

Weaving spiders, come not here;
Hence, you long-legg'd spinners, hence!
Beetles black, approach not near;
Worm nor snail, do no offence.

CHORUS

Philomel, with melody, & c.

SECOND FAIRY

Hence, away! now all is well:
One aloof stand sentinel.

Exeunt Fairies. TITANIA *sleeps*

Enter OBERON *and squeezes
the flower on* TITANIA'S *eyelids*

OBERON

What thou seest when thou dost wake,
Do it for thy true-love take,
Love and languish for his sake:
Be it ounce, or cat, or bear,
Pard, or boar with bristled hair,
In thy eye that shall appear
When thou wakest, it is thy dear:
Wake when some vile thing is near.

Exit

Enter LYSANDER *and* HERMIA

LYSANDER

Fair love, you faint with wandering in the wood;
   And to speak troth, I have forgot our way:
We'll rest us, Hermia, if you think it good,
   And tarry for the comfort of the day.

HERMIA

Be it so, Lysander: find you out a bed;
For I upon this bank will rest my head.

LYSANDER

One turf shall serve as pillow for us both;
One heart, one bed, two bosoms and one troth.

HERMIA

    Nay, good Lysander; for my sake, my dear,

    Lie further off yet, do not lie so near.

LYSANDER

    O, take the sense, sweet, of my innocence!

    Love takes the meaning in love's conference.

    I mean, that my heart unto yours is knit

    So that but one heart we can make of it;

    Two bosoms interchainèd with an oath;

    So then two bosoms and a single troth.

    Then by your side no bed-room me deny;

    For lying so, Hermia, I do not lie.

HERMIA

    Lysander riddles very prettily:

    Now much beshrew my manners and my pride,

    If Hermia meant to say Lysander lied.

    But, gentle friend, for love and courtesy

    Lie further off; in human modesty,

    Such separation as may well be said

    Becomes a virtuous bachelor and a maid,

    So far be distant; and, good night, sweet friend:

    Thy love ne'er alter till thy sweet life end!

LYSANDER

    Amen, amen, to that fair prayer, say I;

    And then end life when I end loyalty!

    Here is my bed: sleep give thee all his rest!

HERMIA

    With half that wish the wisher's eyes be press'd!

They sleep

Enter PUCK

PUCK

    Through the forest have I gone.

    But Athenian found I none,

    On whose eyes I might approve

    This flower's force in stirring love.

    Night and silence.—Who is here?

    Weeds of Athens he doth wear:

This is he, my master said,
Despisèd the Athenian maid;
And here the maiden, sleeping sound,
On the dank and dirty ground.
Pretty soul! she durst not lie
Near this lack-love, this kill-courtesy.
Churl, upon thy eyes I throw
All the power this charm doth owe.
He squeezes the flower on Lysander's eyes
When thou wakest, let love forbid
Sleep his seat on thy eyelid:
So awake when I am gone;
For I must now to Oberon.

Exit

Enter DEMETRIUS *and* HELENA, *running*

HELENA
Stay, though thou kill me, sweet Demetrius.
DEMETRIUS
I charge thee, hence, and do not haunt me thus.
HELENA
O, wilt thou darkling leave me? do not so.
DEMETRIUS
Stay, on thy peril: I alone will go.

Exit

HELENA
O, I am out of breath in this fond chase!
The more my prayer, the lesser is my grace.
Happy is Hermia, wheresoe'er she lies;
For she hath blessèd and attractive eyes.
How came her eyes so bright? Not with salt tears:
If so, my eyes are oftener wash'd than hers.
No, no, I am as ugly as a bear;
For beasts that meet me run away for fear:
Therefore no marvel though Demetrius
Do, as a monster fly my presence thus.
What wicked and dissembling glass of mine
Made me compare with Hermia's sphery eyne?

But who is here? Lysander! on the ground!
Dead? or asleep? I see no blood, no wound.
Lysander if you live, good sir, awake.

LYSANDER

[*Awaking*] And run through fire I will for thy sweet sake.
Transparent Helena! Nature shows art,
That through thy bosom makes me see thy heart.
Where is Demetrius? O, how fit a word
Is that vile name to perish on my sword!

HELENA

Do not say so, Lysander; say not so
What though he love your Hermia? Lord, what though?
Yet Hermia still loves you: then be content.

LYSANDER

Content with Hermia! No; I do repent
The tedious minutes I with her have spent.
Not Hermia but Helena I love:
Who will not change a raven for a dove?
The will of man is by his reason sway'd;
And reason says you are the worthier maid.
Things growing are not ripe until their season
So I, being young, till now ripe not to reason;
And touching now the point of human skill,
Reason becomes the marshal to my will
And leads me to your eyes, where I o'erlook
Love's stories written in love's richest book.

HELENA

Wherefore was I to this keen mockery born?
When at your hands did I deserve this scorn?
Is't not enough, is't not enough, young man,
That I did never, no, nor never can,
Deserve a sweet look from Demetrius' eye,
But you must flout my insufficiency?
Good troth, you do me wrong, good sooth, you do,
In such disdainful manner me to woo.
But fare you well: perforce I must confess
I thought you lord of more true gentleness.

O, that a lady, of one man refused.
Should of another therefore be abused!

Exit

LYSANDER
  She sees not Hermia. Hermia, sleep thou there:
  And never mayst thou come Lysander near!
  For as a surfeit of the sweetest things
  The deepest loathing to the stomach brings,
  Or as tie heresies that men do leave
  Are hated most of those they did deceive,
  So thou, my surfeit and my heresy,
  Of all be hated, but the most of me!
  And, all my powers, address your love and might
  To honour Helen and to be her knight!

Exit

HERMIA
  [*Awaking*] Help me, Lysander, help me! do thy best
  To pluck this crawling serpent from my breast!
  Ay me, for pity! what a dream was here!
  Lysander, look how I do quake with fear:
  Methought a serpent eat my heart away,
  And you sat smiling at his cruel pray.
  Lysander! what, removed? Lysander! lord!
  What, out of hearing? gone? no sound, no word?
  Alack, where are you speak, an if you hear;
  Speak, of all loves! I swoon almost with fear.
  No? then I well perceive you all not nigh
  Either death or you I'll find immediately.

Exit

ACT

III

SCENE I.
THE WOOD. TITANIA LYING ASLEEP.

Enter QUINCE, SNUG, BOTTOM, FLUTE, SNOUT, *and* STARVELING

BOTTOM

Are we all met?

QUINCE

Pat, pat; and here's a marvellous convenient place for our rehearsal. This green plot shall be our stage, this hawthorn-brake our tiring-house; and we will do it in action as we will do it before the duke.

BOTTOM

Peter Quince,—

QUINCE

What sayest thou, bully Bottom?

BOTTOM

There are things in this comedy of Pyramus and Thisbe that will never please. First, Pyramus must draw a sword to kill himself; which the ladies cannot abide. How answer you that?

SNOUT

By'r lakin, a parlous fear.

STARVELING

I believe we must leave the killing out, when all is done.

BOTTOM

Not a whit: I have a device to make all well. Write me a prologue; and let the prologue seem to say, we will do no harm with our swords, and that Pyramus is not killed indeed; and, for the more better assurance, tell them that I, Pyramus, am not Pyramus, but Bottom the weaver: this will put them out of fear.

QUINCE

Well, we will have such a prologue; and it shall be written in eight and six.

BOTTOM

No, make it two more; let it be written in eight and eight.

SNOUT

Will not the ladies be afeard of the lion?

STARVELING

I fear it, I promise you.

BOTTOM

Masters, you ought to consider with yourselves: to bring in—God shield us!—a lion among ladies, is a most dreadful thing; for there is not a more fearful wild-fowl than your lion living; and we ought to look to 't.

SNOUT

Therefore another prologue must tell he is not a lion.

BOTTOM

Nay, you must name his name, and half his face must be seen through the lion's neck: and he himself must speak through, saying thus, or to the same defect,—'Ladies,'—or 'Fair-ladies—I would wish You,'—or 'I would request you,'—or 'I would entreat you,—not to fear, not to tremble: my life for yours. If you think I come hither as a lion, it were pity of my life: no I am no such thing; I am a man as other men are;' and there indeed let him name his name, and tell them plainly he is Snug the joiner.

QUINCE

Well it shall be so. But there is two hard things; that is, to bring the moonlight into a chamber; for, you know, Pyramus and Thisbe meet by moonlight.

SNOUT

Doth the moon shine that night we play our play?

BOTTOM

A calendar, a calendar! look in the almanac; find out moonshine, find out moonshine.

QUINCE

Yes, it doth shine that night.

BOTTOM

Why, then may you leave a casement of the great chamber window, where we play, open, and the moon may shine in at the casement.

QUINCE

Ay; or else one must come in with a bush of thorns and a lanthorn, and say he comes to disfigure, or to present, the person of Moonshine. Then, there is another thing: we must have a wall in the great chamber; for Pyramus and Thisbe says the story, did talk through the chink of a wall.

SNOUT

You can never bring in a wall. What say you, Bottom?

BOTTOM

Some man or other must present Wall: and let him have some plaster, or some loam, or some rough-cast about him, to signify wall; and let him hold his fingers thus, and through that cranny shall Pyramus and Thisbe whisper.

QUINCE

If that may be, then all is well. Come, sit down, every mother's son, and rehearse your parts. Pyramus, you begin: when you have spoken your speech, enter into that brake: and so every one according to his cue.

Enter PUCK *behind*

PUCK

What hempen home-spuns have we swaggering here,
So near the cradle of the Fairy Queen?
What, a play toward! I'll be an auditor;
An actor too, perhaps, if I see cause.

QUINCE

Speak, Pyramus. Thisbe, stand forth.

BOTTOM *as Pyramus*

Thisbe, the flowers of odious savours sweet,—

QUINCE

Odours, odours.

BOTTOM *as Pyramus*

—odours savours sweet:

So hath thy breath, my dearest Thisbe dear.

But hark, a voice! stay thou but here awhile,

And by and by I will to thee appear.

Exit

PUCK

A stranger Pyramus than e'er played here.

Exit

FLUTE

Must I speak now?

QUINCE

Ay, marry, must you; for you must understand he goes but to see a noise that he heard, and is to come again.

FLUTE *as Thisbe*

Most radiant Pyramus, most lily-white of hue,

Of colour like the red rose on triumphant brier,

Most brisky juvenal and eke most lovely Jew,

As true as truest horse that yet would never tire,

I'll meet thee, Pyramus, at Ninny's tomb.

QUINCE

'Ninus' tomb,' man: why, you must not speak that yet; that you answer to Pyramus: you speak all your part at once, cues and all Pyramus enter: your cue is past; it is, 'never tire.'

FLUTE

(*as Thisbe*)

O! As true as truest horse, that yet would never tire.

Re-enter PUCK, *and* BOTTOM *with an ass's head*

BOTTOM

If I were fair, Thisbe, I were only thine.

QUINCE

O monstrous! O strange! we are haunted. Pray, masters! fly, masters! Help!

Exeunt QUINCE, SNUG, FLUTE, SNOUT, *and* STARVELING

PUCK

I'll follow you, I'll lead you about a round,
Through bog, through bush, through brake, through brier:
Sometime a horse I'll be, sometime a hound,
A hog, a headless bear, sometime a fire;
And neigh, and bark, and grunt, and roar, and burn,
Like horse, hound, hog, bear, fire, at every turn.

Exit

BOTTOM

Why do they run away? this is a knavery of them to make me
afeard.

Re-enter SNOUT

SNOUT

O Bottom, thou art changed! what do I see on thee?

BOTTOM

What do you see? you see an asshead of your own, do you?

Exit SNOUT

Re-enter QUINCE

QUINCE

Bless thee, Bottom! bless thee! thou art translated.

Exit

BOTTOM

I see their knavery: this is to make an ass of me; to fright me, if
they could. But I will not stir from this place, do what they can:
I will walk up and down here, and I will sing, that they shall hear
I am not afraid.
[*Sings*]

> The ousel cock so black of hue,
> With orange-tawny bill,
> The throstle with his note so true,
> The wren with little quill,—

TITANIA

[*Awaking*] What angel wakes me from my flowery bed?

BOTTOM

[*Sings*]

> The finch, the sparrow and the lark,

The plain-song cuckoo gray,
Whose note full many a man doth mark,
And dares not answer nay;—

for, indeed, who would set his wit to so foolish a bird? Who
would give a bird the lie, though he cry 'cuckoo' never so?

TITANIA

I pray thee, gentle mortal, sing again:
Mine ear is much enamour'd of thy note;
So is mine eye enthrallèd to thy shape;
And thy fair virtue's force perforce doth move me
On the first view to say, to swear, I love thee.

BOTTOM

Methinks, mistress, you should have little reason for that: and
yet, to say the truth, reason and love keep little company together
now-a-days; the more the pity that some honest neighbours will
not make them friends. Nay, I can gleek upon occasion.

TITANIA

Thou art as wise as thou art beautiful.

BOTTOM

Not so, neither: but if I had wit enough to get out of this wood,
I have enough to serve mine own turn.

TITANIA

Out of this wood do not desire to go:
Thou shalt remain here, whether thou wilt or no.
I am a spirit of no common rate;
The summer still doth tend upon my state;
And I do love thee: therefore, go with me;
I'll give thee fairies to attend on thee,
And they shall fetch thee jewels from the deep,
And sing while thou on pressèd flowers dost sleep;
And I will purge thy mortal grossness so
That thou shalt like an airy spirit go.
Peaseblossom! Cobweb! Moth! and Mustardseed!

Enter PEASEBLOSSOM, COBWEB,
MOTH, *and* MUSTARDSEED

PEASEBLOSSOM

Ready.

COBWEB

And I.

MOTH

And I.

MUSTARDSEED

And I.

ALL

Where shall we go?

TITANIA

Be kind and courteous to this gentleman;
Hop in his walks and gambol in his eyes;
Feed him with apricocks and dewberries,
With purple grapes, green figs, and mulberries;
The honey-bags steal from the humble-bees,
And for night-tapers crop their waxen thighs
And light them at the fiery glow-worm's eyes,
To have my love to bed and to arise;
And pluck the wings from Painted butterflies
To fan the moonbeams from his sleeping eyes:
Nod to him, elves, and do him courtesies.

PEASEBLOSSOM

Hail, mortal!

COBWEB

Hail!

MOTH

Hail!

MUSTARDSEED

Hail!

BOTTOM

I cry your worship's mercy, heartily: I beseech your worship's
name.

COBWEB

Cobweb.

BOTTOM

I shall desire you of more acquaintance, good Master Cobweb: if
I cut my finger, I shall make bold with you. Your name, honest
gentleman?

PEASEBLOSSOM
  Peaseblossom.
BOTTOM
  I pray you, commend me to Mistress Squash, your mother, and
  to Master Peascod, your father. Good Master Peaseblossom, I
  shall desire you of more acquaintance too. Your name, I beseech
  you, sir?
MUSTARDSEED
  Mustardseed.
BOTTOM
  Good Master Mustardseed, I know your patience well: that same
  cowardly, giant-like ox-beef hath devoured many a gentleman
  of your house: I promise you your kindred had made my eyes
  water ere now. I desire your more acquaintance, good Master
  Mustardseed.
TITANIA
  Come, wait upon him; lead him to my bower.
  The moon methinks looks with a watery eye;
  And when she weeps, weeps every little flower,
  Lamenting some enforcèd chastity.
  Tie up my love's tongue bring him silently.

                                                          Exeunt

                          SCENE II.
                  ANOTHER PART OF THE WOOD.

                       Enter OBERON
OBERON
  I wonder if Titania be awaked;
  Then, what it was that next came in her eye,
  Which she must dote on in extremity.
                       Enter PUCK
  Here comes my messenger.
  How now, mad spirit!
  What night rule now about this haunted grove?
PUCK
  My mistress with a monster is in love.

Near to her close and consecrated bower,
While she was in her dull and sleeping hour,
A crew of patches, rude mechanicals,
That work for bread upon Athenian stalls,
Were met together to rehearse a play
Intended for great Theseus' nuptial-day.
The shallowest thick-skin of that barren sort,
Who Pyramus presented, in their sport
Forsook his scene and enter'd in a brake
When I did him at this advantage take,
An ass's nole I fixèd on his head:
Anon his Thisbe must be answerèd,
And forth my mimic comes. When they him spy,
As wild geese that the creeping fowler eye,
Or russet-pated choughs, many in sort,
Rising and cawing at the gun's report,
Sever themselves and madly sweep the sky,
So, at his sight, away his fellows fly;
And, at our stamp, here o'er and o'er one falls;
He murder cries and help from Athens calls.
Their sense thus weak, lost with their fears thus strong,
Made senseless things begin to do them wrong;
For briers and thorns at their apparel snatch;
Some sleeves, some hats, from yielders all things catch.
I led them on in this distracted fear,
And left sweet Pyramus translated there:
When in that moment, so it came to pass,
Titania waked and straightway loved an ass.

OBERON
This falls out better than I could devise.
But hast thou yet latch'd the Athenian's eyes
With the love-juice, as I did bid thee do?

PUCK
I took him sleeping,—that is finish'd too,—
And the Athenian woman by his side:
That, when he waked, of force she must be eyed.
                    Enter HERMIA *and* DEMETRIUS

OBERON
Stand close: this is the same Athenian.

PUCK
This is the woman, but not this the man.

DEMETRIUS
O, why rebuke you him that loves you so?
Lay breath so bitter on your bitter foe.

HERMIA
Now I but chide; but I should use thee worse,
For thou, I fear, hast given me cause to curse,
If thou hast slain Lysander in his sleep,
Being o'er shoes in blood, plunge in the deep,
And kill me too.
The sun was not so true unto the day
As he to me: would he have stolen away
From sleeping Hermia? I'll believe as soon
This whole earth may be bored and that the moon
May through the centre creep and so displease
Her brother's noontide with Antipodes.
It cannot be but thou hast murder'd him;
So should a murderer look, so dead, so grim.

DEMETRIUS
So should the murder'd look, and so should I,
Pierced through the heart with your stern cruelty:
Yet you, the murderer, look as bright, as clear,
As yonder Venus in her glimmering sphere.

HERMIA
What's this to my Lysander? where is he?
Ah, good Demetrius, wilt thou give him me?

DEMETRIUS
I had rather give his carcass to my hounds.

HERMIA
Out, dog! out, cur! thou drivest me past the bounds
Of maiden's patience. Hast thou slain him, then?
Henceforth be never number'd among men!
O, once tell true, tell true, even for my sake!
Durst thou have look'd upon him being awake,

And hast thou kill'd him sleeping? O brave touch!
Could not a worm, an adder, do so much?
An adder did it; for with doubler tongue
Than thine, thou serpent, never adder stung.

DEMETRIUS

You spend your passion on a misprised mood:
I am not guilty of Lysander's blood;
Nor is he dead, for aught that I can tell.

HERMIA

I pray thee, tell me then that he is well.

DEMETRIUS

An if I could, what should I get therefore?

HERMIA

A privilege never to see me more.
And from thy hated presence part I so:
See me no more, whether he be dead or no.

Exit

DEMETRIUS

There is no following her in this fierce vein:
Here therefore for a while I will remain.
So sorrow's heaviness doth heavier grow
For debt that bankrupt sleep doth sorrow owe:
Which now in some slight measure it will pay,
If for his tender here I make some stay.

Lies down and sleeps

OBERON

What hast thou done? thou hast mistaken quite
And laid the love-juice on some true-love's sight:
Of thy misprision must perforce ensue
Some true love turn'd and not a false turn'd true.

PUCK

Then fate o'er-rules, that, one man holding troth,
A million fail, confounding oath on oath.

OBERON

About the wood go swifter than the wind,
And Helena of Athens look thou find:
All fancy-sick she is and pale of cheer,

With sighs of love, that costs the fresh blood dear:
By some illusion see thou bring her here:
I'll charm his eyes against she do appear.

PUCK

I go, I go; look how I go,
Swifter than arrow from the Tartar's bow.

Exit

OBERON

Flower of this purple dye,
Hit with Cupid's archery,
Sink in apple of his eye.
[*He squeezes the flower on Demetrius's eyes*]
When his love he doth espy,
Let her shine as gloriously
As the Venus of the sky.
When thou wakest, if she be by,
Beg of her for remedy.

Re-enter PUCK

PUCK

Captain of our fairy band,
Helena is here at hand;
And the youth, mistook by me,
Pleading for a lover's fee.
Shall we their fond pageant see?
Lord, what fools these mortals be!

OBERON

Stand aside: the noise they make
Will cause Demetrius to awake.

PUCK

Then will two at once woo one;
That must needs be sport alone;
And those things do best please me
That befal preposterously.

Enter LYSANDER *and* HELENA

LYSANDER

Why should you think that I should woo in scorn?
Scorn and derision never come in tears:

Look, when I vow, I weep; and vows so born,
In their nativity all truth appears.
How can these things in me seem scorn to you,
Bearing the badge of faith, to prove them true?

HELENA
You do advance your cunning more and more.
When truth kills truth, O devilish-holy fray!
These vows are Hermia's: will you give her o'er?
Weigh oath with oath, and you will nothing weigh:
Your vows to her and me, put in two scales,
Will even weigh, and both as light as tales.

LYSANDER
I had no judgment when to her I swore.

HELENA
Nor none, in my mind, now you give her o'er.

LYSANDER
Demetrius loves her, and he loves not you.

DEMETRIUS
[*Awaking*] O Helena, goddess, nymph, perfect, divine!
To what, my love, shall I compare thine eyne?
Crystal is muddy. O, how ripe in show
Thy lips, those kissing cherries, tempting grow!
That pure congealèd white, high Taurus snow,
Fann'd with the eastern wind, turns to a crow
When thou hold'st up thy hand: O, let me kiss
This princess of pure white, this seal of bliss!

HELENA
O spite! O hell! I see you all are bent
To set against me for your merriment:
If you we re civil and knew courtesy,
You would not do me thus much injury.
Can you not hate me, as I know you do,
But you must join in souls to mock me too?
If you were men, as men you are in show,
You would not use a gentle lady so;
To vow, and swear, and superpraise my parts,
When I am sure you hate me with your hearts.

You both are rivals, and love Hermia;
And now both rivals, to mock Helena:
A trim exploit, a manly enterprise,
To conjure tears up in a poor maid's eyes
With your derision! none of noble sort
Would so offend a virgin, and extort
A poor soul's patience, all to make you sport.

LYSANDER
You are unkind, Demetrius; be not so;
For you love Hermia; this you know I know:
And here, with all good will, with all my heart,
In Hermia's love I yield you up my part;
And yours of Helena to me bequeath,
Whom I do love and will do till my death.

HELENA
Never did mockers waste more idle breath.

DEMETRIUS
Lysander, keep thy Hermia; I will none:
If e'er I loved her, all that love is gone.
My heart to her but as guest-wise sojourn'd,
And now to Helen is it home return'd,
There to remain.

LYSANDER
Helen, it is not so.

DEMETRIUS
Disparage not the faith thou dost not know,
Lest, to thy peril, thou aby it dear.
Look, where thy love comes; yonder is thy dear.

Re-enter HERMIA

HERMIA
Dark night, that from the eye his function takes,
The ear more quick of apprehension makes;
Wherein it doth impair the seeing sense,
It pays the hearing double recompense.
Thou art not by mine eye, Lysander, found;
Mine ear, I thank it, brought me to thy sound
But why unkindly didst thou leave me so?

LYSANDER

    Why should he stay, whom love doth press to go?

HERMIA

    What love could press Lysander from my side?

LYSANDER

    Lysander's love, that would not let him bide,

    Fair Helena, who more engilds the night

    Than all you fiery oes and eyes of light.

    Why seek'st thou me? Could not this make thee know,

    The hate I bear thee made me leave thee so?

HERMIA

    You speak not as you think: it cannot be.

HELENA

    Lo, she is one of this confederacy!

    Now I perceive they have conjoin'd all three

    To fashion this false sport, in spite of me.

    Injurious Hermia! most ungrateful maid!

    Have you conspired, have you with these contrived

    To bait me with this foul derision?

    Is all the counsel that we two have shared,

    The sisters' vows, the hours that we have spent,

    When we have chid the hasty-footed time

    For parting us,—O, is it all forgot?

    All school-days' friendship, childhood innocence?

    We, Hermia, like two artificial gods,

    Have with our needles created both one flower,

    Both on one sampler, sitting on one cushion,

    Both warbling of one song, both in one key,

    As if our hands, our sides, voices and minds,

    Had been incorporate. So we grow together,

    Like to a double cherry, seeming parted,

    But yet an union in partition;

    Two lovely berries moulded on one stem;

    So, with two seeming bodies, but one heart;

    Two of the first, like coats in heraldry,

    Due but to one and crownèd with one crest.

    And will you rent our ancient love asunder,

To join with men in scorning your poor friend?
It is not friendly, 'tis not maidenly:
Our sex, as well as I, may chide you for it,
Though I alone do feel the injury.

HERMIA

I am amazèd at your passionate words.
I scorn you not: it seems that you scorn me.

HELENA

Have you not set Lysander, as in scorn,
To follow me and praise my eyes and face?
And made your other love, Demetrius,
Who even but now did spurn me with his foot,
To call me goddess, nymph, divine and rare,
Precious, celestial? Wherefore speaks he this
To her he hates? and wherefore doth Lysander
Deny your love, so rich within his soul,
And tender me, forsooth, affection,
But by your setting on, by your consent?
What thought I be not so in grace as you,
So hung upon with love, so fortunate,
But miserable most, to love unloved?
This you should pity rather than despise.

HERNIA

I understand not what you mean by this.

HELENA

Ay, do, persever, counterfeit sad looks,
Make mouths upon me when I turn my back;
Wink each at other; hold the sweet jest up:
This sport, well carried, shall be chroniclèd.
If you have any pity, grace, or manners,
You would not make me such an argument.
But fare ye well: 'tis partly my own fault;
Which death or absence soon shall remedy.

LYSANDER

Stay, gentle Helena; hear my excuse:
My love, my life my soul, fair Helena!

HELENA

O excellent!

HERMIA

[*To Lysander*] Sweet, do not scorn her so.

DEMETRIUS

If she cannot entreat, I can compel.

LYSANDER

Thou canst compel no more than she entreat:

Thy threats have no more strength than her weak prayers.

Helen, I love thee; by my life, I do:

I swear by that which I will lose for thee,

To prove him false that says I love thee not.

DEMETRIUS

I say I love thee more than he can do.

LYSANDER

If thou say so, withdraw, and prove it too.

DEMETRIUS

Quick, come!

HERMIA

Lysander, whereto tends all this?

LYSANDER

Away, you Ethiope!

DEMETRIUS

No, no; he'll

Seem to break loose; take on as you would follow,

But yet come not: [*To Lysander*] you are a tame man, go!

LYSANDER

Hang off, thou cat, thou burr! vile thing, let loose,

Or I will shake thee from me like a serpent!

HERMIA

Why are you grown so rude? what change is this? Sweet love,—

LYSANDER

Thy love! out, tawny Tartar, out!

Out, loathèd medicine! hated potion, hence!

HERMIA

Do you not jest?

HELENA

Yes, sooth; and so do you.

LYSANDER

Demetrius, I will keep my word with thee.

DEMETRIUS

I would I had your bond, for I perceive

A weak bond holds you: I'll not trust your word.

LYSANDER

What, should I hurt her, strike her, kill her dead?

Although I hate her, I'll not harm her so.

HERMIA

What, can you do me greater harm than hate?

Hate me! wherefore? O me! what news, my love!

Am not I Hermia? are not you Lysander?

I am as fair now as I was erewhile.

Since night you loved me; yet since night you left me:

Why, then you left me—O, the gods forbid!—

In earnest, shall I say?

LYSANDER

Ay, by my life;

And never did desire to see thee more.

Therefore be out of hope, of question, of doubt;

Be certain, nothing truer; 'tis no jest

That I do hate thee and love Helena.

HERMIA

O me! you juggler! you canker-blossom!

You thief of love! what, have you come by night

And stolen my love's heart from him?

HELENA

Fine, i'faith!

Have you no modesty, no maiden shame,

No touch of bashfulness? What, will you tear

Impatient answers from my gentle tongue?

Fie, fie! you counterfeit, you puppet, you!

HERMIA

Puppet? why so? ay, that way goes the game.

Now I perceive that she hath made compare

Between our statures; she hath urged her height;
And with her personage, her tall personage,
Her height, forsooth, she hath prevail'd with him.
And are you grown so high in his esteem;
Because I am so dwarfish and so low?
How low am I, thou painted maypole? speak;
How low am I? I am not yet so low
But that my nails can reach unto thine eyes.

HELENA
I pray you, though you mock me, gentlemen,
Let her not hurt me: I was never curst;
I have no gift at all in shrewishness;
I am a right maid for my cowardice:
Let her not strike me. You perhaps may think,
Because she is something lower than myself,
That I can match her.

HERMIA
Lower! hark, again.

HELENA
Good Hermia, do not be so bitter with me.
I evermore did love you, Hermia,
Did ever keep your counsels, never wrong'd you;
Save that, in love unto Demetrius,
I told him of your stealth unto this wood.
He follow'd you; for love I follow'd him;
But he hath chid me hence and threaten'd me
To strike me, spurn me, nay, to kill me too:
And now, so you will let me quiet go,
To Athens will I bear my folly back
And follow you no further: let me go:
You see how simple and how fond I am.

HERMIA
Why, get you gone: who is't that hinders you?

HELENA
A foolish heart, that I leave here behind.

HERMIA
What, with Lysander?

HELENA
    With Demetrius.
LYSANDER
    Be not afraid; she shall not harm thee, Helena.
DEMETRIUS
    No, sir, she shall not, though you take her part.
HELENA
    O, when she's angry, she is keen and shrewd!
    She was a vixen when she went to school;
    And though she be but little, she is fierce.
HERMIA
    'Little' again! nothing but 'low' and 'little'!
    Why will you suffer her to flout me thus?
    Let me come to her.
LYSANDER
    Get you gone, you dwarf;
    You minimus, of hindering knot-grass made;
    You bead, you acorn.
DEMETRIUS
    You are too officious
    In her behalf that scorns your services.
    Let her alone: speak not of Helena;
    Take not her part; for, if thou dost intend
    Never so little show of love to her,
    Thou shalt aby it.
LYSANDER
    Now she holds me not;
    Now follow, if thou darest, to try whose right,
    Of thine or mine, is most in Helena.
DEMETRIUS
    Follow! nay, I'll go with thee, cheek by jole.

                        Exeunt LYSANDER *and* DEMETRIUS
HERMIA
    You, mistress, all this coil is 'long of you:
    Nay, go not back.
HELENA
    I will not trust you, I,

Nor longer stay in your curst company.
Your hands than mine are quicker for a fray,
My legs are longer though, to run away.

Exit

HERMIA
I am amazed, and know not what to say.

Exit

Oberon and Puck come forward

OBERON
This is thy negligence: still thou mistakest,
Or else committ'st thy knaveries wilfully.

PUCK
Believe me, king of shadows, I mistook.
Did not you tell me I should know the man
By the Athenian garment he had on?
And so far blameless proves my enterprise,
That I have 'nointed an Athenian's eyes;
And so far am I glad it so did sort
As this their jangling I esteem a sport.

OBERON
Thou see'st these lovers seek a place to fight:
Hie therefore, Robin, overcast the night;
The starry welkin cover thou anon
With drooping fog as black as Acheron,
And lead these testy rivals so astray
As one come not within another's way.
Like to Lysander sometime frame thy tongue,
Then stir Demetrius up with bitter wrong;
And sometime rail thou like Demetrius;
And from each other look thou lead them thus,
Till o'er their brows death-counterfeiting sleep
With leaden legs and batty wings doth creep:
Then crush this herb into Lysander's eye;
Whose liquor hath this virtuous property,
To take from thence all error with his might,
And make his eyeballs roll with wonted sight.
When they next wake, all this derision

Shall seem a dream and fruitless vision,
And back to Athens shall the lovers wend,
With league whose date till death shall never end.
Whiles I in this affair do thee employ,
I'll to my Queen and beg her Indian boy;
And then I will her charmèd eye release
From monster's view, and all things shall be peace.

PUCK

My fairy lord, this must be done with haste,
For night's swift dragons cut the clouds full fast,
And yonder shines Aurora's harbinger;
At whose approach, ghosts, wandering here and there,
Troop home to churchyards: damnèd spirits all,
That in crossways and floods have burial,
Already to their wormy beds are gone;
For fear lest day should look their shames upon,
They willfully themselves exile from light
And must for aye consort with black-brow'd night.

OBERON

But we are spirits of another sort:
I with the morning's love have oft made sport,
And, like a forester, the groves may tread,
Even till the eastern gate, all fiery-red,
Opening on Neptune with fair blessèd beams,
Turns into yellow gold his salt green streams.
But, notwithstanding, haste; make no delay:
We may effect this business yet ere day.

Exit

PUCK

Up and down, up and down,
I will lead them up and down:
I am fear'd in field and town:
Goblin, lead them up and down.
Here comes one.

Re-enter LYSANDER

LYSANDER

Where art thou, proud Demetrius? speak thou now.

PUCK

[*in Demetrius' voice*] Here, villain; drawn and ready. Where art
thou?

LYSANDER

I will be with thee straight.

PUCK

[*in Demetrius' voice*] Follow me, then,
To plainer ground.

Exit LYSANDER, *as following the voice*
Re-enter DEMETRIUS

DEMETRIUS

Lysander! speak again:
Thou runaway, thou coward, art thou fled?
Speak! In some bush? Where dost thou hide thy head?

PUCK

[*in Lysander's voice*] Thou coward, art thou bragging to the stars,
Telling the bushes that thou look'st for wars,
And wilt not come? Come, recreant; come, thou child;
I'll whip thee with a rod: he is defiled
That draws a sword on thee.

DEMETRIUS

Yea, art thou there?

PUCK

[*in Lysander's voice*] Follow my voice: we'll try no manhood here.

Exeunt

Re-enter LYSANDER

LYSANDER

He goes before me and still dares me on:
When I come where he calls, then he is gone.
The villain is much lighter-heel'd than I:
I follow'd fast, but faster he did fly;
That fallen am I in dark uneven way,
And here will rest me.

Lies down

Come, thou gentle day!
For if but once thou show me thy grey light,
I'll find Demetrius and revenge this spite.

Sleeps
Re-enter PUCK *and* DEMETRIUS

PUCK

[*in Lysander's voice*] Ho, ho, ho! Coward, why comest thou not?

DEMETRIUS

Abide me, if thou darest; for well I wot
Thou runn'st before me, shifting every place,
And darest not stand, nor look me in the face.
Where art thou now?

PUCK

[*in Lysander's voice*] Come hither: I am here.

DEMETRIUS

Nay, then, thou mock'st me. Thou shalt buy this dear,
If ever I thy face by daylight see:
Now, go thy way. Faintness constraineth me
To measure out my length on this cold bed.
By day's approach look to be visited.

Lies down and sleeps
Re-enter HELENA

HELENA

O weary night, O long and tedious night,
Abate thy hour! Shine comforts from the east,
That I may back to Athens by daylight,
From these that my poor company detest:
And sleep, that sometimes shuts up sorrow's eye,
Steal me awhile from mine own company.

Lies down and sleeps

PUCK

Yet but three? Come one more;
Two of both kinds make up four.
Here she comes, curst and sad:
Cupid is a knavish lad,
Thus to make poor females mad.

Re-enter HERMIA

HERMIA

Never so weary, never so in woe,
Bedabbled with the dew and torn with briers,

I can no further crawl, no further go;
My legs can keep no pace with my desires.
Here will I rest me till the break of day.
Heavens shield Lysander, if they mean a fray!

Lies down and sleeps

PUCK

On the ground
Sleep sound:
I'll apply
To your eye,
Gentle lover, remedy.

Squeezing the juice on Lysander's eyes

When thou wakest,
Thou takest
True delight
In the sight
Of thy former lady's eye:
And the country proverb known,
That every man should take his own,
In your waking shall be shown:
Jack shall have Jill;
Nought shall go ill;
The man shall have his mare again, and all shall be well.

Exit

ACT

IV

SCENE I.
THE WOOD. LYSANDER, DEMETRIUS,
HELENA, AND HERMIA LYING ASLEEP.

Enter TITANIA *and* BOTTOM; PEASEBLOSSOM, COBWEB, MOTH,
MUSTARDSEED, *and other Fairies attending;* OBERON *behind unseen*

TITANIA

Come, sit thee down upon this flowery bed,
While I thy amiable cheeks do coy,
And stick musk-roses in thy sleek smooth head,
And kiss thy fair large ears, my gentle joy.

BOTTOM

Where's Peaseblossom?

PEASEBLOSSOM

Ready.

BOTTOM

Scratch my head Peaseblossom. Where's Mounsieur
Cobweb?

COBWEB

Ready.

BOTTOM

Mounsieur Cobweb, good mounsieur, get you your

weapons in your hand, and kill me a red-hipped humble-bee on the top of a thistle; and, good mounsieur, bring me the honey-bag. Do not fret yourself too much in the action, mounsieur; and, good mounsieur, have a care the honey-bag break not; I would be loath to have you overflown with a honey-bag, signior. Where's Mounsieur Mustardseed?

MUSTARDSEED

Ready.

BOTTOM

Give me your neaf, Mounsieur Mustardseed. Pray you, leave your courtesy, good mounsieur.

MUSTARDSEED

What's your Will?

BOTTOM

Nothing, good mounsieur, but to help Cavalery Cobweb to scratch. I must to the barber's, monsieur; for methinks I am marvellous hairy about the face; and I am such a tender ass, if my hair do but tickle me, I must scratch.

TITANIA

What, wilt thou hear some music, my sweet love?

BOTTOM

I have a reasonable good ear in music. Let's have the tongs and the bones.

TITANIA

Or say, sweet love, what thou desirest to eat.

BOTTOM

Truly, a peck of provender: I could munch your good dry oats. Methinks I have a great desire to a bottle of hay: good hay, sweet hay, hath no fellow.

TITANIA

I have a venturous fairy that shall seek
The squirrel's hoard, and fetch thee new nuts.

BOTTOM

I had rather have a handful or two of dried peas. But, I pray you, let none of your people stir me: I have an exposition of sleep come upon me.

TITANIA

Sleep thou, and I will wind thee in my arms.
Fairies, begone, and be all ways away.

Exeunt Fairies

So doth the woodbine the sweet honeysuckle
Gently entwist; the female ivy so
Enrings the barky fingers of the elm.
O, how I love thee! how I dote on thee!

They sleep
Enter PUCK

OBERON

[*Advancing*] Welcome, good Robin.
See'st thou this sweet sight?
Her dotage now I do begin to pity:
For, meeting her of late behind the wood,
Seeking sweet favours from this hateful fool,
I did upbraid her and fall out with her;
For she his hairy temples then had rounded
With a coronet of fresh and fragrant flowers;
And that same dew, which sometime on the buds
Was wont to swell like round and orient pearls,
Stood now within the pretty flowerets' eyes
Like tears that did their own disgrace bewail.
When I had at my pleasure taunted her
And she in mild terms begg'd my patience,
I then did ask of her her changeling child;
Which straight she gave me, and her fairy sent
To bear him to my bower in fairy land.
And now I have the boy, I will undo
This hateful imperfection of her eyes:
And, gentle Puck, take this transformed scalp
From off the head of this Athenian swain;
That, he awaking when the other do,
May all to Athens back again repair
And think no more of this night's accidents
But as the fierce vexation of a dream.
But first I will release the Fairy Queen.

[*To Titania*] Be as thou wast wont to be;
See as thou wast wont to see:
Dian's bud o'er Cupid's flower
Hath such force and blessed power.
Now, my Titania; wake you, my sweet Queen.

TITANIA
[*Awaking*] My Oberon! what visions have I seen!
Methought I was enamour'd of an ass.

OBERON
There lies your love.

TITANIA
How came these things to pass?
O, how mine eyes do loathe his visage now!

OBERON
Silence awhile. Robin, take off this head.
Titania, music call; and strike more dead
Than common sleep of all these five the sense.

TITANIA
Music, ho! Music, such as charmeth sleep!

Music, still

PUCK
[*To Bottom, removing the ass's head*]
Now, when thou wakest, with thine own fool's eyes peep.

OBERON
Sound, music! [*Music*] Come, my queen, take hands with me,
And rock the ground whereon these sleepers be.

They dance

Now thou and I are new in amity,
And will to-morrow midnight solemnly
Dance in Duke Theseus' house triumphantly,
And bless it to all fair prosperity:
There shall the pairs of faithful lovers be
Wedded, with Theseus, all in jollity.

PUCK
Fairy king, attend, and mark:
I do hear the morning lark.

OBERON

    Then, my queen, in silence sad,
    Trip we after the night's shade:
    We the globe can compass soon,
    Swifter than the wandering moon.

TITANIA

    Come, my lord, and in our flight
    Tell me how it came this night
    That I sleeping here was found
    With these mortals on the ground.

Exeunt

Horns winded within
Enter THESEUS, HIPPOLYTA, EGEUS, *and train*

THESEUS

    Go, one of you, find out the forester;
    For now our observation is perform'd;
    And since we have the vaward of the day,
    My love shall hear the music of my hounds.
    Uncouple in the western valley; let them go:
    Dispatch, I say, and find the forester.

Exit an Attendant

    We will, fair queen, up to the mountain's top,
    And mark the musical confusion
    Of hounds and echo in conjunction.

HIPPOLYTA

    I was with Hercules and Cadmus once,
    When in a wood of Crete they bay'd the bear
    With hounds of Sparta: never did I hear
    Such gallant chiding: for, besides the groves,
    The skies, the fountains, every region near
    Seem'd all one mutual cry: I never heard
    So musical a discord, such sweet thunder.

THESEUS

    My hounds are bred out of the Spartan kind,
    So flew'd, so sanded, and their heads are hung
    With ears that sweep away the morning dew;
    Crook-knee'd, and dew-lapp'd like Thessalian bulls;

Slow in pursuit, but match'd in mouth like bells,
Each under each. A cry more tuneable
Was never holla'd to, nor cheer'd with horn,
In Crete, in Sparta, nor in Thessaly:
Judge when you hear.

He sees the sleepers

But, soft! what nymphs are these?

EGEUS

My lord, this is my daughter here asleep;
And this, Lysander; this Demetrius is;
This Helena, old Nedar's Helena:
I wonder of their being here together.

THESEUS

No doubt they rose up early to observe
The rite of May, and hearing our intent,
Came here in grace our solemnity.
But speak, Egeus; is not this the day
That Hermia should give answer of her choice?

EGEUS

It is, my lord.

THESEUS

Go, bid the huntsmen wake them with their horns.

*Horns and shout within. Lysander, Demetrius, Helena, and Hermia
wake and start up*

Good morrow, friends. Saint Valentine is past:
Begin these wood-birds but to couple now?

LYSANDER

Pardon, my lord.

THESEUS

I pray you all, stand up.
I know you two are rival enemies:
How comes this gentle concord in the world,
That hatred is so far from jealousy,
To sleep by hate, and fear no enmity?

LYSANDER

My lord, I shall reply amazedly,
Half sleep, half waking: but as yet, I swear,

I cannot truly say how I came here;
But, as I think,—for truly would I speak,
And now do I bethink me, so it is,—
I came with Hermia hither: our intent
Was to be gone from Athens, where we might,
Without the peril of the Athenian law.

EGEUS

Enough, enough, my lord; you have enough:
I beg the law, the law, upon his head.
They would have stolen away; they would, Demetrius,
Thereby to have defeated you and me,
You of your wife and me of my consent,
Of my consent that she should be your wife.

DEMETRIUS

My lord, fair Helen told me of their stealth,
Of this their purpose hither to this wood;
And I in fury hither follow'd them,
Fair Helena in fancy following me.
But, my good lord, I wot not by what power,—
But by some power it is,—my love to Hermia,
Melted as the snow, seems to me now
As the remembrance of an idle gaud
Which in my childhood I did dote upon;
And all the faith, the virtue of my heart,
The object and the pleasure of mine eye,
Is only Helena. To her, my lord,
Was I betroth'd ere I saw Hermia:
But, like in sickness, did I loathe this food;
But, as in health, come to my natural taste,
Now I do wish it, love it, long for it,
And will for evermore be true to it.

THESEUS

Fair lovers, you are fortunately met:
Of this discourse we more will hear anon.
Egeus, I will overbear your will,
For in the temple by and by with us
These couples shall eternally be knit:

And, for the morning now is something worn,
Our purposed hunting shall be set aside.
Away with us to Athens; three and three,
We'll hold a feast in great solemnity.
Come, Hippolyta.

Exeunt THESEUS, HIPPOLYTA,
EGEUS, *and train*

DEMETRIUS

These things seem small and undistinguishable,
Like far-off mountains turnèd into clouds.

HERMIA

Methinks I see these things with parted eye,
When every thing seems double.

HELENA

So methinks:
And I have found Demetrius like a jewel,
Mine own, and not mine own.

DEMETRIUS

Are you sure
That we are awake? It seems to me
That yet we sleep, we dream. Do not you think
The duke was here, and bid us follow him?

HERMIA

Yea; and my father.

HELENA

And Hippolyta.

LYSANDER

And he did bid us follow to the temple.

DEMETRIUS

Why, then, we are awake: let's follow him
And by the way let us recount our dreams.

Exeunt

BOTTOM

[*Awaking*] When my cue comes, call me, and I will answer: my
next is, 'Most fair Pyramus.' Heigh-ho! Peter Quince! Flute, the
bellows-mender! Snout, the tinker! Starveling! God's my life,
stolen hence, and left me asleep! I have had a most rare vision.

I have had a dream, past the wit of man to say what dream it was: man is but an ass, if he go about to expound this dream. Methought I was—there is no man can tell what. Methought I was,—and methought I had,—but man is but a patched fool, if he will offer to say what methought I had. The eye of man hath not heard, the ear of man hath not seen, man's hand is not able to taste, his tongue to conceive, nor his heart to report, what my dream was. I will get Peter Quince to write a ballad of this dream: it shall be called Bottom's Dream, because it hath no bottom; and I will sing it in the latter end of a play, before the duke: peradventure, to make it the more gracious, I shall sing it at her death.

Exit

SCENE II.
ATHENS. QUINCE'S HOUSE.

Enter QUINCE, FLUTE, SNOUT, *and* STARVELING

QUINCE

Have you sent to Bottom's house ? is he come home yet?

STARVELING

He cannot be heard of. Out of doubt he is transported.

FLUTE

If he come not, then the play is marred: it goes not forward, doth it?

QUINCE

It is not possible: you have not a man in all
Athens able to discharge Pyramus but he.

FLUTE

No, he hath simply the best wit of any handicraft man in Athens.

QUINCE

Yea and the best person too; and he is a very paramour for a sweet voice.

FLUTE

You must say 'paragon:' a paramour is, God bless us, a thing of naught.

Enter SNUG

SNUG

Masters, the duke is coming from the temple, and there is two or three lords and ladies more married: if our sport had gone forward, we had all been made men.

FLUTE

O sweet bully Bottom! Thus hath he lost sixpence a day during his life; he could not have 'scaped sixpence a day: an the duke had not given him sixpence a day for playing Pyramus, I'll be hanged; he would have deserved it: sixpence a day in Pyramus, or nothing.

Enter BOTTOM

BOTTOM

Where are these lads? where are these hearts?

QUINCE

Bottom! O most courageous day! O most happy hour!

BOTTOM

Masters, I am to discourse wonders: but ask me not what; for if I tell you, I am no true Athenian. I will tell you every thing, right as it fell out.

QUINCE

Let us hear, sweet Bottom.

BOTTOM

Not a word of me. All that I will tell you is, that the duke hath dined. Get your apparel together, good strings to your beards, new ribbons to your pumps; meet presently at the palace; every man look o'er his part; for the short and the long is, our play is preferred. In any case, let Thisbe have clean linen; and let not him that plays the lion pair his nails, for they shall hang out for the lion's claws. And, most dear actors, eat no onions nor garlic, for we are to utter sweet breath; and I do not doubt but to hear them say, it is a sweet comedy. No more words: away! go, away!

Exeunt

ACT

V

SCENE I.
ATHENS. THE PALACE OF THESEUS.

Enter THESEUS, HIPPOLYTA, PHILOSTRATE,
Lords and Attendants

HIPPOLYTA
    'Tis strange my Theseus, that these lovers speak of.

THESEUS
    More strange than true: I never may believe
    These antique fables, nor these fairy toys.
    Lovers and madmen have such seething brains,
    Such shaping fantasies, that apprehend
    More than cool reason ever comprehends.
    The lunatic, the lover and the poet
    Are of imagination all compact:
    One sees more devils than vast hell can hold,
    That is, the madman: the lover, all as frantic,
    Sees Helen's beauty in a brow of Egypt:
    The poet's eye, in fine frenzy rolling,
    Doth glance from heaven to earth, from earth to heaven;
    And as imagination bodies forth
    The forms of things unknown, the poet's pen

Turns them to shapes and gives to airy nothing
A local habitation and a name.
Such tricks hath strong imagination,
That if it would but apprehend some joy,
It comprehends some bringer of that joy;
Or in the night, imagining some fear,
How easy is a bush supposed a bear!

HIPPOLYTA

But all the story of the night told over,
And all their minds transfigured so together,
More witnesseth than fancy's images
And grows to something of great constancy;
But, howsoever, strange and admirable.

THESEUS

Here come the lovers, full of joy and mirth.

Enter LYSANDER, DEMETRIUS, HERMIA, *and* HELENA

Joy, gentle friends! joy and fresh days of love
Accompany your hearts!

LYSANDER

More than to us
Wait in your royal walks, your board, your bed!

THESEUS

Come now; what masques, what dances shall we have,
To wear away this long age of three hours
Between our after-supper and bed-time?
Where is our usual manager of mirth?
What revels are in hand? Is there no play,
To ease the anguish of a torturing hour?
Call Philostrate.

PHILOSTRATE

Here, mighty Theseus.

THESEUS

Say, what abridgement have you for this evening?
What masque? what music? How shall we beguile
The lazy time, if not with some delight?

PHILOSTRATE

There is a brief how many sports are ripe:

• 81 •

Make choice of which your highness will see first.

Giving a paper

THESEUS

    [*Reads*] 'The battle with the Centaurs, to be sung
    By an Athenian eunuch to the harp.'
    We'll none of that: that have I told my love,
    In glory of my kinsman Hercules.
    Reads
    'The riot of the tipsy Bacchanals,
    Tearing the Thracian singer in their rage.'
    That is an old device; and it was play'd
    When I from Thebes came last a conqueror.
    Reads
    'The thrice three Muses mourning for the death
    Of Learning, late deceased in beggary.'
    That is some satire, keen and critical,
    Not sorting with a nuptial ceremony.
    Reads
    'A tedious brief scene of young Pyramus
    And his love Thisbe; very tragical mirth.'
    Merry and tragical! tedious and brief!
    That is, hot ice and wondrous strange snow.
    How shall we find the concord of this discord?

PHILOSTRATE

    A play there is, my lord, some ten words long,
    Which is as brief as I have known a play;
    But by ten words, my lord, it is too long,
    Which makes it tedious; for in all the play
    There is not one word apt, one player fitted:
    And tragical, my noble lord, it is;
    For Pyramus therein doth kill himself.
    Which, when I saw rehearsed, I must confess,
    Made mine eyes water; but more merry tears
    The passion of loud laughter never shed.

THESEUS

    What are they that do play it?

PHILOSTRATE

    Hard-handed men that work in Athens here,
    Which never labour'd in their minds till now,
    And now have toil'd their unbreathed memories
    With this same play, against your nuptial.

THESEUS

    And we will hear it.

PHILOSTRATE

    No, my noble lord;
    It is not for you: I have heard it over,
    And it is nothing, nothing in the world;
    Unless you can find sport in their intents,
    Extremely stretch'd and conn'd with cruel pain,
    To do you service.

THESEUS

    I will hear that play;
    For never anything can be amiss,
    When simpleness and duty tender it.
    Go, bring them in: and take your places, ladies.

                                 Exit PHILOSTRATE

HIPPOLYTA

    I love not to see wretchedness o'er charged
    And duty in his service perishing.

THESEUS

    Why, gentle sweet, you shall see no such thing.

HIPPOLYTA

    He says they can do nothing in this kind.

THESEUS

    The kinder we, to give them thanks for nothing.
    Our sport shall be to take what they mistake:
    And what poor duty cannot do, noble respect
    Takes it in might, not merit.
    Where I have come, great clerks have purposed
    To greet me with premeditated welcomes;
    Where I have seen them shiver and look pale,
    Make periods in the midst of sentences,

Throttle their practised accent in their fears
And in conclusion dumbly have broke off,
Not paying me a welcome. Trust me, sweet,
Out of this silence yet I pick'd a welcome;
And in the modesty of fearful duty
I read as much as from the rattling tongue
Of saucy and audacious eloquence.
Love, therefore, and tongue-tied simplicity
In least speak most, to my capacity.

Re-enter PHILOSTRATE

PHILOSTRATE

So please your grace, the Prologue is address'd.

THESEUS

Let him approach.

Flourish of trumpets
Enter QUINCE *for the Prologue*

PROLOGUE

If we offend, it is with our good will.
That you should think, we come not to offend,
But with good will. To show our simple skill,
That is the true beginning of our end.
Consider then we come but in despite.
We do not come as minding to contest you,
Our true intent is. All for your delight
We are not here. That you should here repent you,
The actors are at hand and by their show
You shall know all that you are like to know.

THESEUS

This fellow doth not stand upon points.

LYSANDER

He hath rid his prologue like a rough colt; he knows not the
stop. A good moral, my lord: it is not enough to speak, but to
speak true.

HIPPOLYTA

Indeed he hath playcd on his prologue like a child on a recorder;
a sound, but not in government.

THESEUS

> His speech, was like a tangled chain; nothing impaired, but all
> disordered. Who is next?

Enter PYRAMUS *and* THISBE, WALL,
MOONSHINE, *and* LION

PROLOGUE

> Gentles, perchance you wonder at this show;
> But wonder on, till truth make all things plain.
> This man is Pyramus, if you would know;
> This beauteous lady Thisbe is certain.
> This man, with lime and rough-cast, doth present
> Wall, that vile Wall which did these lovers sunder;
> And through Wall's chink, poor souls, they are content
> To whisper. At the which let no man wonder.
> This man, with lanthorn, dog, and bush of thorn,
> Presenteth Moonshine; for, if you will know,
> By moonshine did these lovers think no scorn
> To meet at Ninus' tomb, there, there to woo.
> This grisly beast, which Lion hight by name,
> The trusty Thisbe, coming first by night,
> Did scare away, or rather did affright;
> And, as she fled, her mantle she did fall,
> Which Lion vile with bloody mouth did stain.
> Anon comes Pyramus, sweet youth and tall,
> And finds his trusty Thisbe's mantle slain:
> Whereat, with blade, with bloody blameful blade,
> He bravely broach'd is boiling bloody breast;
> And Thisbe, tarrying in mulberry shade,
> His dagger drew, and died. For all the rest,
> Let Lion, Moonshine, Wall, and lovers twain
> At large discourse, while here they do remain.

Exeunt PROLOGUE, THISBE,
LION, *and* MOONSHINE

THESEUS

> I wonder if the lion be to speak.

DEMETRIUS

> No wonder, my lord: one lion may, when many asses do.

• 85 •

SNOUT *as Wall*

    In this same interlude it doth befall
    That I, one Snout by name, present a wall;
    And such a wall, as I would have you think,
    That had in it a crannied hole or chink,
    Through which the lovers, Pyramus and Thisbe,
    Did whisper often very secretly.
    This loam, this rough-cast and this stone doth show
    That I am that same wall; the truth is so:
    And this the cranny is, right and sinister,
    Through which the fearful lovers are to whisper.

THESEUS

    Would you desire lime and hair to speak better?

DEMETRIUS

    It is the wittiest partition that ever I heard discourse, my lord.

                  Enter BOTTOM *as* PYRAMUS

THESEUS

    Pyramus draws near the wall: silence!

BOTTOM *as Pyramus*

    O grim-look'd night! O night with hue so black!
    O night, which ever art when day is not!
    O night, O night! alack, alack, alack,
    I fear my Thisbe's promise is forgot!
    And thou, O wall, O sweet, O lovely wall,
    That stand'st between her father's ground and mine!
    Thou wall, O wall, O sweet and lovely wall,
    Show me thy chink, to blink through with mine eyne!

                  Wall holds up his fingers

    Thanks, courteous wall: Jove shield thee well for this!
    But what see I? No Thisbe do I see.
    O wicked wall, through whom I see no bliss!
    Cursed be thy stones for thus deceiving me!

THESEUS

    The wall, methinks, being sensible, should curse again.

BOTTOM *as Pyramus*

    No, in truth, sir, he should not. 'Deceiving me' is Thisbe's cue:

she is to enter now, and I am to spy her through the wall. You shall see, it will fall pat as I told you. Yonder she comes.

Enter FLUTE *as* THISBE

FLUTE *as Thisbe*

O wall, full often hast thou heard my moans,
For parting my fair Pyramus and me!
My cherry lips have often kiss'd thy stones,
Thy stones with lime and hair knit up in thee.

BOTTOM *as Pyramus*

I see a voice: now will I to the chink,
To spy an I can hear my Thisbe's face. Thisbe!

FLUTE *as Thisbe*

My love thou art, my love I think.

BOTTOM *as Pyramus*

Think what thou wilt, I am thy lover's grace;
And, like Limander, am I trusty still.

FLUTE *as Thisbe*

And I like Helen, till the Fates me kill.

BOTTOM *as Pyramus*

Not Shafalus to Procrus was so true.

FLUTE *as Thisbe*

As Shafalus to Procrus, I to you.

BOTTOM *as Pyramus*

O kiss me through the hole of this vile wall!

FLUTE *as Thisbe*

I kiss the wall's hole, not your lips at all.

BOTTOM *as Pyramus*

Wilt thou at Ninny's tomb meet me straightway?

FLUTE *as Thisbe*

'Tide life, 'tide death, I come without delay.

Exeunt PYRAMUS *and* THISBE

SNOUT *as Wall*

Thus have I, Wall, my part dischargèd so;
And, being done, thus Wall away doth go.

Exit

THESEUS

Now is the mural down between the two neighbours.

DEMETRIUS

No remedy, my lord, when walls are so wilful to hear without warning.

HIPPOLYTA

This is the silliest stuff that ever I heard.

THESEUS

The best in this kind are but shadows; and the worst are no worse, if imagination amend them.

HIPPOLYTA

It must be your imagination then, and not theirs.

THESEUS

If we imagine no worse of them than they of themselves, they may pass for excellent men. Here come two noble beasts in, a man and a lion.

Enter LION *and* MOONSHINE

SNUG *as Lion*

You, ladies, you, whose gentle hearts do fear
The smallest monstrous mouse that creeps on floor,
May now perchance both quake and tremble here,
When lion rough in wildest rage doth roar.
Then know that I, one Snug the joiner, am
A lion-fell, nor else no lion's dam;
For, if I should as lion come in strife
Into this place, 'twere pity on my life.

THESEUS

A very gentle beast, of a good conscience.

DEMETRIUS

The very best at a beast, my lord, that e'er I saw.

LYSANDER

This lion is a very fox for his valour.

THESEUS

True; and a goose for his discretion.

DEMETRIUS

Not so, my lord; for his valour cannot carry his discretion; and the fox carries the goose.

THESEUS

His discretion, I am sure, cannot carry his valour; for the goose carries not the fox. It is well: leave it to his discretion, and let us listen to the moon.

STARVELING *as Moonshine*

This lanthorn doth the hornèd moon present;—

DEMETRIUS

He should have worn the horns on his head.

THESEUS

He is no crescent, and his horns are invisible within the circumference.

STARVELING *as Moonshine*

This lanthorn doth the horned moon present;
Myself the man i' the moon do seem to be.

THESEUS

This is the greatest error of all the rest: the man should be put into the lanthorn. How is it else the man i' the moon?

DEMETRIUS

He dares not come there for the candle; for, you see, it is already in snuff.

HIPPOLYTA

I am aweary of this moon: would he would change!

THESEUS

It appears, by his small light of discretion, that he is in the wane; but yet, in courtesy, in all reason, we must stay the time.

LYSANDER

Proceed, Moon.

STARVELING *as Moonshine*

All that I have to say, is, to tell you that the lanthorn is the moon; I, the man in the moon; this thorn-bush, my thorn-bush; and this dog, my dog.

DEMETRIUS

Why, all these should be in the lanthorn; for all these are in the moon. But, silence! here comes Thisbe.

Enter FLUTE *as* THISBE

FLUTE *as Thisbe*

This is old Ninny's tomb. Where is my love?

SNUG *as Lion*

[*Roaring*] Oh—

Thisbe runs off

DEMETRIUS

Well roared, Lion.

THESEUS

Well run, Thisbe.

HIPPOLYTA

Well shone, Moon. Truly, the moon shines with a good grace.

The LION *shakes* THISBE'S *mantle, and Exit*

THESEUS

Well moused, Lion.

LYSANDER

And so the lion vanished.

DEMETRIUS

And then came Pyramus.

Enter PYRAMUS

BOTTOM *as Pyramus*

Sweet Moon, I thank thee for thy sunny beams;
I thank thee, Moon, for shining now so bright;
For, by thy gracious, golden, glittering gleams,
I trust to take of truest Thisbe sight.
　　　　　　　But stay, O spite!
　　　　　　　But mark, poor knight,
　　　　What dreadful dole is here!
　　　　　　　Eyes, do you see?
　　　　　　　How can it be?
　　　　O dainty duck! O dear!
　　　　　　　Thy mantle good,
　　　　What, stain'd with blood!
　　　　Approach, ye Furies fell!
　　　　　　　O Fates, come, come,
　　　　　　　Cut thread and thrum;
　　　　Quail, crush, conclude, and quell!

THESEUS

This passion, and the death of a dear friend, would go near to make a man look sad.

HIPPOLYTA

Beshrew my heart, but I pity the man.

BOTTOM *as Pyramus*

O wherefore, Nature, didst thou lions frame?
Since lion vile hath here deflower'd my dear:
Which is—no, no—which was the fairest dame
That lived, that loved, that liked, that look'd with cheer.

Come, tears, confound;
Out, sword, and wound
The pap of Pyramus;
Ay, that left pap,
Where heart doth hop:

Stabs himself

Thus die I, thus, thus, thus.
Now am I dead,
Now am I fled;
My soul is in the sky:
Tongue, lose thy light;
Moon take thy flight:

Exit MOONSHINE

Now die, die, die, die, die.

Dies

DEMETRIUS

No die, but an ace, for him; for he is but one.

LYSANDER

Less than an ace, man; for he is dead; he is nothing.

THESEUS

With the help of a surgeon he might yet recover, and prove an
ass.

HIPPOLYTA

How chance Moonshine is gone before Thisbe comes back and
finds her lover?

THESEUS

She will find him by starlight. Here she comes; and her passion
ends the play.

Re-enter THISBE

HIPPOLYTA

Methinks she should not use a long one for such a Pyramus: I
hope she will be brief.

DEMETRIUS

A mote will turn the balance, which Pyramus, which Thisbe, is the
better; he for a man, God warrant us; she for a woman, God bless us.

LYSANDER

She hath spied him already with those sweet eyes.

DEMETRIUS

And thus she means, videlicet:—

FLUTE *as Thisbe*

Asleep, my love?
What, dead, my dove?
O Pyramus, arise!
Speak, speak. Quite dumb?
Dead, dead? A tomb
Must cover thy sweet eyes.
These My lips,
This cherry nose,
These yellow cowslip cheeks,
Are gone, are gone:
Lovers, make moan:
His eyes were green as leeks.
O Sisters Three,
Come, come to me,
With hands as pale as milk;
Lay them in gore,
Since you have shore
With shears his thread of silk.
Tongue, not a word:
Come, trusty sword;
Come, blade, my breast imbrue:

Stabs herself

And, farewell, friends;
Thus Thisbe ends:
Adieu, adieu, adieu.

Dies

THESEUS

Moonshine and Lion are left to bury the dead.

DEMETRIUS

Ay, and Wall too.

BOTTOM

[*Starting up*] No assure you; the wall is down that parted their fathers. Will it please you to see the epilogue, or to hear a Bergomask dance between two of our company?

THESEUS

No epilogue, I pray you; for your play needs no excuse. Never excuse; for when the players are all dead, there needs none to be blamed. Marry, if he that writ it had played Pyramus and hanged himself in Thisbe's garter, it would have been a fine tragedy: and so it is, truly; and very notably discharged. But come, your Bergomask: let your epilogue alone.

A dance

The iron tongue of midnight hath told twelve:
Lovers, to bed; 'tis almost fairy time.
I fear we shall out-sleep the coming morn
As much as we this night have overwatch'd.
This palpable-gross play hath well beguiled
The heavy gait of night. Sweet friends, to bed.
A fortnight hold we this solemnity,
In nightly revels and new jollity.

Exeunt

Enter PUCK

PUCK

Now the hungry lion roars,
And the wolf behowls the moon;
Whilst the heavy ploughman snores,
All with weary task fordone.
Now the wasted brands do glow,
Whilst the screech-owl, screeching loud,
Puts the wretch that lies in woe
In remembrance of a shroud.
Now it is the time of night
That the graves all gaping wide,

Every one lets forth his sprite,
In the church-way paths to glide:
And we fairies, that do run
By the triple Hecate's team,
From the presence of the sun,
Following darkness like a dream,
Now are frolic: not a mouse
Shall disturb this hallow'd house:
I am sent with broom before,
To sweep the dust behind the door.

Enter OBERON *and* TITANIA *with their train*

OBERON

Through the house give gathering light,
By the dead and drowsy fire:
Every elf and fairy sprite
Hop as light as bird from brier;
And this ditty, after me,
Sing, and dance it trippingly.

TITANIA

First, rehearse your song by rote
To each word a warbling note:
Hand in hand, with fairy grace,
Will we sing, and bless this place.

Song and dance

OBERON

Now, until the break of day,
Through this house each fairy stray.
To the best bride-bed will we,
Which by us shall blessed be;
And the issue there create
Ever shall be fortunate.
So shall all the couples three
Ever true in loving be;
And the blots of Nature's hand
Shall not in their issue stand;
Never mole, hare lip, nor scar,
Nor mark prodigious, such as are

Despisèd in nativity,
Shall upon their children be.
With this field-dew consecrate,
Every fairy take his gait;
And each several chamber bless,
Through this palace, with sweet peace;
And the owner of it blest
Ever shall in safety rest.
Trip away; make no stay;
Meet me all by break of day.

Exeunt OBERON, TITANIA, *and train*

PUCK

[*To the audience*]
If we shadows have offended,
Think but this, and all is mended,
That you have but slumber'd here
While these visions did appear.
And this weak and idle theme,
No more yielding but a dream,
Gentles, do not reprehend:
if you pardon, we will mend:
And, as I am an honest Puck,
If we have unearned luck
Now to 'scape the serpent's tongue,
We will make amends ere long;
Else the Puck a liar call;
So, good night unto you all.
Give me your hands, if we be friends,
And Robin shall restore amends.

The Merchant of Venice

"But love is blind, and lovers cannot see
The pretty follies that themselves commit"

Characters of the Play

THE DUKE OF VENICE
THE PRINCE OF MOROCCO ⎫ suitors to Portia
THE PRINCE OF ARRAGON ⎭
ANTONIO, a merchant of Venice
BASSANIO, his friend
SALANIO ⎫
SALARINO ⎬ friends to Antonio and Bassanio
GRATIANO ⎭
LORENZO, in love with Jessica
SHYLOCK, a rich Jew
TUBAL, a Jew, his friend
LAUNCELOT GOBBO, a clown, servant to Shylock
OLD GOBBO, father to Launcelot
LEONARDO, servant to Bassanio
BALTHASAR ⎫ servants to Portia
STEPHANO ⎭
PORTIA, a rich heiress
NERISSA, her waiting-maid
JESSICA, daughter to Shylock
Magnificoes of Venice, Officers of the Court of Justice,
Gaoler, Servants to Portia, and other Attendants.

SCENE:
Partly at Venice, and partly at Belmont,
the seat of PORTIA, on the Continent

ACT

I

SCENE I.
VENICE. A STREET.

Enter ANTONIO, SALARINO, *and* SALANIO

ANTONIO

    In sooth, I know not why I am so sad;
    It wearies me; you say it wearies you;
    But how I caught it, found it, or came by it,
    What stuff 'tis made of, whereof it is born,
    I am to learn;
    And such a want-wit sadness makes of me
    That I have much ado to know myself.

SALARINO

    Your mind is tossing on the ocean;
    There where your argosies, with portly sail—
    Like signiors and rich burghers on the flood,
    Or as it were the pageants of the sea—
    Do overpeer the petty traffickers,
    That curtsy to them, do them reverence,
    As they fly by them with their woven wings.

SALANIO

    Believe me, sir, had I such venture forth,

The better part of my affections would
Be with my hopes abroad. I should be still
Plucking the grass to know where sits the wind,
Peering in maps for ports, and piers, and roads;
And every object that might make me fear
Misfortune to my ventures, out of doubt
Would make me sad.

SALARINO

My wind, cooling my broth
Would blow me to an ague, when I thought
What harm a wind too great might do at sea.
I should not see the sandy hour-glass run
But I should think of shallows and of flats,
And see my wealthy Andrew dock'd in sand,
Vailing her high top lower than her ribs
To kiss her burial. Should I go to church
And see the holy edifice of stone,
And not bethink me straight of dangerous rocks,
Which, touching but my gentle vessel's side,
Would scatter all her spices on the stream,
Enrobe the roaring waters with my silks,
And, in a word, but even now worth this,
And now worth nothing? Shall I have the thought
To think on this, and shall I lack the thought
That such a thing bechanc'd would make me sad?
But tell not me; I know Antonio
Is sad to think upon his merchandise.

ANTONIO

Believe me, no; I thank my fortune for it,
My ventures are not in one bottom trusted,
Nor to one place; nor is my whole estate
Upon the fortune of this present year;
Therefore my merchandise makes me not sad.

SALARINO

Why, then you are in love.

ANTONIO

Fie, fie!

SALARINO

    Not in love neither? Then let us say you are sad
    Because you are not merry; and 'twere as easy
    For you to laugh and leap and say you are merry,
    Because you are not sad. Now, by two-headed Janus,
    Nature hath fram'd strange fellows in her time:
    Some that will evermore peep through their eyes,
    And laugh like parrots at a bag-piper;
    And other of such vinegar aspect
    That they'll not show their teeth in way of smile
    Though Nestor swear the jest be laughable.

             Enter BASSANIO, LORENZO, *and* GRATIANO

SALANIO

    Here comes Bassanio, your most noble kinsman,
    Gratiano, and Lorenzo. Fare ye well;
    We leave you now with better company.

SALARINO

    I would have stay'd till I had made you merry,
    If worthier friends had not prevented me.

ANTONIO

    Your worth is very dear in my regard.
    I take it your own business calls on you,
    And you embrace th' occasion to depart.

SALARINO

    Good morrow, my good lords.

BASSANIO

    Good signiors both, when shall we laugh? Say when.
    You grow exceeding strange; must it be so?

SALARINO

    We'll make our leisures to attend on yours.

             Exeunt SALARINO *and* SALANIO

LORENZO

    My Lord Bassanio, since you have found Antonio,
    We two will leave you; but at dinner-time,
    I pray you, have in mind where we must meet.

BASSANIO

    I will not fail you.

GRATIANO

    You look not well, Signior Antonio;
    You have too much respect upon the world;
    They lose it that do buy it with much care.
    Believe me, you are marvellously chang'd.

ANTONIO

    I hold the world but as the world, Gratiano;
    A stage, where every man must play a part,
    And mine a sad one.

GRATIANO

    Let me play the fool;
    With mirth and laughter let old wrinkles come;
    And let my liver rather heat with wine
    Than my heart cool with mortifying groans.
    Why should a man whose blood is warm within
    Sit like his grandsire cut in alabaster,
    Sleep when he wakes, and creep into the jaundice
    By being peevish? I tell thee what, Antonio—
    I love thee, and 'tis my love that speaks—
    There are a sort of men whose visages
    Do cream and mantle like a standing pond,
    And do a wilful stillness entertain,
    With purpose to be dress'd in an opinion
    Of wisdom, gravity, profound conceit;
    As who should say 'I am Sir Oracle,
    And when I ope my lips let no dog bark.'
    O my Antonio, I do know of these
    That therefore only are reputed wise
    For saying nothing; when, I am very sure,
    If they should speak, would almost damn those ears
    Which, hearing them, would call their brothers fools.
    I'll tell thee more of this another time.
    But fish not with this melancholy bait,
    For this fool gudgeon, this opinion.
    Come, good Lorenzo. Fare ye well awhile;
    I'll end my exhortation after dinner.

LORENZO

    Well, we will leave you then till dinner-time.
    I must be one of these same dumb wise men,
    For Gratiano never lets me speak.

GRATIANO

    Well, keep me company but two years moe,
    Thou shalt not know the sound of thine own tongue.

ANTONIO

    Fare you well; I'll grow a talker for this gear.

GRATIANO

    Thanks, i' faith, for silence is only commendable
    In a neat's tongue dried, and a maid not vendible.

                            Exeunt GRATIANO *and* LORENZO

ANTONIO

    Is that anything now?

BASSANIO

    Gratiano speaks an infinite deal of nothing, more than any man
    in all Venice. His reasons are as two grains of wheat hid in, two
    bushels of chaff: you shall seek all day ere you find them, and
    when you have them they are not worth the search.

ANTONIO

    Well; tell me now what lady is the same
    To whom you swore a secret pilgrimage,
    That you to-day promis'd to tell me of?

BASSANIO

    'Tis not unknown to you, Antonio,
    How much I have disabled mine estate
    By something showing a more swelling port
    Than my faint means would grant continuance;
    Nor do I now make moan to be abridg'd
    From such a noble rate; but my chief care
    Is to come fairly off from the great debts
    Wherein my time, something too prodigal,
    Hath left me gag'd. To you, Antonio,
    I owe the most, in money and in love;
    And from your love I have a warranty

To unburden all my plots and purposes
How to get clear of all the debts I owe.

ANTONIO

I pray you, good Bassanio, let me know it;
And if it stand, as you yourself still do,
Within the eye of honour, be assur'd
My purse, my person, my extremest means,
Lie all unlock'd to your occasions.

BASSANIO

In my school-days, when I had lost one shaft,
I shot his fellow of the self-same flight
The self-same way, with more advised watch,
To find the other forth; and by adventuring both
I oft found both. I urge this childhood proof,
Because what follows is pure innocence.
I owe you much; and, like a wilful youth,
That which I owe is lost; but if you please
To shoot another arrow that self way
Which you did shoot the first, I do not doubt,
As I will watch the aim, or to find both,
Or bring your latter hazard back again
And thankfully rest debtor for the first.

ANTONIO

You know me well, and herein spend but time
To wind about my love with circumstance;
And out of doubt you do me now more wrong
In making question of my uttermost
Than if you had made waste of all I have.
Then do but say to me what I should do
That in your knowledge may by me be done,
And I am prest unto it; therefore, speak.

BASSANIO

In Belmont is a lady richly left,
And she is fair and, fairer than that word,
Of wondrous virtues. Sometimes from her eyes
I did receive fair speechless messages:
Her name is Portia—nothing undervalu'd

To Cato's daughter, Brutus' Portia:
Nor is the wide world ignorant of her worth,
For the four winds blow in from every coast
Renowned suitors, and her sunny locks
Hang on her temples like a golden fleece;
Which makes her seat of Belmont Colchos' strond,
And many Jasons come in quest of her.
O my Antonio! had I but the means
To hold a rival place with one of them,
I have a mind presages me such thrift
That I should questionless be fortunate.

ANTONIO
Thou know'st that all my fortunes are at sea;
Neither have I money nor commodity
To raise a present sum; therefore go forth,
Try what my credit can in Venice do;
That shall be rack'd, even to the uttermost,
To furnish thee to Belmont to fair Portia.
Go presently inquire, and so will I,
Where money is; and I no question make
To have it of my trust or for my sake.

Exeunt

SCENE II.
BELMONT. A ROOM IN PORTIA'S HOUSE.

Enter PORTIA *and* NERISSA

PORTIA
By my troth, Nerissa, my little body is aweary of this great world.

NERISSA
You would be, sweet madam, if your miseries were in the same
abundance as your good fortunes are; and yet, for aught I see,
they are as sick that surfeit with too much as they that starve with
nothing. It is no mean happiness, therefore, to be seated in the
mean: superfluity come sooner by white hairs, but competency
lives longer.

PORTIA

Good sentences, and well pronounced.

NERISSA

They would be better, if well followed.

PORTIA

If to do were as easy as to know what were good to do, chapels
had been churches, and poor men's cottages princes' palaces. It
is a good divine that follows his own instructions; I can easier
teach twenty what were good to be done than to be one of the
twenty to follow mine own teaching. The brain may devise laws
for the blood, but a hot temper leaps o'er a cold decree; such
a hare is madness the youth, to skip o'er the meshes of good
counsel the cripple. But this reasoning is not in the fashion to
choose me a husband. O me, the word 'choose'! I may neither
choose who I would nor refuse who I dislike; so is the will of a
living daughter curb'd by the will of a dead father. Is it not hard,
Nerissa, that I cannot choose one, nor refuse none?

NERISSA

Your father was ever virtuous, and holy men at their death have
good inspirations; therefore the lott'ry that he hath devised in
these three chests, of gold, silver, and lead, whereof who chooses
his meaning chooses you, will no doubt never be chosen by any
rightly but one who you shall rightly love. But what warmth is
there in your affection towards any of these princely suitors that
are already come?

PORTIA

I pray thee over-name them; and as thou namest them, I will
describe them; and according to my description, level at my
affection.

NERISSA

First, there is the Neapolitan prince.

PORTIA

Ay, that's a colt indeed, for he doth nothing but talk of his horse;
and he makes it a great appropriation to his own good parts that
he can shoe him himself; I am much afeard my lady his mother
play'd false with a smith.

NERISSA

Then is there the County Palatine.

PORTIA

He doth nothing but frown, as who should say 'An you will not
have me, choose.' He hears merry tales and smiles not: I fear he
will prove the weeping philosopher when he grows old, being so
full of unmannerly sadness in his youth. I had rather be married
to a death's-head with a bone in his mouth than to either of
these. God defend me from these two!

NERISSA

How say you by the French lord, Monsieur Le Bon?

PORTIA

God made him, and therefore let him pass for a man. In truth,
I know it is a sin to be a mocker, but he! why, he hath a horse
better than the Neapolitan's, a better bad habit of frowning than
the Count Palatine; he is every man in no man. If a throstle sing
he falls straight a-capering; he will fence with his own shadow;
if I should marry him, I should marry twenty husbands. If he
would despise me, I would forgive him; for if he love me to
madness, I shall never requite him.

NERISSA

What say you, then, to Falconbridge, the young baron of
England?

PORTIA

You know I say nothing to him, for he understands not me, nor
I him: he hath neither Latin, French, nor Italian, and you will
come into the court and swear that I have a poor pennyworth
in the English. He is a proper man's picture; but alas, who can
converse with a dumb-show? How oddly he is suited! I think he
bought his doublet in Italy, his round hose in France, his bonnet
in Germany, and his behaviour everywhere.

NERISSA

What think you of the Scottish lord, his neighbour?

PORTIA

That he hath a neighbourly charity in him, for he borrowed
a box of the ear of the Englishman, and swore he would pay

him again when he was able; I think the Frenchman became his surety, and sealed under for another.

NERISSA

How like you the young German, the Duke of Saxony's nephew?

PORTIA

Very vilely in the morning when he is sober, and most vilely in the afternoon when he is drunk: when he is best, he is a little worse than a man, and when he is worst, he is little better than a beast. An the worst fall that ever fell, I hope I shall make shift to go without him.

NERISSA

If he should offer to choose, and choose the right casket, you should refuse to perform your father's will, if you should refuse to accept him.

PORTIA

Therefore, for fear of the worst, I pray thee set a deep glass of Rhenish wine on the contrary casket; for if the devil be within and that temptation without, I know he will choose it. I will do anything, Nerissa, ere I will be married to a sponge.

NERISSA

You need not fear, lady, the having any of these lords; they have acquainted me with their determinations, which is indeed to return to their home, and to trouble you with no more suit, unless you may be won by some other sort than your father's imposition, depending on the caskets.

PORTIA

If I live to be as old as Sibylla, I will die as chaste as Diana, unless I be obtained by the manner of my father's will. I am glad this parcel of wooers are so reasonable; for there is not one among them but I dote on his very absence, and I pray God grant them a fair departure.

NERISSA

Do you not remember, lady, in your father's time, a Venetian, a scholar and a soldier, that came hither in company of the Marquis of Montferrat?

PORTIA

Yes, yes, it was Bassanio; as I think, so was he called.

NERISSA

True, madam; he, of all the men that ever my foolish eyes looked upon, was the best deserving a fair lady.

PORTIA

I remember him well, and I remember him worthy of thy praise.

Enter a SERVANT

How now! what news?

SERVANT

The four strangers seek for you, madam, to take their leave; and there is a forerunner come from a fifth, the Prince of Morocco, who brings word the Prince his master will be here to-night.

PORTIA

If I could bid the fifth welcome with so good heart as I can bid the other four farewell, I should be glad of his approach; if he have the condition of a saint and the complexion of a devil, I had rather he should shrive me than wive me. Come, Nerissa. Sirrah, go before. Whiles we shut the gate upon one wooer, another knocks at the door.

Exeunt

SCENE III.
VENICE. A PUBLIC PLACE.

Enter BASSANIO *and* SHYLOCK

SHYLOCK

Three thousand ducats; well?

BASSANIO

Ay, sir, for three months.

SHYLOCK

For three months; well?

BASSANIO

For the which, as I told you, Antonio shall be bound.

SHYLOCK

Antonio shall become bound; well?

BASSANIO

May you stead me? Will you pleasure me? Shall I know your answer?

SHYLOCK

Three thousand ducats, for three months, and Antonio bound.

BASSANIO

Your answer to that.

SHYLOCK

Antonio is a good man.

BASSANIO

Have you heard any imputation to the contrary?

SHYLOCK

Ho, no, no, no, no: my meaning in saying he is a good man is to have you understand me that he is sufficient; yet his means are in supposition: he hath an argosy bound to Tripolis, another to the Indies; I understand, moreover, upon the Rialto, he hath a third at Mexico, a fourth for England, and other ventures he hath, squandered abroad. But ships are but boards, sailors but men; there be land-rats and water-rats, land-thieves and water-thieves—I mean pirates; and then there is the peril of waters, winds, and rocks. The man is, notwithstanding, sufficient. Three thousand ducats— I think I may take his bond.

BASSANIO

Be assured you may.

SHYLOCK

I will be assured I may; and, that I may be assured, I will bethink me. May I speak with Antonio?

BASSANIO

If it please you to dine with us.

SHYLOCK

Yes, to smell pork; to eat of the habitation which your prophet, the Nazarite, conjured the devil into. I will buy with you, sell with you, talk with you, walk with you, and so following; but I will not eat with you, drink with you, nor pray with you. What news on the Rialto? Who is he comes here?

Enter ANTONIO

BASSANIO

This is Signior Antonio.

SHYLOCK

[*Aside*] How like a fawning publican he looks!

I hate him for he is a Christian;
But more for that in low simplicity
He lends out money gratis, and brings down
The rate of usance here with us in Venice.
If I can catch him once upon the hip,
I will feed fat the ancient grudge I bear him.
He hates our sacred nation; and he rails,
Even there where merchants most do congregate,
On me, my bargains, and my well-won thrift,
Which he calls interest. Cursed be my tribe
If I forgive him!

BASSANIO
Shylock, do you hear?

SHYLOCK
I am debating of my present store,
And, by the near guess of my memory,
I cannot instantly raise up the gross
Of full three thousand ducats. What of that?
Tubal, a wealthy Hebrew of my tribe,
Will furnish me. But soft! how many months
Do you desire? [To ANTONIO] Rest you fair, good signior;
Your worship was the last man in our mouths.

ANTONIO
Shylock, albeit I neither lend nor borrow
By taking nor by giving of excess,
Yet, to supply the ripe wants of my friend,
I'll break a custom. [To BASSANIO] Is he yet possess'd
How much ye would?

SHYLOCK
Ay, ay, three thousand ducats.

ANTONIO
And for three months.

SHYLOCK
I had forgot; three months; you told me so.
Well then, your bond; and, let me see. But hear you,
Methought you said you neither lend nor borrow
Upon advantage.

ANTONIO

    I do never use it.

SHYLOCK

    When Jacob graz'd his uncle Laban's sheep—
    This Jacob from our holy Abram was,
    As his wise mother wrought in his behalf,
    The third possessor; ay, he was the third—

ANTONIO

    And what of him? Did he take interest?

SHYLOCK

    No, not take interest; not, as you would say,
    Directly interest; mark what Jacob did.
    When Laban and himself were compromis'd
    That all the eanlings which were streak'd and pied
    Should fall as Jacob's hire, the ewes, being rank,
    In end of autumn turned to the rams;
    And when the work of generation was
    Between these woolly breeders in the act,
    The skilful shepherd pill'd me certain wands,
    And, in the doing of the deed of kind,
    He stuck them up before the fulsome ewes,
    Who, then conceiving, did in eaning time
    Fall parti-colour'd lambs, and those were Jacob's.
    This was a way to thrive, and he was blest;
    And thrift is blessing, if men steal it not.

ANTONIO

    This was a venture, sir, that Jacob serv'd for;
    A thing not in his power to bring to pass,
    But sway'd and fashion'd by the hand of heaven.
    Was this inserted to make interest good?
    Or is your gold and silver ewes and rams?

SHYLOCK

    I cannot tell; I make it breed as fast.
    But note me, signior.

ANTONIO

    Mark you this, Bassanio,
    The devil can cite Scripture for his purpose.

An evil soul producing holy witness
Is like a villain with a smiling cheek,
A goodly apple rotten at the heart.
O, what a goodly outside falsehood hath!

SHYLOCK

Three thousand ducats; 'tis a good round sum.
Three months from twelve; then let me see the rate.

ANTONIO

Well, Shylock, shall we be beholding to you?

SHYLOCK

Signior Antonio, many a time and oft
In the Rialto you have rated me
About my moneys and my usances;
Still have I borne it with a patient shrug,
For suff'rance is the badge of all our tribe;
You call me misbeliever, cut-throat dog,
And spit upon my Jewish gaberdine,
And all for use of that which is mine own.
Well then, it now appears you need my help;
Go to, then; you come to me, and you say
'Shylock, we would have moneys.' You say so:
You that did void your rheum upon my beard,
And foot me as you spurn a stranger cur
Over your threshold; moneys is your suit.
What should I say to you? Should I not say
'Hath a dog money? Is it possible
A cur can lend three thousand ducats?' Or
Shall I bend low and, in a bondman's key,
With bated breath and whisp'ring humbleness,
Say this:—
'Fair sir, you spit on me on Wednesday last;
You spurn'd me such a day; another time
You call'd me dog; and for these courtesies
I'll lend you thus much moneys?'

ANTONIO

I am as like to call thee so again,
To spit on thee again, to spurn thee too.

If thou wilt lend this money, lend it not
As to thy friends—for when did friendship take
A breed for barren metal of his friend?—
But lend it rather to thine enemy;
Who if he break thou mayst with better face
Exact the penalty.

SHYLOCK

Why, look you, how you storm!
I would be friends with you, and have your love,
Forget the shames that you have stain'd me with,
Supply your present wants, and take no doit
Of usance for my moneys, and you'll not hear me:
This is kind I offer.

BASSANIO

This were kindness.

SHYLOCK

This kindness will I show.
Go with me to a notary, seal me there
Your single bond; and, in a merry sport,
If you repay me not on such a day,
In such a place, such sum or sums as are
Express'd in the condition, let the forfeit
Be nominated for an equal pound
Of your fair flesh, to be cut off and taken
In what part of your body pleaseth me.

ANTONIO

Content, in faith; I'll seal to such a bond,
And say there is much kindness in the Jew.

BASSANIO

You shall not seal to such a bond for me;
I'll rather dwell in my necessity.

ANTONIO

Why, fear not, man; I will not forfeit it;
Within these two months, that's a month before
This bond expires, I do expect return
Of thrice three times the value of this bond.

SHYLOCK
> O father Abram, what these Christians are,
> Whose own hard dealings teaches them suspect
> The thoughts of others. Pray you, tell me this;
> If he should break his day, what should I gain
> By the exaction of the forfeiture?
> A pound of man's flesh, taken from a man,
> Is not so estimable, profitable neither,
> As flesh of muttons, beefs, or goats. I say,
> To buy his favour, I extend this friendship;
> If he will take it, so; if not, adieu;
> And, for my love, I pray you wrong me not.

ANTONIO
> Yes, Shylock, I will seal unto this bond.

SHYLOCK
> Then meet me forthwith at the notary's;
> Give him direction for this merry bond,
> And I will go and purse the ducats straight,
> See to my house, left in the fearful guard
> Of an unthrifty knave, and presently
> I'll be with you.

ANTONIO
> Hie thee, gentle Jew.

Exit SHYLOCK

> This Hebrew will turn Christian: he grows kind.

BASSANIO
> I like not fair terms and a villain's mind.

ANTONIO
> Come on; in this there can be no dismay;
> My ships come home a month before the day.

Exeunt

ACT

II

SCENE I.
BELMONT. A ROOM IN
PORTIA'S HOUSE.

Flourish of cornets. Enter the PRINCE OF MOROCCO, *and
his Followers;* PORTIA, NERISSA, *and Others of her train*

PRINCE OF MOROCCO
    Mislike me not for my complexion,
    The shadow'd livery of the burnish'd sun,
    To whom I am a neighbour, and near bred.
    Bring me the fairest creature northward born,
    Where Phoebus' fire scarce thaws the icicles,
    And let us make incision for your love
    To prove whose blood is reddest, his or mine.
    I tell thee, lady, this aspect of mine
    Hath fear'd the valiant; by my love, I swear
    The best-regarded virgins of our clime
    Have lov'd it too. I would not change this hue,
    Except to steal your thoughts, my gentle queen.
PORTIA
    In terms of choice I am not solely led
    By nice direction of a maiden's eyes;

Besides, the lottery of my destiny
Bars me the right of voluntary choosing;
But, if my father had not scanted me
And hedg'd me by his wit, to yield myself
His wife who wins me by that means I told you,
Yourself, renowned Prince, then stood as fair
As any comer I have look'd on yet
For my affection.

PRINCE OF MOROCCO
Even for that I thank you:
Therefore, I pray you, lead me to the caskets
To try my fortune. By this scimitar,
That slew the Sophy and a Persian prince,
That won three fields of Sultan Solyman,
I would o'erstare the sternest eyes that look,
Outbrave the heart most daring on the earth,
Pluck the young sucking cubs from the she-bear,
Yea, mock the lion when he roars for prey,
To win thee, lady. But, alas the while!
If Hercules and Lichas play at dice
Which is the better man, the greater throw
May turn by fortune from the weaker hand.
So is Alcides beaten by his page;
And so may I, blind Fortune leading me,
Miss that which one unworthier may attain,
And die with grieving.

PORTIA
You must take your chance,
And either not attempt to choose at all,
Or swear before you choose, if you choose wrong,
Never to speak to lady afterward
In way of marriage; therefore be advis'd.

PRINCE OF MOROCCO
Nor will not; come, bring me unto my chance.

PORTIA
First, forward to the temple: after dinner
Your hazard shall be made.

PRINCE OF MOROCCO
    Good fortune then!
    To make me blest or cursed'st among men!

                                    Cornets, and Exeunt

SCENE II.
VENICE. A STREET.

Enter LAUNCELOT GOBBO

LAUNCELOT
    Certainly my conscience will serve me to run from this Jew my
    master. The fiend is at mine elbow and tempts me, saying to me
    'Gobbo, Launcelot Gobbo, good Launcelot' or 'good Gobbo' or
    'good Launcelot Gobbo, use your legs, take the start, run away.' My
    conscience says 'No; take heed, honest Launcelot, take heed, honest
    Gobbo' or, as aforesaid, 'honest Launcelot Gobbo, do not run; scorn
    running with thy heels.' Well, the most courageous fiend bids me
    pack. 'Via!' says the fiend; 'away!' says the fiend. 'For the heavens,
    rouse up a brave mind,' says the fiend 'and run.' Well, my conscience,
    hanging about the neck of my heart, says very wisely to me 'My
    honest friend Launcelot, being an honest man's son'—or rather 'an
    honest woman's son'; for indeed my father did something smack,
    something grow to, he had a kind of taste—well, my conscience
    says 'Launcelot, budge not.' 'Budge,' says the fiend. 'Budge not,' says
    my conscience. 'Conscience,' say I, 'you counsel well.' 'Fiend,' say
    I, 'you counsel well.' To be ruled by my conscience, I should stay
    with the Jew my master, who—God bless the mark!—is a kind of
    devil; and, to run away from the Jew, I should be ruled by the fiend,
    who—saving your reverence!—is the devil himself. Certainly
    the Jew is the very devil incarnation; and, in my conscience, my
    conscience is but a kind of hard conscience, to offer to counsel me
    to stay with the Jew. The fiend gives the more friendly counsel: I
    will run, fiend; my heels are at your commandment; I will run.

                Enter OLD GOBBO, *with a basket*

OLD GOBBO
    Master young man, you, I pray you; which is the way to Master
    Jew's?

LAUNCELOT

[*Aside*] O heavens! This is my true-begotten father, who, being more than sand-blind, high-gravel blind, knows me not: I will try confusions with him.

OLD GOBBO

Master young gentleman, I pray you, which is the way to Master Jew's?

LAUNCELOT

Turn up on your right hand at the next turning, but, at the next turning of all, on your left; marry, at the very next turning, turn of no hand, but turn down indirectly to the Jew's house.

OLD GOBBO

Be God's sonties, 'twill be a hard way to hit. Can you tell me whether one Launcelot, that dwells with him, dwell with him or no?

LAUNCELOT

Talk you of young Master Launcelot? [*Aside*] Mark me now; now will I raise the waters. Talk you of young Master Launcelot?

OLD GOBBO

No master, sir, but a poor man's son; his father, though I say't, is an honest exceeding poor man, and, God be thanked, well to live.

LAUNCELOT

Well, let his father be what a will, we talk of young Master Launcelot.

OLD GOBBO

Your worship's friend, and Launcelot, sir.

LAUNCELOT

But I pray you, ergo, old man, ergo, I beseech you, talk you of young Master Launcelot?

OLD GOBBO

Of Launcelot, an't please your mastership.

LAUNCELOT

Ergo, Master Launcelot. Talk not of Master Launcelot, father; for the young gentleman, according to Fates and Destinies and such odd sayings, the Sisters Three and such branches of learning, is indeed deceased; or, as you would say in plain terms, gone to heaven.

OLD GOBBO

Marry, God forbid! The boy was the very staff of my age, my very prop.

LAUNCELOT

Do I look like a cudgel or a hovelpost, a staff or a prop? Do you know me, father?

OLD GOBBO

Alack the day! I know you not, young gentleman; but I pray you tell me, is my boy—God rest his soul!—alive or dead?

LAUNCELOT

Do you not know me, father?

OLD GOBBO

Alack, sir, I am sand-blind; I know you not.

LAUNCELOT

Nay, indeed, if you had your eyes, you might fail of the knowing me: it is a wise father that knows his own child. Well, old man, I will tell you news of your son. Give me your blessing; truth will come to light; murder cannot be hid long; a man's son may, but in the end truth will out.

OLD GOBBO

Pray you, sir, stand up; I am sure you are not Launcelot, my boy.

LAUNCELOT

Pray you, let's have no more fooling about it, but give me your blessing; I am Launcelot, your boy that was, your son that is, your child that shall be.

OLD GOBBO

I cannot think you are my son.

LAUNCELOT

I know not what I shall think of that; but I am Launcelot, the Jew's man, and I am sure Margery your wife is my mother.

OLD GOBBO

Her name is Margery, indeed. I'll be sworn, if thou be Launcelot, thou art mine own flesh and blood. Lord worshipped might he be, what a beard hast thou got! Thou hast got more hair on thy chin than Dobbin my thill-horse has on his tail.

LAUNCELOT

It should seem, then, that Dobbin's tail grows backward; I am

sure he had more hair on his tail than I have on my face when
I last saw him.

OLD GOBBO
Lord! how art thou changed! How dost thou and thy master
agree? I have brought him a present. How 'gree you now?

LAUNCELOT
Well, well; but, for mine own part, as I have set up my rest to
run away, so I will not rest till I have run some ground. My
master's a very Jew. Give him a present! Give him a halter. I am
famished in his service; you may tell every finger I have with
my ribs. Father, I am glad you are come; give me your present
to one Master Bassanio, who indeed gives rare new liveries. If I
serve not him, I will run as far as God has any ground. O rare
fortune! Here comes the man: to him, father; for I am a Jew, if I
serve the Jew any longer.

Enter BASSANIO, *with* LEONARDO,
with other Followers

BASSANIO
You may do so; but let it be so hasted that supper be ready at
the farthest by five of the clock. See these letters delivered, put
the liveries to making, and desire Gratiano to come anon to my
lodging.

Exit a SERVANT

LAUNCELOT
To him, father.

OLD GOBBO
God bless your worship!

BASSANIO
Gramercy; wouldst thou aught with me?

OLD GOBBO
Here's my son, sir, a poor boy—

LAUNCELOT
Not a poor boy, sir, but the rich Jew's man, that would, sir, as my
father shall specify—

OLD GOBBO
He hath a great infection, sir, as one would say, to serve—

LAUNCELOT

Indeed the short and the long is, I serve the Jew, and have a desire, as my father shall specify—

OLD GOBBO

His master and he, saving your worship's reverence, are scarce cater-cousins—

LAUNCELOT

To be brief, the very truth is that the Jew, having done me wrong, doth cause me, as my father, being I hope an old man, shall frutify unto you—

OLD GOBBO

I have here a dish of doves that I would bestow upon your worship; and my suit is—

LAUNCELOT

In very brief, the suit is impertinent to myself, as your worship shall know by this honest old man; and, though I say it, though old man, yet poor man, my father.

BASSANIO

One speak for both. What would you?

LAUNCELOT

Serve you, sir.

OLD GOBBO

That is the very defect of the matter, sir.

BASSANIO

I know thee well; thou hast obtain'd thy suit.
Shylock thy master spoke with me this day,
And hath preferr'd thee, if it be preferment
To leave a rich Jew's service to become
The follower of so poor a gentleman.

LAUNCELOT

The old proverb is very well parted between my master Shylock and you, sir: you have the grace of God, sir, and he hath enough.

BASSANIO

Thou speak'st it well. Go, father, with thy son.
Take leave of thy old master, and inquire
My lodging out. [*To a* SERVANT] Give him a livery
More guarded than his fellows'; see it done.

LAUNCELOT

Father, in. I cannot get a service, no! I have ne'er a tongue in my head! [*Looking on his palm*] Well; if any man in Italy have a fairer table which doth offer to swear upon a book, I shall have good fortune. Go to; here's a simple line of life: here's a small trifle of wives; alas, fifteen wives is nothing; a'leven widows and nine maids is a simple coming-in for one man. And then to scape drowning thrice, and to be in peril of my life with the edge of a feather-bed; here are simple scapes. Well, if Fortune be a woman, she's a good wench for this gear. Father, come; I'll take my leave of the Jew in the twinkling of an eye.

Exeunt LAUNCELOT *and*
OLD GOBBO

BASSANIO

I pray thee, good Leonardo, think on this:
These things being bought and orderly bestow'd,
Return in haste, for I do feast to-night
My best esteem'd acquaintance; hie thee, go.

LEONARDO

My best endeavours shall be done herein.

Enter GRATIANO

GRATIANO

Where's your master?

LEONARDO

Yonder, sir, he walks.

Exit

GRATIANO

Signior Bassanio!

BASSANIO

Gratiano!

GRATIANO

I have suit to you.

BASSANIO

You have obtain'd it.

GRATIANO

You must not deny me: I must go with you to Belmont.

BASSANIO

    Why, then you must. But hear thee, Gratiano;
    Thou art too wild, too rude, and bold of voice;
    Parts that become thee happily enough,
    And in such eyes as ours appear not faults;
    But where thou art not known, why there they show
    Something too liberal. Pray thee, take pain
    To allay with some cold drops of modesty
    Thy skipping spirit, lest through thy wild behaviour
    I be misconstrued in the place I go to,
    And lose my hopes.

GRATIANO

    Signior Bassanio, hear me:
    If I do not put on a sober habit,
    Talk with respect, and swear but now and then,
    Wear prayer-books in my pocket, look demurely,
    Nay more, while grace is saying, hood mine eyes
    Thus with my hat, and sigh, and say 'amen';
    Use all the observance of civility,
    Like one well studied in a sad ostent
    To please his grandam, never trust me more.

BASSANIO

    Well, we shall see your bearing.

GRATIANO

    Nay, but I bar to-night; you shall not gauge me
    By what we do to-night.

BASSANIO

    No, that were pity;
    I would entreat you rather to put on
    Your boldest suit of mirth, for we have friends
    That purpose merriment. But fare you well;
    I have some business.

GRATIANO

    And I must to Lorenzo and the rest;
    But we will visit you at supper-time.

Exeunt

SCENE III.
VENICE. A ROOM IN SHYLOCK'S HOUSE.

Enter JESSICA *and* LAUNCELOT

JESSICA

    I am sorry thou wilt leave my father so:
    Our house is hell, and thou, a merry devil,
    Didst rob it of some taste of tediousness.
    But fare thee well; there is a ducat for thee;
    And, Launcelot, soon at supper shalt thou see
    Lorenzo, who is thy new master's guest:
    Give him this letter; do it secretly.
    And so farewell. I would not have my father
    See me in talk with thee.

LAUNCELOT

    Adieu! tears exhibit my tongue. Most beautiful pagan, most
    sweet Jew! If a Christian do not play the knave and get thee, I
    am much deceived. But, adieu! these foolish drops do something
    drown my manly spirit; adieu!

JESSICA

    Farewell, good Launcelot.

                                       Exit LAUNCELOT

    Alack, what heinous sin is it in me
    To be asham'd to be my father's child!
    But though I am a daughter to his blood,
    I am not to his manners. O Lorenzo!
    If thou keep promise, I shall end this strife,
    Become a Christian and thy loving wife.

                                             Exit

SCENE IV.
VENICE. A STREET.

Enter GRATIANO, LORENZO,
SALARINO, *and* SALANIO

LORENZO

    Nay, we will slink away in supper-time,

Disguise us at my lodging, and return
All in an hour.

GRATIANO

We have not made good preparation.

SALARINO

We have not spoke us yet of torch-bearers.

SALANIO

'Tis vile, unless it may be quaintly order'd,
And better in my mind not undertook.

LORENZO

'Tis now but four o'clock; we have two hours
To furnish us.

Enter LAUNCELOT, *with a letter*

Friend Launcelot, what's the news?

LAUNCELOT

An it shall please you to break up this, it shall seem to signify.

LORENZO

I know the hand; in faith, 'tis a fair hand,
And whiter than the paper it writ on
Is the fair hand that writ.

GRATIANO

Love news, in faith.

LAUNCELOT

By your leave, sir.

LORENZO

Whither goest thou?

LAUNCELOT

Marry, sir, to bid my old master, the Jew, to sup to-night with
my new master, the Christian.

LORENZO

Hold, here, take this. Tell gentle Jessica
I will not fail her; speak it privately.
Go, gentlemen,

Exit LAUNCELOT

Will you prepare you for this masque to-night?
I am provided of a torch-bearer.

SALARINO
    Ay, marry, I'll be gone about it straight.
SALANIO
    And so will I.
LORENZO
    Meet me and Gratiano
    At Gratiano's lodging some hour hence.
SALARINO
    'Tis good we do so.

Exeunt SALARINO *and* SALANIO

GRATIANO
    Was not that letter from fair Jessica?
LORENZO
    I must needs tell thee all. She hath directed
    How I shall take her from her father's house;
    What gold and jewels she is furnish'd with;
    What page's suit she hath in readiness.
    If e'er the Jew her father come to heaven,
    It will be for his gentle daughter's sake;
    And never dare misfortune cross her foot,
    Unless she do it under this excuse,
    That she is issue to a faithless Jew.
    Come, go with me, peruse this as thou goest;
    Fair Jessica shall be my torch-bearer.

Exeunt

SCENE V.
VENICE. BEFORE SHYLOCK'S HOUSE.

Enter SHYLOCK *and* LAUNCELOT

SHYLOCK
    Well, thou shalt see; thy eyes shall be thy judge,
    The difference of old Shylock and Bassanio:—
    What, Jessica!—Thou shalt not gormandize,
    As thou hast done with me—What, Jessica!—
    And sleep and snore, and rend apparel out—
    Why, Jessica, I say!

LAUNCELOT
Why, Jessica!
SHYLOCK
Who bids thee call? I do not bid thee call.
LAUNCELOT
Your worship was wont to tell me I could do nothing without
bidding.

Enter JESSICA

JESSICA
Call you? What is your will?
SHYLOCK
I am bid forth to supper, Jessica:
There are my keys. But wherefore should I go?
I am not bid for love; they flatter me;
But yet I'll go in hate, to feed upon
The prodigal Christian. Jessica, my girl,
Look to my house. I am right loath to go;
There is some ill a-brewing towards my rest,
For I did dream of money-bags to-night.
LAUNCELOT
I beseech you, sir, go: my young master doth expect your
reproach.
SHYLOCK
So do I his.
LAUNCELOT
And they have conspired together; I will not say you shall see
a masque, but if you do, then it was not for nothing that my
nose fell a-bleeding on Black Monday last at six o'clock i' the
morning, falling out that year on Ash Wednesday was four year
in the afternoon.
SHYLOCK
What! are there masques? Hear you me, Jessica:
Lock up my doors, and when you hear the drum,
And the vile squealing of the wry neck'd fife,
Clamber not you up to the casements then,
Nor thrust your head into the public street

To gaze on Christian fools with varnish'd faces;
But stop my house's ears—I mean my casements;
Let not the sound of shallow fopp'ry enter
My sober house. By Jacob's staff, I swear
I have no mind of feasting forth to-night;
But I will go. Go you before me, sirrah;
Say I will come.

LAUNCELOT

I will go before, sir. Mistress, look out at window for all this;
There will come a Christian by
Will be worth a Jewess' eye.

Exit LAUNCELOT

SHYLOCK

What says that fool of Hagar's offspring, ha?

JESSICA

His words were 'Farewell, mistress'; nothing else.

SHYLOCK

The patch is kind enough, but a huge feeder;
Snail-slow in profit, and he sleeps by day
More than the wild-cat; drones hive not with me,
Therefore I part with him; and part with him
To one that I would have him help to waste
His borrow'd purse. Well, Jessica, go in;
Perhaps I will return immediately:
Do as I bid you, shut doors after you:
'Fast bind, fast find,'
A proverb never stale in thrifty mind.

Exit

JESSICA

Farewell; and if my fortune be not crost,
I have a father, you a daughter, lost.

Exit

SCENE VI.
VENICE. BEFORE SHYLOCK'S HOUSE.

Enter GRATIANO *and* SALARINO, *masqued*

GRATIANO

    This is the pent-house under which Lorenzo
    Desir'd us to make stand.

SALARINO

    His hour is almost past.

GRATIANO

    And it is marvel he out-dwells his hour,
    For lovers ever run before the clock.

SALARINO

    O! ten times faster Venus' pigeons fly
    To seal love's bonds new made than they are wont
    To keep obliged faith unforfeited!

GRATIANO

    That ever holds: who riseth from a feast
    With that keen appetite that he sits down?
    Where is the horse that doth untread again
    His tedious measures with the unbated fire
    That he did pace them first? All things that are
    Are with more spirit chased than enjoy'd.
    How like a younker or a prodigal
    The scarfed bark puts from her native bay,
    Hugg'd and embraced by the strumpet wind!
    How like the prodigal doth she return,
    With over-weather'd ribs and ragged sails,
    Lean, rent, and beggar'd by the strumpet wind!

SALARINO

    Here comes Lorenzo; more of this hereafter.

Enter LORENZO

LORENZO

    Sweet friends, your patience for my long abode;
    Not I, but my affairs, have made you wait:
    When you shall please to play the thieves for wives,

I'll watch as long for you then. Approach;
Here dwells my father Jew. Ho! who's within?

Enter JESSICA, *above, in boy's clothes*

JESSICA
Who are you? Tell me, for more certainty,
Albeit I'll swear that I do know your tongue.

LORENZO
Lorenzo, and thy love.

JESSICA
Lorenzo, certain; and my love indeed,
For who love I so much? And now who knows
But you, Lorenzo, whether I am yours?

LORENZO
Heaven and thy thoughts are witness that thou art.

JESSICA
Here, catch this casket; it is worth the pains.
I am glad 'tis night, you do not look on me,
For I am much asham'd of my exchange;
But love is blind, and lovers cannot see
The pretty follies that themselves commit,
For, if they could, Cupid himself would blush
To see me thus transformed to a boy.

LORENZO
Descend, for you must be my torch-bearer.

JESSICA
What! must I hold a candle to my shames?
They in themselves, good sooth, are too too light.
Why, 'tis an office of discovery, love,
And I should be obscur'd.

LORENZO
So are you, sweet,
Even in the lovely garnish of a boy.
But come at once;
For the close night doth play the runaway,
And we are stay'd for at Bassanio's feast.

JESSICA

    I will make fast the doors, and gild myself

    With some moe ducats, and be with you straight.

Exit above

GRATIANO

    Now, by my hood, a Gentile, and no Jew.

LORENZO

    Beshrew me, but I love her heartily;

    For she is wise, if I can judge of her,

    And fair she is, if that mine eyes be true,

    And true she is, as she hath prov'd herself;

    And therefore, like herself, wise, fair, and true,

    Shall she be placed in my constant soul.

Enter JESSICA

    What, art thou come? On, gentlemen, away!

    Our masquing mates by this time for us stay.

Exit with JESSICA *and*

SALARINO

Enter ANTONIO

ANTONIO

    Who's there?

GRATIANO

    Signior Antonio!

ANTONIO

    Fie, fie, Gratiano! where are all the rest?

    'Tis nine o'clock; our friends all stay for you.

    No masque to-night: the wind is come about;

    Bassanio presently will go aboard:

    I have sent twenty out to seek for you.

GRATIANO

    I am glad on't: I desire no more delight

    Than to be under sail and gone to-night.

Exeunt

SCENE VII.
BELMONT. A ROOM IN PORTIA'S HOUSE.

Flourish of cornets. Enter PORTIA,
with the PRINCE OF MOROCCO, *and their trains*

PORTIA

Go draw aside the curtains and discover
The several caskets to this noble prince.
Now make your choice.

PRINCE OF MOROCCO

The first, of gold, who this inscription bears:
'Who chooseth me shall gain what many men desire.'
The second, silver, which this promise carries:
'Who chooseth me shall get as much as he deserves.'
This third, dull lead, with warning all as blunt:
'Who chooseth me must give and hazard all he hath.'
How shall I know if I do choose the right?

PORTIA

The one of them contains my picture, prince;
If you choose that, then I am yours withal.

PRINCE OF MOROCCO

Some god direct my judgment! Let me see;
I will survey the inscriptions back again.
What says this leaden casket?
'Who chooseth me must give and hazard all he hath.'
Must give: for what? For lead? Hazard for lead!
This casket threatens; men that hazard all
Do it in hope of fair advantages:
A golden mind stoops not to shows of dross;
I'll then nor give nor hazard aught for lead.
What says the silver with her virgin hue?
'Who chooseth me shall get as much as he deserves.'
As much as he deserves! Pause there, Morocco,
And weigh thy value with an even hand.
If thou be'st rated by thy estimation,
Thou dost deserve enough, and yet enough
May not extend so far as to the lady;

And yet to be afeard of my deserving
Were but a weak disabling of myself.
As much as I deserve? Why, that's the lady!
I do in birth deserve her, and in fortunes,
In graces, and in qualities of breeding;
But more than these, in love I do deserve.
What if I stray'd no farther, but chose here?
Let's see once more this saying grav'd in gold:
'Who chooseth me shall gain what many men desire.'
Why, that's the lady: all the world desires her;
From the four corners of the earth they come,
To kiss this shrine, this mortal-breathing saint:
The Hyrcanian deserts and the vasty wilds
Of wide Arabia are as throughfares now
For princes to come view fair Portia:
The watery kingdom, whose ambitious head
Spits in the face of heaven, is no bar
To stop the foreign spirits, but they come
As o'er a brook to see fair Portia.
One of these three contains her heavenly picture.
Is't like that lead contains her? 'Twere damnation
To think so base a thought; it were too gross
To rib her cerecloth in the obscure grave.
Or shall I think in silver she's immur'd,
Being ten times undervalu'd to tried gold?
O sinful thought! Never so rich a gem
Was set in worse than gold. They have in England
A coin that bears the figure of an angel
Stamped in gold; but that's insculp'd upon;
But here an angel in a golden bed
Lies all within. Deliver me the key;
Here do I choose, and thrive I as I may!

PORTIA

There, take it, prince, and if my form lie there,
Then I am yours.
[*He unlocks the golden casket.*]

PRINCE OF MOROCCO
    O hell! what have we here?
    A carrion Death, within whose empty eye
    There is a written scroll! I'll read the writing.
                'All that glisters is not gold,
                Often have you heard that told;
                Many a man his life hath sold
                But my outside to behold:
                Gilded tombs do worms infold.
                Had you been as wise as bold,
                Young in limbs, in judgment old,
                Your answer had not been inscroll'd:
                Fare you well, your suit is cold.'
    Cold indeed; and labour lost:
    Then, farewell, heat, and welcome, frost!
    Portia, adieu! I have too griev'd a heart
    To take a tedious leave; thus losers part.
                        Exit with his train. Flourish of cornets

PORTIA
    A gentle riddance. Draw the curtains: go.
    Let all of his complexion choose me so.
                                        Exeunt

SCENE VIII.
VENICE. A STREET.

Enter SALARINO *and* SALANIO

SALARINO
    Why, man, I saw Bassanio under sail;
    With him is Gratiano gone along;
    And in their ship I am sure Lorenzo is not.

SALANIO
    The villain Jew with outcries rais'd the Duke,
    Who went with him to search Bassanio's ship.

SALARINO
    He came too late, the ship was under sail;

But there the Duke was given to understand
That in a gondola were seen together
Lorenzo and his amorous Jessica.
Besides, Antonio certified the Duke
They were not with Bassanio in his ship.

SALANIO

I never heard a passion so confus'd,
So strange, outrageous, and so variable,
As the dog Jew did utter in the streets.
'My daughter! O my ducats! O my daughter!
Fled with a Christian! O my Christian ducats!
Justice! the law! my ducats and my daughter!
A sealed bag, two sealed bags of ducats,
Of double ducats, stol'n from me by my daughter!
And jewels! two stones, two rich and precious stones,
Stol'n by my daughter! Justice! find the girl!
She hath the stones upon her and the ducats.'

SALARINO

Why, all the boys in Venice follow him,
Crying, his stones, his daughter, and his ducats.

SALANIO

Let good Antonio look he keep his day,
Or he shall pay for this.

SALARINO

Marry, well remember'd.
I reason'd with a Frenchman yesterday,
Who told me—in the narrow seas that part
The French and English—there miscarried
A vessel of our country richly fraught.
I thought upon Antonio when he told me,
And wish'd in silence that it were not his.

SALANIO

You were best to tell Antonio what you hear;
Yet do not suddenly, for it may grieve him.

SALARINO

A kinder gentleman treads not the earth.

I saw Bassanio and Antonio part:
Bassanio told him he would make some speed
Of his return. He answer'd 'Do not so;
Slubber not business for my sake, Bassanio,
But stay the very riping of the time;
And for the Jew's bond which he hath of me,
Let it not enter in your mind of love:
Be merry, and employ your chiefest thoughts
To courtship, and such fair ostents of love
As shall conveniently become you there.'
And even there, his eye being big with tears,
Turning his face, he put his hand behind him,
And with affection wondrous sensible
He wrung Bassanio's hand; and so they parted.

SALANIO
I think he only loves the world for him.
I pray thee, let us go and find him out,
And quicken his embraced heaviness
With some delight or other.

SALARINO
Do we so.

Exeunt

SCENE IX.
BELMONT. A ROOM IN PORTIA'S HOUSE.

Enter NERISSA, *with a* SERVITOR

NERISSA
Quick, quick, I pray thee, draw the curtain straight;
The Prince of Arragon hath ta'en his oath,
And comes to his election presently.

Flourish of cornets. Enter the PRINCE OF ARRAGON,
PORTIA, *and their Trains*

PORTIA
Behold, there stand the caskets, noble Prince:
If you choose that wherein I am contain'd,

Straight shall our nuptial rites be solemniz'd;
But if you fail, without more speech, my lord,
You must be gone from hence immediately.

ARRAGON
I am enjoin'd by oath to observe three things:
First, never to unfold to any one
Which casket 'twas I chose; next, if I fail
Of the right casket, never in my life
To woo a maid in way of marriage;
Lastly,
If I do fail in fortune of my choice,
Immediately to leave you and be gone.

PORTIA
To these injunctions every one doth swear
That comes to hazard for my worthless self.

ARRAGON
And so have I address'd me. Fortune now
To my heart's hope! Gold, silver, and base lead.
'Who chooseth me must give and hazard all he hath.'
You shall look fairer ere I give or hazard.
What says the golden chest? Ha! let me see:
'Who chooseth me shall gain what many men desire.'
What many men desire! that 'many' may be meant
By the fool multitude, that choose by show,
Not learning more than the fond eye doth teach;
Which pries not to th' interior, but, like the martlet,
Builds in the weather on the outward wall,
Even in the force and road of casualty.
I will not choose what many men desire,
Because I will not jump with common spirits
And rank me with the barbarous multitudes.
Why, then to thee, thou silver treasure-house;
Tell me once more what title thou dost bear:
'Who chooseth me shall get as much as he deserves.'
And well said too; for who shall go about
To cozen fortune, and be honourable

Without the stamp of merit? Let none presume
To wear an undeserved dignity.
O! that estates, degrees, and offices
Were not deriv'd corruptly, and that clear honour
Were purchas'd by the merit of the wearer!
How many then should cover that stand bare!
How many be commanded that command!
How much low peasantry would then be glean'd
From the true seed of honour; and how much honour
Pick'd from the chaff and ruin of the times
To be new varnish'd! Well, but to my choice:
'Who chooseth me shall get as much as he deserves.'
I will assume desert. Give me a key for this,
And instantly unlock my fortunes here.
[*He opens the silver casket.*]

PORTIA
[*Aside*] Too long a pause for that which you find there.

ARRAGON
What's here? The portrait of a blinking idiot,
Presenting me a schedule! I will read it.
How much unlike art thou to Portia!
How much unlike my hopes and my deservings!
'Who chooseth me shall have as much as he deserves.'
Did I deserve no more than a fool's head?
Is that my prize? Are my deserts no better?

PORTIA.
To offend, and judge, are distinct offices,
And of opposed natures.

ARRAGON
What is here? [*Reads.*]
'The fire seven times tried this;
Seven times tried that judgment is
That did never choose amiss.
Some there be that shadows kiss;
Such have but a shadow's bliss;
There be fools alive, I wis,

Silver'd o'er, and so was this.
Take what wife you will to bed,
I will ever be your head:
So be gone; you are sped.'
Still more fool I shall appear
By the time I linger here;
With one fool's head I came to woo,
But I go away with two.
Sweet, adieu! I'll keep my oath,
Patiently to bear my wroth.

Exit ARRAGON *with his train.*

PORTIA

Thus hath the candle sing'd the moth.
O, these deliberate fools! When they do choose,
They have the wisdom by their wit to lose.

NERISSA

The ancient saying is no heresy:
'Hanging and wiving goes by destiny.'

PORTIA

Come, draw the curtain, Nerissa.

Enter a SERVANT

SERVANT

Where is my lady?

PORTIA

Here; what would my lord?

SERVANT

Madam, there is alighted at your gate
A young Venetian, one that comes before
To signify th' approaching of his lord;
From whom he bringeth sensible regreets;
To wit, besides commends and courteous breath,
Gifts of rich value. Yet I have not seen
So likely an ambassador of love.
A day in April never came so sweet,
To show how costly summer was at hand,
As this fore-spurrer comes before his lord.

PORTIA
No more, I pray thee; I am half afeard
Thou wilt say anon he is some kin to thee,
Thou spend'st such high-day wit in praising him.
Come, come, Nerissa, for I long to see
Quick Cupid's post that comes so mannerly.

NERISSA
Bassanio, lord Love, if thy will it be!

Exeunt

ACT

SCENE I.
VENICE. A STREET.

Enter SALANIO *and* SALARINO

SALANIO

Now, what news on the Rialto?

SALARINO

Why, yet it lives there unchecked that Antonio hath a ship of rich lading wrack'd on the narrow seas; the Goodwins, I think they call the place, a very dangerous flat and fatal, where the carcasses of many a tall ship lie buried, as they say, if my gossip Report be an honest woman of her word.

SALANIO

I would she were as lying a gossip in that as ever knapped ginger or made her neighbours believe she wept for the death of a third husband. But it is true, without any slips of prolixity or crossing the plain highway of talk, that the good Antonio, the honest Antonio. O that I had a title good enough to keep his name company!—

SALARINO

Come, the full stop.

SALANIO
Ha! What sayest thou? Why, the end is, he hath lost a ship.

SALARINO
I would it might prove the end of his losses.

SALANIO
Let me say 'amen' betimes, lest the devil cross my prayer, for here he comes in the likeness of a Jew.

Enter SHYLOCK

How now, Shylock! What news among the merchants?

SHYLOCK
You knew, none so well, none so well as you, of my daughter's flight.

SALARINO
That's certain; I, for my part, knew the tailor that made the wings she flew withal.

SALANIO
And Shylock, for his own part, knew the bird was fledged; and then it is the complexion of them all to leave the dam.

SHYLOCK
She is damned for it.

SALARINO
That's certain, if the devil may be her judge.

SHYLOCK
My own flesh and blood to rebel!

SALANIO
Out upon it, old carrion! Rebels it at these years?

SHYLOCK
I say my daughter is my flesh and my blood.

SALARINO
There is more difference between thy flesh and hers than between jet and ivory; more between your bloods than there is between red wine and Rhenish. But tell us, do you hear whether Antonio have had any loss at sea or no?

SHYLOCK
There I have another bad match: a bankrupt, a prodigal, who dare scarce show his head on the Rialto; a beggar, that used to come so smug upon the mart; let him look to his bond: he was

wont to call me usurer; let him look to his bond: he was wont to lend money for a Christian courtesy; let him look to his bond.

SALARINO

Why, I am sure, if he forfeit, thou wilt not take his flesh: what's that good for?

SHYLOCK

To bait fish withal: if it will feed nothing else, it will feed my revenge. He hath disgrac'd me and hind'red me half a million; laugh'd at my losses, mock'd at my gains, scorned my nation, thwarted my bargains, cooled my friends, heated mine enemies. And what's his reason? I am a Jew. Hath not a Jew eyes? Hath not a Jew hands, organs, dimensions, senses, affections, passions, fed with the same food, hurt with the same weapons, subject to the same diseases, healed by the same means, warmed and cooled by the same winter and summer, as a Christian is? If you prick us, do we not bleed? If you tickle us, do we not laugh? If you poison us, do we not die? And if you wrong us, shall we not revenge? If we are like you in the rest, we will resemble you in that. If a Jew wrong a Christian, what is his humility? Revenge. If a Christian wrong a Jew, what should his sufferance be by Christian example? Why, revenge. The villainy you teach me I will execute; and it shall go hard but I will better the instruction.

Enter a Servant

SERVANT

Gentlemen, my master Antonio is at his house, and desires to speak with you both.

SALARINO

We have been up and down to seek him.

Enter TUBAL

SALANIO

Here comes another of the tribe: a third cannot be match'd, unless the devil himself turn Jew.

Exeunt SALANIO,
SALARINO, *and Servant*

SHYLOCK

How now, Tubal! what news from Genoa? Hast thou found my daughter?

TUBAL

    I often came where I did hear of her, but cannot find her.

SHYLOCK

    Why there, there, there, there! A diamond gone, cost me two
    thousand ducats in Frankfort! The curse never fell upon our
    nation till now; I never felt it till now. Two thousand ducats in
    that, and other precious, precious jewels. I would my daughter
    were dead at my foot, and the jewels in her ear; would she were
    hearsed at my foot, and the ducats in her coffin! No news of
    them? Why, so—and I know not what's spent in the search.
    Why, thou—loss upon loss! The thief gone with so much, and
    so much to find the thief; and no satisfaction, no revenge; nor
    no ill luck stirring but what lights on my shoulders; no sighs but
    of my breathing; no tears but of my shedding.

TUBAL

    Yes, other men have ill luck too. Antonio, as I heard in Genoa—

SHYLOCK

    What, what, what? Ill luck, ill luck?

TUBAL

    Hath an argosy cast away, coming from Tripolis.

SHYLOCK

    I thank God! I thank God! Is it true, is it true?

TUBAL

    I spoke with some of the sailors that escaped the wrack.

SHYLOCK

    I thank thee, good Tubal. Good news, good news! ha, ha!
    Where? in Genoa?

TUBAL

    Your daughter spent in Genoa, as I heard, one night, fourscore
    ducats.

SHYLOCK

    Thou stick'st a dagger in me—I shall never see my gold again:
    fourscore ducats at a sitting! Fourscore ducats!

TUBAL

    There came divers of Antonio's creditors in my company to
    Venice that swear he cannot choose but break.

SHYLOCK

I am very glad of it; I'll plague him, I'll torture him; I am glad of it.

TUBAL

One of them showed me a ring that he had of your daughter for a monkey.

SHYLOCK

Out upon her! Thou torturest me, Tubal: It was my turquoise; I had it of Leah when I was a bachelor; I would not have given it for a wilderness of monkeys.

TUBAL

But Antonio is certainly undone.

SHYLOCK

Nay, that's true; that's very true. Go, Tubal, fee me an officer; bespeak him a fortnight before. I will have the heart of him, if he forfeit; for, were he out of Venice, I can make what merchandise I will. Go, Tubal, and meet me at our synagogue; go, good Tubal; at our synagogue, Tubal.

Exeunt

SCENE II.
BELMONT. A ROOM IN PORTIA'S HOUSE.

Enter BASSANIO, PORTIA, GRATIANO,
NERISSA, *and Attendants*

PORTIA

I pray you tarry; pause a day or two
Before you hazard; for, in choosing wrong,
I lose your company; therefore forbear a while.
There's something tells me, but it is not love,
I would not lose you; and you know yourself
Hate counsels not in such a quality.
But lest you should not understand me well—
And yet a maiden hath no tongue but thought—
I would detain you here some month or two
Before you venture for me. I could teach you
How to choose right, but then I am forsworn;

So will I never be; so may you miss me;
But if you do, you'll make me wish a sin,
That I had been forsworn. Beshrew your eyes!
They have o'erlook'd me and divided me:
One half of me is yours, the other half yours,
Mine own, I would say; but if mine, then yours,
And so all yours. O! these naughty times
Puts bars between the owners and their rights;
And so, though yours, not yours. Prove it so,
Let fortune go to hell for it, not I.
I speak too long, but 'tis to peize the time,
To eke it, and to draw it out in length,
To stay you from election.

BASSANIO

Let me choose;
For as I am, I live upon the rack.

PORTIA

Upon the rack, Bassanio! Then confess
What treason there is mingled with your love.

BASSANIO

None but that ugly treason of mistrust,
Which makes me fear th' enjoying of my love:
There may as well be amity and life
'Tween snow and fire as treason and my love.

PORTIA

Ay, but I fear you speak upon the rack,
Where men enforced do speak anything.

BASSANIO

Promise me life, and I'll confess the truth.

PORTIA

Well then, confess and live.

BASSANIO

'Confess' and 'love'
Had been the very sum of my confession:
O happy torment, when my torturer
Doth teach me answers for deliverance!
But let me to my fortune and the caskets.

PORTIA

    Away, then! I am lock'd in one of them:
    If you do love me, you will find me out.
    Nerissa and the rest, stand all aloof;
    Let music sound while he doth make his choice;
    Then, if he lose, he makes a swan-like end,
    Fading in music: that the comparison
    May stand more proper, my eye shall be the stream
    And watery death-bed for him. He may win;
    And what is music then? Then music is
    Even as the flourish when true subjects bow
    To a new-crowned monarch; such it is
    As are those dulcet sounds in break of day
    That creep into the dreaming bridegroom's ear
    And summon him to marriage. Now he goes,
    With no less presence, but with much more love,
    Than young Alcides when he did redeem
    The virgin tribute paid by howling Troy
    To the sea-monster: I stand for sacrifice;
    The rest aloof are the Dardanian wives,
    With bleared visages come forth to view
    The issue of th' exploit. Go, Hercules!
    Live thou, I live. With much much more dismay
    I view the fight than thou that mak'st the fray.
    [*A Song, whilst* BASSANIO *comments on the caskets to himself.*]

            Tell me where is fancy bred,
            Or in the heart or in the head,
            How begot, how nourished?
                Reply, reply.
            It is engend'red in the eyes,
            With gazing fed; and fancy dies
            In the cradle where it lies.
            Let us all ring fancy's knell:
            I'll begin it.—Ding, dong, bell.

ALL

    Ding, dong, bell.

BASSANIO

    So may the outward shows be least themselves:
    The world is still deceiv'd with ornament.
    In law, what plea so tainted and corrupt
    But, being season'd with a gracious voice,
    Obscures the show of evil? In religion,
    What damned error but some sober brow
    Will bless it, and approve it with a text,
    Hiding the grossness with fair ornament?
    There is no vice so simple but assumes
    Some mark of virtue on his outward parts.
    How many cowards, whose hearts are all as false
    As stairs of sand, wear yet upon their chins
    The beards of Hercules and frowning Mars;
    Who, inward search'd, have livers white as milk;
    And these assume but valour's excrement
    To render them redoubted! Look on beauty
    And you shall see 'tis purchas'd by the weight:
    Which therein works a miracle in nature,
    Making them lightest that wear most of it:
    So are those crisped snaky golden locks
    Which make such wanton gambols with the wind,
    Upon supposed fairness, often known
    To be the dowry of a second head,
    The skull that bred them, in the sepulchre.
    Thus ornament is but the guiled shore
    To a most dangerous sea; the beauteous scarf
    Veiling an Indian beauty; in a word,
    The seeming truth which cunning times put on
    To entrap the wisest. Therefore, thou gaudy gold,
    Hard food for Midas, I will none of thee;
    Nor none of thee, thou pale and common drudge
    'Tween man and man: but thou, thou meagre lead,
    Which rather threaten'st than dost promise aught,
    Thy plainness moves me more than eloquence,
    And here choose I: joy be the consequence!

PORTIA

    [*Aside*] How all the other passions fleet to air,
    As doubtful thoughts, and rash-embrac'd despair,
    And shuddering fear, and green-ey'd jealousy!
    O love! be moderate; allay thy ecstasy;
    In measure rain thy joy; scant this excess;
    I feel too much thy blessing; make it less,
    For fear I surfeit!

BASSANIO

    What find I here? [*Opening the leaden casket.*]
    Fair Portia's counterfeit! What demi-god
    Hath come so near creation? Move these eyes?
    Or whether riding on the balls of mine,
    Seem they in motion? Here are sever'd lips,
    Parted with sugar breath; so sweet a bar
    Should sunder such sweet friends. Here in her hairs
    The painter plays the spider, and hath woven
    A golden mesh t' entrap the hearts of men
    Faster than gnats in cobwebs: but her eyes!—
    How could he see to do them? Having made one,
    Methinks it should have power to steal both his,
    And leave itself unfurnish'd: yet look, how far
    The substance of my praise doth wrong this shadow
    In underprizing it, so far this shadow
    Doth limp behind the substance. Here's the scroll,
    The continent and summary of my fortune.

        'You that choose not by the view,
        Chance as fair and choose as true!
          Since this fortune falls to you,
            Be content and seek no new.
            If you be well pleas'd with this,
        And hold your fortune for your bliss,
            Turn to where your lady is
          And claim her with a loving kiss.'
    A gentle scroll. Fair lady, by your leave; [*Kissing her.*]
    I come by note, to give and to receive.
    Like one of two contending in a prize,

That thinks he hath done well in people's eyes,
Hearing applause and universal shout,
Giddy in spirit, still gazing in a doubt
Whether those peals of praise be his or no;
So, thrice-fair lady, stand I, even so,
As doubtful whether what I see be true,
Until confirm'd, sign'd, ratified by you.

PORTIA

You see me, Lord Bassanio, where I stand,
Such as I am: though for myself alone
I would not be ambitious in my wish
To wish myself much better, yet for you
I would be trebled twenty times myself,
A thousand times more fair, ten thousand times more rich;
That only to stand high in your account,
I might in virtues, beauties, livings, friends,
Exceed account. But the full sum of me
Is sum of something which, to term in gross,
Is an unlesson'd girl, unschool'd, unpractis'd;
Happy in this, she is not yet so old
But she may learn; happier than this,
She is not bred so dull but she can learn;
Happiest of all is that her gentle spirit
Commits itself to yours to be directed,
As from her lord, her governor, her king.
Myself and what is mine to you and yours
Is now converted. But now I was the lord
Of this fair mansion, master of my servants,
Queen o'er myself; and even now, but now,
This house, these servants, and this same myself,
Are yours—my lord's. I give them with this ring,
Which when you part from, lose, or give away,
Let it presage the ruin of your love,
And be my vantage to exclaim on you.

BASSANIO

Madam, you have bereft me of all words,
Only my blood speaks to you in my veins;

And there is such confusion in my powers
As, after some oration fairly spoke
By a beloved prince, there doth appear
Among the buzzing pleased multitude;
Where every something, being blent together,
Turns to a wild of nothing, save of joy,
Express'd and not express'd. But when this ring
Parts from this finger, then parts life from hence:
O! then be bold to say Bassanio's dead.

NERISSA
My lord and lady, it is now our time,
That have stood by and seen our wishes prosper,
To cry, 'Good joy'. Good joy, my lord and lady!

GRATIANO
My Lord Bassanio, and my gentle lady,
I wish you all the joy that you can wish;
For I am sure you can wish none from me;
And when your honours mean to solemnize
The bargain of your faith, I do beseech you
Even at that time I may be married too.

BASSANIO
With all my heart, so thou canst get a wife.

GRATIANO
I thank your lordship, you have got me one.
My eyes, my lord, can look as swift as yours:
You saw the mistress, I beheld the maid;
You lov'd, I lov'd; for intermission
No more pertains to me, my lord, than you.
Your fortune stood upon the caskets there,
And so did mine too, as the matter falls;
For wooing here until I sweat again,
And swearing till my very roof was dry
With oaths of love, at last, if promise last,
I got a promise of this fair one here
To have her love, provided that your fortune
Achiev'd her mistress.

PORTIA

Is this true, Nerissa?

NERISSA

Madam, it is, so you stand pleas'd withal.

BASSANIO

And do you, Gratiano, mean good faith?

GRATIANO

Yes, faith, my lord.

BASSANIO

Our feast shall be much honour'd in your marriage.

GRATIANO

We'll play with them the first boy for a thousand ducats.

NERISSA

What! and stake down?

GRATIANO

No; we shall ne'er win at that sport, and stake down.
But who comes here? Lorenzo and his infidel?
What, and my old Venetian friend, Salanio!

Enter LORENZO, JESSICA, *and* SALANIO

BASSANIO

Lorenzo and Salanio, welcome hither,
If that the youth of my new interest here
Have power to bid you welcome. By your leave,
I bid my very friends and countrymen,
Sweet Portia, welcome.

PORTIA

So do I, my lord;
They are entirely welcome.

LORENZO

I thank your honour. For my part, my lord,
My purpose was not to have seen you here;
But meeting with Salanio by the way,
He did entreat me, past all saying nay,
To come with him along.

SALANIO

I did, my lord,
And I have reason for it. Signior Antonio

Commends him to you.

Gives BASSANIO *a letter*

BASSANIO

Ere I ope his letter,
I pray you tell me how my good friend doth.

SALANIO

Not sick, my lord, unless it be in mind;
Nor well, unless in mind; his letter there
Will show you his estate.

BASSANIO *opens the letter*

GRATIANO

Nerissa, cheer yon stranger; bid her welcome.
Your hand, Salanio. What's the news from Venice?
How doth that royal merchant, good Antonio?
I know he will be glad of our success:
We are the Jasons, we have won the fleece.

SALANIO

I would you had won the fleece that he hath lost.

PORTIA

There are some shrewd contents in yon same paper.
That steal the colour from Bassanio's cheek:
Some dear friend dead, else nothing in the world
Could turn so much the constitution
Of any constant man. What, worse and worse!
With leave, Bassanio: I am half yourself,
And I must freely have the half of anything
That this same paper brings you.

BASSANIO

O sweet Portia!
Here are a few of the unpleasant'st words
That ever blotted paper. Gentle lady,
When I did first impart my love to you,
I freely told you all the wealth I had
Ran in my veins, I was a gentleman,
And then I told you true. And yet, dear lady,
Rating myself at nothing, you shall see
How much I was a braggart. When I told you

My state was nothing, I should then have told you
That I was worse than nothing; for indeed
I have engag'd myself to a dear friend,
Engag'd my friend to his mere enemy,
To feed my means. Here is a letter, lady,
The paper as the body of my friend,
And every word in it a gaping wound
Issuing life-blood. But is it true, Salanio?
Hath all his ventures fail'd? What, not one hit?
From Tripolis, from Mexico, and England,
From Lisbon, Barbary, and India?
And not one vessel scape the dreadful touch
Of merchant-marring rocks?

SALANIO

Not one, my lord.
Besides, it should appear that, if he had
The present money to discharge the Jew,
He would not take it. Never did I know
A creature that did bear the shape of man,
So keen and greedy to confound a man.
He plies the Duke at morning and at night,
And doth impeach the freedom of the state,
If they deny him justice. Twenty merchants,
The Duke himself, and the magnificoes
Of greatest port, have all persuaded with him;
But none can drive him from the envious plea
Of forfeiture, of justice, and his bond.

JESSICA

When I was with him, I have heard him swear
To Tubal and to Chus, his countrymen,
That he would rather have Antonio's flesh
Than twenty times the value of the sum
That he did owe him; and I know, my lord,
If law, authority, and power, deny not,
It will go hard with poor Antonio.

PORTIA

Is it your dear friend that is thus in trouble?

BASSANIO

> The dearest friend to me, the kindest man,
> The best condition'd and unwearied spirit
> In doing courtesies; and one in whom
> The ancient Roman honour more appears
> Than any that draws breath in Italy.

PORTIA

> What sum owes he the Jew?

BASSANIO

> For me, three thousand ducats.

PORTIA

> What! no more?
> Pay him six thousand, and deface the bond;
> Double six thousand, and then treble that,
> Before a friend of this description
> Shall lose a hair through Bassanio's fault.
> First go with me to church and call me wife,
> And then away to Venice to your friend;
> For never shall you lie by Portia's side
> With an unquiet soul. You shall have gold
> To pay the petty debt twenty times over:
> When it is paid, bring your true friend along.
> My maid Nerissa and myself meantime,
> Will live as maids and widows. Come, away!
> For you shall hence upon your wedding day.
> Bid your friends welcome, show a merry cheer;
> Since you are dear bought, I will love you dear.
> But let me hear the letter of your friend.

BASSANIO

> [Reads] 'Sweet Bassanio, my ships have all miscarried, my creditors grow cruel, my estate is very low, my bond to the Jew is forfeit; and since, in paying it, it is impossible I should live, all debts are clear'd between you and I, if I might but see you at my death. Notwithstanding, use your pleasure; if your love do not persuade you to come, let not my letter.'

PORTIA

> O love, dispatch all business and be gone!

BASSANIO

> Since I have your good leave to go away,
> I will make haste; but, till I come again,
> No bed shall e'er be guilty of my stay,
> Nor rest be interposer 'twixt us twain.

Exeunt

SCENE III.
VENICE. A STREET.

Enter SHYLOCK, SALARINO,
ANTONIO, *and Gaoler*

SHYLOCK

> Gaoler, look to him. Tell not me of mercy;
> This is the fool that lent out money gratis:
> Gaoler, look to him.

ANTONIO

> Hear me yet, good Shylock.

SHYLOCK

> I'll have my bond; speak not against my bond.
> I have sworn an oath that I will have my bond.
> Thou call'dst me dog before thou hadst a cause,
> But, since I am a dog, beware my fangs;
> The Duke shall grant me justice. I do wonder,
> Thou naughty gaoler, that thou art so fond
> To come abroad with him at his request.

ANTONIO

> I pray thee hear me speak.

SHYLOCK

> I'll have my bond. I will not hear thee speak;
> I'll have my bond; and therefore speak no more.
> I'll not be made a soft and dull-eyed fool,
> To shake the head, relent, and sigh, and yield
> To Christian intercessors. Follow not;
> I'll have no speaking; I will have my bond.

Exit

SALARINO

 It is the most impenetrable cur
 That ever kept with men.

ANTONIO

 Let him alone;
 I'll follow him no more with bootless prayers.
 He seeks my life; his reason well I know:
 I oft deliver'd from his forfeitures
 Many that have at times made moan to me;
 Therefore he hates me.

SALARINO

 I am sure the Duke
 Will never grant this forfeiture to hold.

ANTONIO

 The Duke cannot deny the course of law;
 For the commodity that strangers have
 With us in Venice, if it be denied,
 'Twill much impeach the justice of the state,
 Since that the trade and profit of the city
 Consisteth of all nations. Therefore, go;
 These griefs and losses have so bated me
 That I shall hardly spare a pound of flesh
 To-morrow to my bloody creditor.
 Well, gaoler, on; pray God Bassanio come
 To see me pay his debt, and then I care not.

Exeunt

SCENE IV.
BELMONT. A ROOM IN PORTIA'S HOUSE.

Enter PORTIA, NERISSA, LORENZO,
JESSICA, *and* BALTHASAR

LORENZO

 Madam, although I speak it in your presence,
 You have a noble and a true conceit
 Of godlike amity, which appears most strongly
 In bearing thus the absence of your lord.

But if you knew to whom you show this honour,
How true a gentleman you send relief,
How dear a lover of my lord your husband,
I know you would be prouder of the work
Than customary bounty can enforce you.

PORTIA

I never did repent for doing good,
Nor shall not now; for in companions
That do converse and waste the time together,
Whose souls do bear an equal yoke of love,
There must be needs a like proportion
Of lineaments, of manners, and of spirit,
Which makes me think that this Antonio,
Being the bosom lover of my lord,
Must needs be like my lord. If it be so,
How little is the cost I have bestowed
In purchasing the semblance of my soul
From out the state of hellish cruelty!
This comes too near the praising of myself;
Therefore, no more of it; hear other things.
Lorenzo, I commit into your hands
The husbandry and manage of my house
Until my lord's return; for mine own part,
I have toward heaven breath'd a secret vow
To live in prayer and contemplation,
Only attended by Nerissa here,
Until her husband and my lord's return.
There is a monastery two miles off,
And there we will abide. I do desire you
Not to deny this imposition,
The which my love and some necessity
Now lays upon you.

LORENZO

Madam, with all my heart
I shall obey you in all fair commands.

PORTIA

My people do already know my mind,

And will acknowledge you and Jessica
In place of Lord Bassanio and myself.
So fare you well till we shall meet again.

LORENZO
Fair thoughts and happy hours attend on you!

JESSICA
I wish your ladyship all heart's content.

PORTIA
I thank you for your wish, and am well pleas'd
To wish it back on you. Fare you well, Jessica.

Exeunt JESSICA *and* LORENZO

Now, Balthasar,
As I have ever found thee honest-true,
So let me find thee still. Take this same letter,
And use thou all th' endeavour of a man
In speed to Padua; see thou render this
Into my cousin's hands, Doctor Bellario;
And look what notes and garments he doth give thee,
Bring them, I pray thee, with imagin'd speed
Unto the traject, to the common ferry
Which trades to Venice. Waste no time in words,
But get thee gone; I shall be there before thee.

BALTHASAR
Madam, I go with all convenient speed.

Exit

PORTIA
Come on, Nerissa, I have work in hand
That you yet know not of; we'll see our husbands
Before they think of us.

NERISSA
Shall they see us?

PORTIA
They shall, Nerissa; but in such a habit
That they shall think we are accomplished
With that we lack. I'll hold thee any wager,
When we are both accoutred like young men,
I'll prove the prettier fellow of the two,

And wear my dagger with the braver grace,
And speak between the change of man and boy
With a reed voice; and turn two mincing steps
Into a manly stride; and speak of frays
Like a fine bragging youth; and tell quaint lies,
How honourable ladies sought my love,
Which I denying, they fell sick and died;
I could not do withal. Then I'll repent,
And wish for all that, that I had not kill'd them.
And twenty of these puny lies I'll tell,
That men shall swear I have discontinu'd school
About a twelvemonth. I have within my mind
A thousand raw tricks of these bragging Jacks,
Which I will practise.

NERISSA
Why, shall we turn to men?

PORTIA
Fie, what a question's that,
If thou wert near a lewd interpreter!
But come, I'll tell thee all my whole device
When I am in my coach, which stays for us
At the park gate; and therefore haste away,
For we must measure twenty miles to-day.

Exeunt

SCENE V.
BELMONT. A GARDEN.

Enter LAUNCELOT *and* JESSICA

LAUNCELOT
Yes, truly; for, look you, the sins of the father are to be laid upon
the children; therefore, I promise you, I fear you. I was always
plain with you, and so now I speak my agitation of the matter;
therefore be of good cheer, for truly I think you are damn'd.
There is but one hope in it that can do you any good, and that is
but a kind of bastard hope neither.

JESSICA

And what hope is that, I pray thee?

LAUNCELOT

Marry, you may partly hope that your father got you not, that you are not the Jew's daughter.

JESSICA

That were a kind of bastard hope indeed; so the sins of my mother should be visited upon me.

LAUNCELOT

Truly then I fear you are damn'd both by father and mother; thus when I shun Scylla, your father, I fall into Charybdis, your mother; well, you are gone both ways.

JESSICA

I shall be saved by my husband; he hath made me a Christian.

LAUNCELOT

Truly, the more to blame he; we were Christians enow before, e'en as many as could well live one by another. This making of Christians will raise the price of hogs; if we grow all to be pork-eaters, we shall not shortly have a rasher on the coals for money.

JESSICA

I'll tell my husband, Launcelot, what you say; here he comes.

Enter LORENZO

LORENZO

I shall grow jealous of you shortly, Launcelot, if you thus get my wife into corners.

JESSICA

Nay, you need nor fear us, Lorenzo; Launcelot and I are out; he tells me flatly there's no mercy for me in heaven, because I am a Jew's daughter; and he says you are no good member of the commonwealth, for in converting Jews to Christians you raise the price of pork.

LORENZO

I shall answer that better to the commonwealth than you can the getting up of the negro's belly; the Moor is with child by you, Launcelot.

LAUNCELOT

It is much that the Moor should be more than reason; but if she

be less than an honest woman, she is indeed more than I took
her for.

LORENZO

How every fool can play upon the word! I think the best
grace of wit will shortly turn into silence, and discourse grow
commendable in none only but parrots. Go in, sirrah; bid them
prepare for dinner.

LAUNCELOT

That is done, sir; they have all stomachs.

LORENZO

Goodly Lord, what a wit-snapper are you! Then bid them
prepare dinner.

LAUNCELOT

That is done too, sir, only 'cover' is the word.

LORENZO

Will you cover, then, sir?

LAUNCELOT

Not so, sir, neither; I know my duty.

LORENZO

Yet more quarrelling with occasion! Wilt thou show the whole
wealth of thy wit in an instant? I pray thee understand a plain
man in his plain meaning: go to thy fellows, bid them cover the
table, serve in the meat, and we will come in to dinner.

LAUNCELOT

For the table, sir, it shall be served in; for the meat, sir, it shall
be covered; for your coming in to dinner, sir, why, let it be as
humours and conceits shall govern.

Exit

LORENZO

O dear discretion, how his words are suited!
The fool hath planted in his memory
An army of good words; and I do know
A many fools that stand in better place,
Garnish'd like him, that for a tricksy word
Defy the matter. How cheer'st thou, Jessica?
And now, good sweet, say thy opinion,
How dost thou like the Lord Bassanio's wife?

JESSICA
    Past all expressing. It is very meet
    The Lord Bassanio live an upright life,
    For, having such a blessing in his lady,
    He finds the joys of heaven here on earth;
    And if on earth he do not merit it,
    In reason he should never come to heaven.
    Why, if two gods should play some heavenly match,
    And on the wager lay two earthly women,
    And Portia one, there must be something else
    Pawn'd with the other; for the poor rude world
    Hath not her fellow.
LORENZO
    Even such a husband
    Hast thou of me as she is for a wife.
JESSICA
    Nay, but ask my opinion too of that.
LORENZO
    I will anon; first let us go to dinner.
JESSICA
    Nay, let me praise you while I have a stomach.
LORENZO
    No, pray thee, let it serve for table-talk;
    Then howsoe'er thou speak'st, 'mong other things
    I shall digest it.
JESSICA
    Well, I'll set you forth.

                                              Exeunt

ACT

IV

SCENE I.
VENICE. A COURT OF JUSTICE.

Enter the DUKE: *the Magnificoes;* ANTONIO, BASSANIO,
GRATIANO, SALARINO, SALANIO, *and Others*

DUKE

What, is Antonio here?

ANTONIO

Ready, so please your Grace.

DUKE

I am sorry for thee; thou art come to answer
A stony adversary, an inhuman wretch,
Uncapable of pity, void and empty
From any dram of mercy.

ANTONIO

I have heard
Your Grace hath ta'en great pains to qualify
His rigorous course; but since he stands obdurate,
And that no lawful means can carry me
Out of his envy's reach, I do oppose
My patience to his fury, and am arm'd

To suffer with a quietness of spirit
The very tyranny and rage of his.

DUKE

Go one, and call the Jew into the court.

SALARINO

He is ready at the door; he comes, my lord.

Enter SHYLOCK

DUKE

Make room, and let him stand before our face.
Shylock, the world thinks, and I think so too,
That thou but leadest this fashion of thy malice
To the last hour of act; and then, 'tis thought,
Thou'lt show thy mercy and remorse, more strange
Than is thy strange apparent cruelty;
And where thou now exacts the penalty,
Which is a pound of this poor merchant's flesh,
Thou wilt not only loose the forfeiture,
But, touch'd with human gentleness and love,
Forgive a moiety of the principal,
Glancing an eye of pity on his losses,
That have of late so huddled on his back,
Enow to press a royal merchant down,
And pluck commiseration of his state
From brassy bosoms and rough hearts of flint,
From stubborn Turks and Tartars, never train'd
To offices of tender courtesy.
We all expect a gentle answer, Jew.

SHYLOCK

I have possess'd your Grace of what I purpose,
And by our holy Sabbath have I sworn
To have the due and forfeit of my bond.
If you deny it, let the danger light
Upon your charter and your city's freedom.
You'll ask me why I rather choose to have
A weight of carrion flesh than to receive
Three thousand ducats. I'll not answer that,
But say it is my humour: is it answer'd?

What if my house be troubled with a rat,
And I be pleas'd to give ten thousand ducats
To have it ban'd? What, are you answer'd yet?
Some men there are love not a gaping pig;
Some that are mad if they behold a cat;
And others, when the bagpipe sings i' the nose,
Cannot contain their urine; for affection,
Mistress of passion, sways it to the mood
Of what it likes or loathes. Now, for your answer:
As there is no firm reason to be render'd,
Why he cannot abide a gaping pig;
Why he, a harmless necessary cat;
Why he, a wauling bagpipe; but of force
Must yield to such inevitable shame
As to offend, himself being offended;
So can I give no reason, nor I will not,
More than a lodg'd hate and a certain loathing
I bear Antonio, that I follow thus
A losing suit against him. Are you answered?

BASSANIO
This is no answer, thou unfeeling man,
To excuse the current of thy cruelty.

SHYLOCK
I am not bound to please thee with my answer.

BASSANIO
Do all men kill the things they do not love?

SHYLOCK
Hates any man the thing he would not kill?

BASSANIO
Every offence is not a hate at first.

SHYLOCK
What! wouldst thou have a serpent sting thee twice?

ANTONIO
I pray you, think you question with the Jew.
You may as well go stand upon the beach,
And bid the main flood bate his usual height;
You may as well use question with the wolf,

Why he hath made the ewe bleat for the lamb;
You may as well forbid the mountain pines
To wag their high tops and to make no noise
When they are fretten with the gusts of heaven;
You may as well do anything most hard
As seek to soften that—than which what's harder?—
His Jewish heart: therefore, I do beseech you,
Make no moe offers, use no farther means,
But with all brief and plain conveniency.
Let me have judgment, and the Jew his will.

BASSANIO
For thy three thousand ducats here is six.

SHYLOCK
If every ducat in six thousand ducats
Were in six parts, and every part a ducat,
I would not draw them; I would have my bond.

DUKE
How shalt thou hope for mercy, rendering none?

SHYLOCK
What judgment shall I dread, doing no wrong?
You have among you many a purchas'd slave,
Which, like your asses and your dogs and mules,
You use in abject and in slavish parts,
Because you bought them; shall I say to you
'Let them be free, marry them to your heirs—
Why sweat they under burdens?—let their beds
Be made as soft as yours, and let their palates
Be season'd with such viands'? You will answer
'The slaves are ours.' So do I answer you:
The pound of flesh which I demand of him
Is dearly bought; 'tis mine, and I will have it.
If you deny me, fie upon your law!
There is no force in the decrees of Venice.
I stand for judgment: answer; shall I have it?

DUKE
Upon my power I may dismiss this court,
Unless Bellario, a learned doctor,

Whom I have sent for to determine this,
Come here to-day.

SALARINO
My lord, here stays without
A messenger with letters from the doctor,
New come from Padua.

DUKE
Bring us the letters; call the messenger.

BASSANIO
Good cheer, Antonio! What, man, courage yet!
The Jew shall have my flesh, blood, bones, and all,
Ere thou shalt lose for me one drop of blood.

ANTONIO
I am a tainted wether of the flock,
Meetest for death; the weakest kind of fruit
Drops earliest to the ground, and so let me.
You cannot better be employ'd, Bassanio,
Than to live still, and write mine epitaph.

Enter NERISSA *dressed like a lawyer's clerk.*

DUKE
Came you from Padua, from Bellario?

NERISSA
From both, my lord. Bellario greets your Grace.
[*Presents a letter.*]

BASSANIO
Why dost thou whet thy knife so earnestly?

SHYLOCK
To cut the forfeiture from that bankrupt there.

GRATIANO
Not on thy sole, but on thy soul, harsh Jew,
Thou mak'st thy knife keen; but no metal can,
No, not the hangman's axe, bear half the keenness
Of thy sharp envy. Can no prayers pierce thee?

SHYLOCK
No, none that thou hast wit enough to make.

GRATIANO
O, be thou damn'd, inexecrable dog!

And for thy life let justice be accus'd.
Thou almost mak'st me waver in my faith,
To hold opinion with Pythagoras
That souls of animals infuse themselves
Into the trunks of men. Thy currish spirit
Govern'd a wolf who, hang'd for human slaughter,
Even from the gallows did his fell soul fleet,
And, whilst thou lay'st in thy unhallow'd dam,
Infus'd itself in thee; for thy desires
Are wolfish, bloody, starv'd and ravenous.

SHYLOCK

Till thou canst rail the seal from off my bond,
Thou but offend'st thy lungs to speak so loud;
Repair thy wit, good youth, or it will fall
To cureless ruin. I stand here for law.

DUKE

This letter from Bellario doth commend
A young and learned doctor to our court.
Where is he?

NERISSA

He attendeth here hard by,
To know your answer, whether you'll admit him.

DUKE OF VENICE

With all my heart: some three or four of you
Go give him courteous conduct to this place.
Meantime, the court shall hear Bellario's letter.

CLERK

[*Reads*] 'Your Grace shall understand that at the receipt of your letter I am very sick; but in the instant that your messenger came, in loving visitation was with me a young doctor of Rome; his name is Balthazar. I acquainted him with the cause in controversy between the Jew and Antonio the merchant; we turn'd o'er many books together; he is furnished with my opinion which, bettered with his own learning—the greatness whereof I cannot enough commend—comes with him at my importunity to fill up your Grace's request in my stead. I beseech you let his lack of years be no impediment to let him lack a reverend estimation, for I never knew so young a body with so old a head. I leave him to your gracious acceptance, whose trial shall better publish his commendation.'

DUKE

You hear the learn'd Bellario, what he writes;
And here, I take it, is the doctor come.

Enter PORTIA, *dressed like a doctor of laws.*

Give me your hand; come you from old Bellario?

PORTIA

I did, my lord.

DUKE

You are welcome; take your place.
Are you acquainted with the difference
That holds this present question in the court?

PORTIA

I am informed throughly of the cause.
Which is the merchant here, and which the Jew?

DUKE OF VENICE

Antonio and old Shylock, both stand forth.

PORTIA

Is your name Shylock?

SHYLOCK

Shylock is my name.

PORTIA

Of a strange nature is the suit you follow;
Yet in such rule that the Venetian law
Cannot impugn you as you do proceed.
[*To* ANTONIO.] You stand within his danger, do you not?

ANTONIO

Ay, so he says.

PORTIA

Do you confess the bond?

ANTONIO

I do.

PORTIA

Then must the Jew be merciful.

SHYLOCK

    On what compulsion must I? Tell me that.

PORTIA

    The quality of mercy is not strain'd;
    It droppeth as the gentle rain from heaven
    Upon the place beneath. It is twice blest:
    It blesseth him that gives and him that takes.
    'Tis mightiest in the mightiest; it becomes
    The throned monarch better than his crown;
    His sceptre shows the force of temporal power,
    The attribute to awe and majesty,
    Wherein doth sit the dread and fear of kings;
    But mercy is above this sceptred sway,
    It is enthroned in the hearts of kings,
    It is an attribute to God himself;
    And earthly power doth then show likest God's
    When mercy seasons justice. Therefore, Jew,
    Though justice be thy plea, consider this,
    That in the course of justice none of us
    Should see salvation; we do pray for mercy,
    And that same prayer doth teach us all to render
    The deeds of mercy. I have spoke thus much
    To mitigate the justice of thy plea,
    Which if thou follow, this strict court of Venice
    Must needs give sentence 'gainst the merchant there.

SHYLOCK

    My deeds upon my head! I crave the law,
    The penalty and forfeit of my bond.

PORTIA

    Is he not able to discharge the money?

BASSANIO

    Yes; here I tender it for him in the court;
    Yea, twice the sum; if that will not suffice,
    I will be bound to pay it ten times o'er
    On forfeit of my hands, my head, my heart;
    If this will not suffice, it must appear
    That malice bears down truth. And, I beseech you,

Wrest once the law to your authority;
To do a great right do a little wrong,
And curb this cruel devil of his will.

PORTIA

It must not be; there is no power in Venice
Can alter a decree established;
'Twill be recorded for a precedent,
And many an error by the same example
Will rush into the state. It cannot be.

SHYLOCK

A Daniel come to judgment! Yea, a Daniel!
O wise young judge, how I do honour thee!

PORTIA

I pray you, let me look upon the bond.

SHYLOCK

Here 'tis, most reverend doctor; here it is.

PORTIA

Shylock, there's thrice thy money offer'd thee.

SHYLOCK

An oath, an oath! I have an oath in heaven.
Shall I lay perjury upon my soul?
No, not for Venice.

PORTIA

Why, this bond is forfeit;
And lawfully by this the Jew may claim
A pound of flesh, to be by him cut off
Nearest the merchant's heart. Be merciful.
Take thrice thy money; bid me tear the bond.

SHYLOCK

When it is paid according to the tenour.
It doth appear you are a worthy judge;
You know the law; your exposition
Hath been most sound; I charge you by the law,
Whereof you are a well-deserving pillar,
Proceed to judgment. By my soul I swear
There is no power in the tongue of man
To alter me. I stay here on my bond.

ANTONIO
Most heartily I do beseech the court
To give the judgment.
PORTIA
Why then, thus it is:
You must prepare your bosom for his knife.
SHYLOCK
O noble judge! O excellent young man!
PORTIA
For the intent and purpose of the law
Hath full relation to the penalty,
Which here appeareth due upon the bond.
SHYLOCK
'Tis very true. O wise and upright judge,
How much more elder art thou than thy looks!
PORTIA
Therefore, lay bare your bosom.
SHYLOCK
Ay, his breast—
So says the bond; doth it not, noble judge?
'Nearest his heart', those are the very words.
PORTIA
It is so. Are there balance here to weigh
The flesh?
SHYLOCK
I have them ready.
PORTIA
Have by some surgeon, Shylock, on your charge,
To stop his wounds, lest he do bleed to death.
SHYLOCK
Is it so nominated in the bond?
PORTIA
It is not so express'd; but what of that?
'Twere good you do so much for charity.
SHYLOCK
I cannot find it; 'tis not in the bond.

PORTIA

You, merchant, have you anything to say?

ANTONIO

But little: I am arm'd and well prepar'd.
Give me your hand, Bassanio: fare you well.!
Grieve not that I am fallen to this for you,
For herein Fortune shows herself more kind
Than is her custom: it is still her use
To let the wretched man outlive his wealth,
To view with hollow eye and wrinkled brow
An age of poverty; from which lingering penance
Of such misery doth she cut me off.
Commend me to your honourable wife:
Tell her the process of Antonio's end;
Say how I lov'd you; speak me fair in death;
And, when the tale is told, bid her be judge
Whether Bassanio had not once a love.
Repent but you that you shall lose your friend,
And he repents not that he pays your debt;
For if the Jew do cut but deep enough,
I'll pay it instantly with all my heart.

BASSANIO

Antonio, I am married to a wife
Which is as dear to me as life itself;
But life itself, my wife, and all the world,
Are not with me esteem'd above thy life;
I would lose all, ay, sacrifice them all
Here to this devil, to deliver you.

PORTIA

Your wife would give you little thanks for that,
If she were by to hear you make the offer.

GRATIANO

I have a wife whom, I protest, I love;
I would she were in heaven, so she could
Entreat some power to change this currish Jew.

NERISSA
    'Tis well you offer it behind her back;
    The wish would make else an unquiet house.
SHYLOCK
    [*Aside*] These be the Christian husbands! I have a daughter;
    Would any of the stock of Barabbas
    Had been her husband, rather than a Christian!
    We trifle time; I pray thee, pursue sentence.
PORTIA
    A pound of that same merchant's flesh is thine.
    The court awards it and the law doth give it.
SHYLOCK
    Most rightful judge!
PORTIA
    And you must cut this flesh from off his breast.
    The law allows it and the court awards it.
SHYLOCK
    Most learned judge! A sentence! Come, prepare.
PORTIA
    Tarry a little; there is something else.
    This bond doth give thee here no jot of blood;
    The words expressly are 'a pound of flesh':
    Take then thy bond, take thou thy pound of flesh;
    But, in the cutting it, if thou dost shed
    One drop of Christian blood, thy lands and goods
    Are, by the laws of Venice, confiscate
    Unto the state of Venice.
GRATIANO
    O upright judge! Mark, Jew: O learned judge!
SHYLOCK
    Is that the law?
PORTIA
    Thyself shalt see the act;
    For, as thou urgest justice, be assur'd
    Thou shalt have justice, more than thou desir'st.
GRATIANO
    O learned judge! Mark, Jew: a learned judge!

SHYLOCK

> I take this offer then: pay the bond thrice,
> And let the Christian go.

BASSANIO

> Here is the money.

PORTIA

> Soft!
> The Jew shall have all justice. Soft! No haste.
> He shall have nothing but the penalty.

GRATIANO

> O Jew! an upright judge, a learned judge!

PORTIA

> Therefore, prepare thee to cut off the flesh.
> Shed thou no blood; nor cut thou less nor more,
> But just a pound of flesh: if thou tak'st more,
> Or less, than a just pound, be it but so much
> As makes it light or heavy in the substance,
> Or the division of the twentieth part
> Of one poor scruple; nay, if the scale do turn
> But in the estimation of a hair,
> Thou diest, and all thy goods are confiscate.

GRATIANO

> A second Daniel, a Daniel, Jew!
> Now, infidel, I have you on the hip.

PORTIA

> Why doth the Jew pause? Take thy forfeiture.

SHYLOCK

> Give me my principal, and let me go.

BASSANIO

> I have it ready for thee; here it is.

PORTIA

> He hath refus'd it in the open court;
> He shall have merely justice, and his bond.

GRATIANO

> A Daniel still say I; a second Daniel!
> I thank thee, Jew, for teaching me that word.

SHYLOCK

    Shall I not have barely my principal?

PORTIA

    Thou shalt have nothing but the forfeiture

    To be so taken at thy peril, Jew.

SHYLOCK

    Why, then the devil give him good of it!

    I'll stay no longer question.

PORTIA

    Tarry, Jew.

    The law hath yet another hold on you.

    It is enacted in the laws of Venice,

    If it be prov'd against an alien

    That by direct or indirect attempts

    He seek the life of any citizen,

    The party 'gainst the which he doth contrive

    Shall seize one half his goods; the other half

    Comes to the privy coffer of the state;

    And the offender's life lies in the mercy

    Of the Duke only, 'gainst all other voice.

    In which predicament, I say, thou stand'st;

    For it appears by manifest proceeding

    That indirectly, and directly too,

    Thou hast contrived against the very life

    Of the defendant; and thou hast incurr'd

    The danger formerly by me rehears'd.

    Down, therefore, and beg mercy of the Duke.

GRATIANO

    Beg that thou mayst have leave to hang thyself;

    And yet, thy wealth being forfeit to the state,

    Thou hast not left the value of a cord;

    Therefore thou must be hang'd at the state's charge.

DUKE

    That thou shalt see the difference of our spirits,

    I pardon thee thy life before thou ask it.

    For half thy wealth, it is Antonio's;

The other half comes to the general state,
Which humbleness may drive unto a fine.

PORTIA

Ay, for the state; not for Antonio.

SHYLOCK

Nay, take my life and all, pardon not that:
You take my house when you do take the prop
That doth sustain my house; you take my life
When you do take the means whereby I live.

PORTIA

What mercy can you render him, Antonio?

GRATIANO

A halter gratis; nothing else, for God's sake!

ANTONIO

So please my lord the Duke and all the court
To quit the fine for one half of his goods;
I am content, so he will let me have
The other half in use, to render it
Upon his death unto the gentleman
That lately stole his daughter:
Two things provided more, that, for this favour,
He presently become a Christian;
The other, that he do record a gift,
Here in the court, of all he dies possess'd
Unto his son Lorenzo and his daughter.

DUKE

He shall do this, or else I do recant
The pardon that I late pronounced here.

PORTIA

Art thou contented, Jew? What dost thou say?

SHYLOCK

I am content.

PORTIA

Clerk, draw a deed of gift.

SHYLOCK

I pray you, give me leave to go from hence;

I am not well; send the deed after me
And I will sign it.

DUKE

Get thee gone, but do it.

GRATIANO

In christening shalt thou have two god-fathers;
Had I been judge, thou shouldst have had ten more,
To bring thee to the gallows, not to the font.

Exit SHYLOCK

DUKE

Sir, I entreat you home with me to dinner.

PORTIA

I humbly do desire your Grace of pardon;
I must away this night toward Padua,
And it is meet I presently set forth.

DUKE

I am sorry that your leisure serves you not.
Antonio, gratify this gentleman,
For in my mind you are much bound to him.

Exeunt DUKE, *Magnificoes, and Train*

BASSANIO

Most worthy gentleman, I and my friend
Have by your wisdom been this day acquitted
Of grievous penalties; in lieu whereof
Three thousand ducats, due unto the Jew,
We freely cope your courteous pains withal.

ANTONIO

And stand indebted, over and above,
In love and service to you evermore.

PORTIA

He is well paid that is well satisfied;
And I, delivering you, am satisfied,
And therein do account myself well paid:
My mind was never yet more mercenary.
I pray you, know me when we meet again:
I wish you well, and so I take my leave.

BASSANIO

 Dear sir, of force I must attempt you further;
 Take some remembrance of us, as a tribute,
 Not as fee. Grant me two things, I pray you,
 Not to deny me, and to pardon me.

PORTIA

 You press me far, and therefore I will yield.
 [*To ANTONIO*]
 Give me your gloves, I'll wear them for your sake.
 [*To BASSANIO*]
 And, for your love, I'll take this ring from you.
 Do not draw back your hand; I'll take no more;
 And you in love shall not deny me this.

BASSANIO

 This ring, good sir? alas, it is a trifle;
 I will not shame myself to give you this.

PORTIA

 I will have nothing else but only this;
 And now, methinks, I have a mind to it.

BASSANIO

 There's more depends on this than on the value.
 The dearest ring in Venice will I give you,
 And find it out by proclamation:
 Only for this, I pray you, pardon me.

PORTIA

 I see, sir, you are liberal in offers;
 You taught me first to beg, and now methinks
 You teach me how a beggar should be answer'd.

BASSANIO

 Good sir, this ring was given me by my wife;
 And, when she put it on, she made me vow
 That I should neither sell, nor give, nor lose it.

PORTIA

 That 'scuse serves many men to save their gifts.
 And if your wife be not a mad woman,
 And know how well I have deserv'd this ring,

She would not hold out enemy for ever
For giving it to me. Well, peace be with you!

Exeunt PORTIA *and* NERISSA

ANTONIO

My Lord Bassanio, let him have the ring:
Let his deservings, and my love withal,
Be valued 'gainst your wife's commandment.

BASSANIO

Go, Gratiano, run and overtake him;
Give him the ring, and bring him, if thou canst,
Unto Antonio's house. Away! make haste.

Exit GRATIANO

Come, you and I will thither presently;
And in the morning early will we both
Fly toward Belmont. Come, Antonio.

Exeunt

SCENE II.
VENICE. A STREET.

Enter PORTIA *and* NERISSA

PORTIA

Inquire the Jew's house out, give him this deed,
And let him sign it; we'll away to-night,
And be a day before our husbands home.
This deed will be well welcome to Lorenzo.

Enter GRATIANO

GRATIANO

Fair sir, you are well o'erta'en.
My Lord Bassanio, upon more advice,
Hath sent you here this ring, and doth entreat
Your company at dinner.

PORTIA

That cannot be:
His ring I do accept most thankfully;
And so, I pray you, tell him: furthermore,
I pray you show my youth old Shylock's house.

GRATIANO

    That will I do.

NERISSA

    Sir, I would speak with you.

    [*Aside to* PORTIA]

    I'll see if I can get my husband's ring,

    Which I did make him swear to keep for ever.

PORTIA

    [*To* NERISSA]

    Thou mayst, I warrant. We shall have old swearing

    That they did give the rings away to men;

    But we'll outface them, and outswear them too.

    Away! make haste: thou know'st where I will tarry.

NERISSA

    Come, good sir, will you show me to this house?

                            Exeunt

ACT

V

SCENE I.
BELMONT. THE AVENUE TO
PORTIA'S HOUSE.

Enter LORENZO *and* JESSICA

LORENZO

    The moon shines bright: in such a night as this,
    When the sweet wind did gently kiss the trees,
    And they did make no noise, in such a night,
    Troilus methinks mounted the Troyan walls,
    And sigh'd his soul toward the Grecian tents,
    Where Cressid lay that night.

JESSICA

    In such a night
    Did Thisby fearfully o'ertrip the dew,
    And saw the lion's shadow ere himself,
    And ran dismay'd away.

LORENZO

    In such a night
    Stood Dido with a willow in her hand
    Upon the wild sea-banks, and waft her love
    To come again to Carthage.

JESSICA
    In such a night
    Medea gather'd the enchanted herbs
    That did renew old Aeson.
LORENZO
    In such a night
    Did Jessica steal from the wealthy Jew,
    And with an unthrift love did run from Venice
    As far as Belmont.
JESSICA
    In such a night
    Did young Lorenzo swear he lov'd her well,
    Stealing her soul with many vows of faith,
    And ne'er a true one.
LORENZO
    In such a night
    Did pretty Jessica, like a little shrew,
    Slander her love, and he forgave it her.
JESSICA
    I would out-night you, did no body come;
    But, hark, I hear the footing of a man.
                                    Enter STEPHANO
LORENZO
    Who comes so fast in silence of the night?
STEPHANO
    A friend.
LORENZO
    A friend! What friend? Your name, I pray you, friend?
STEPHANO
    Stephano is my name, and I bring word
    My mistress will before the break of day
    Be here at Belmont; she doth stray about
    By holy crosses, where she kneels and prays
    For happy wedlock hours.
LORENZO
    Who comes with her?

STEPHANO
    None but a holy hermit and her maid.
    I pray you, is my master yet return'd?
LORENZO
    He is not, nor we have not heard from him.
    But go we in, I pray thee, Jessica,
    And ceremoniously let us prepare
    Some welcome for the mistress of the house.

                 Enter LAUNCELOT

LAUNCELOT
    Sola, sola! wo ha, ho! sola, sola!
LORENZO
    Who calls?
LAUNCELOT
    Sola! Did you see Master Lorenzo? Master Lorenzo! Sola, sola!
LORENZO
    Leave holloaing, man. Here!
LAUNCELOT
    Sola! Where? Where?
LORENZO
    Here!
LAUNCELOT
    Tell him there's a post come from my master with his horn full
    of good news; my master will be here ere morning.

                                                       Exit

LORENZO
    Sweet soul, let's in, and there expect their coming.
    And yet no matter; why should we go in?
    My friend Stephano, signify, I pray you,
    Within the house, your mistress is at hand;
    And bring your music forth into the air.

                                        Exit STEPHANO

    How sweet the moonlight sleeps upon this bank!
    Here will we sit and let the sounds of music
    Creep in our ears; soft stillness and the night
    Become the touches of sweet harmony.
    Sit, Jessica. Look how the floor of heaven

Is thick inlaid with patines of bright gold;
There's not the smallest orb which thou behold'st
But in his motion like an angel sings,
Still quiring to the young-eyed cherubins;
Such harmony is in immortal souls;
But, whilst this muddy vesture of decay
Doth grossly close it in, we cannot hear it.

Enter Musicians

Come, ho! and wake Diana with a hymn;
With sweetest touches pierce your mistress' ear.
And draw her home with music.

Music

JESSICA

I am never merry when I hear sweet music.

LORENZO

The reason is, your spirits are attentive;
For do but note a wild and wanton herd,
Or race of youthful and unhandled colts,
Fetching mad bounds, bellowing and neighing loud,
Which is the hot condition of their blood;
If they but hear perchance a trumpet sound,
Or any air of music touch their ears,
You shall perceive them make a mutual stand,
Their savage eyes turn'd to a modest gaze
By the sweet power of music: therefore the poet
Did feign that Orpheus drew trees, stones, and floods;
Since nought so stockish, hard, and full of rage,
But music for the time doth change his nature.
The man that hath no music in himself,
Nor is not mov'd with concord of sweet sounds,
Is fit for treasons, stratagems, and spoils;
The motions of his spirit are dull as night,
And his affections dark as Erebus.
Let no such man be trusted. Mark the music.

Enter PORTIA *and* NERISSA, *at a distance.*

PORTIA

That light we see is burning in my hall.

How far that little candle throws his beams!
So shines a good deed in a naughty world.

NERISSA

When the moon shone, we did not see the candle.

PORTIA

So doth the greater glory dim the less:
A substitute shines brightly as a king
Until a king be by, and then his state
Empties itself, as doth an inland brook
Into the main of waters. Music! hark!

NERISSA

It is your music, madam, of the house.

PORTIA

Nothing is good, I see, without respect:
Methinks it sounds much sweeter than by day.

NERISSA

Silence bestows that virtue on it, madam.

PORTIA

The crow doth sing as sweetly as the lark
When neither is attended; and I think
The nightingale, if she should sing by day,
When every goose is cackling, would be thought
No better a musician than the wren.
How many things by season season'd are
To their right praise and true perfection!
Peace, ho! The moon sleeps with Endymion,
And would not be awak'd!
[Music ceases.]

LORENZO

That is the voice,
Or I am much deceiv'd, of Portia.

PORTIA

He knows me as the blind man knows the cuckoo,
By the bad voice.

LORENZO

Dear lady, welcome home.

PORTIA

    We have been praying for our husbands' welfare,

    Which speed, we hope, the better for our words.

    Are they return'd?

LORENZO

    Madam, they are not yet;

    But there is come a messenger before,

    To signify their coming.

PORTIA

    Go in, Nerissa:

    Give order to my servants that they take

    No note at all of our being absent hence;

    Nor you, Lorenzo; Jessica, nor you.

    [*A tucket sounds.*]

LORENZO

    Your husband is at hand; I hear his trumpet.

    We are no tell-tales, madam, fear you not.

PORTIA

    This night methinks is but the daylight sick;

    It looks a little paler; 'tis a day

    Such as the day is when the sun is hid.

              Enter BASSANIO, ANTONIO,

             GRATIANO, *and their Followers.*

BASSANIO

    We should hold day with the Antipodes,

    If you would walk in absence of the sun.

PORTIA

    Let me give light, but let me not be light,

    For a light wife doth make a heavy husband,

    And never be Bassanio so for me:

    But God sort all! You are welcome home, my lord.

BASSANIO

    I thank you, madam; give welcome to my friend:

    This is the man, this is Antonio,

    To whom I am so infinitely bound.

PORTIA

You should in all sense be much bound to him,
For, as I hear, he was much bound for you.

ANTONIO

No more than I am well acquitted of.

PORTIA

Sir, you are very welcome to our house.
It must appear in other ways than words,
Therefore I scant this breathing courtesy.

GRATIANO

[To NERISSA]

By yonder moon I swear you do me wrong;
In faith, I gave it to the judge's clerk.
Would he were gelt that had it, for my part,
Since you do take it, love, so much at heart.

PORTIA

A quarrel, ho, already! What's the matter?

GRATIANO

About a hoop of gold, a paltry ring
That she did give me, whose posy was
For all the world like cutlers' poetry
Upon a knife, 'Love me, and leave me not.'

NERISSA

What talk you of the posy, or the value?
You swore to me, when I did give it you,
That you would wear it till your hour of death,
And that it should lie with you in your grave;
Though not for me, yet for your vehement oaths,
You should have been respective and have kept it.
Gave it a judge's clerk! No, God's my judge,
The clerk will ne'er wear hair on's face that had it.

GRATIANO

He will, an if he live to be a man.

NERISSA

Ay, if a woman live to be a man.

GRATIANO

Now, by this hand, I gave it to a youth,

A kind of boy, a little scrubbed boy
No higher than thyself, the judge's clerk;
A prating boy that begg'd it as a fee;
I could not for my heart deny it him.

PORTIA

You were to blame, I must be plain with you,
To part so slightly with your wife's first gift,
A thing stuck on with oaths upon your finger,
And so riveted with faith unto your flesh.
I gave my love a ring, and made him swear
Never to part with it, and here he stands,
I dare be sworn for him he would not leave it
Nor pluck it from his finger for the wealth
That the world masters. Now, in faith, Gratiano,
You give your wife too unkind a cause of grief;
An 'twere to me, I should be mad at it.

BASSANIO

[Aside] Why, I were best to cut my left hand off,
And swear I lost the ring defending it.

GRATIANO

My Lord Bassanio gave his ring away
Unto the judge that begg'd it, and indeed
Deserv'd it too; and then the boy, his clerk,
That took some pains in writing, he begg'd mine;
And neither man nor master would take aught
But the two rings.

PORTIA

What ring gave you, my lord?
Not that, I hope, which you receiv'd of me.

BASSANIO

If I could add a lie unto a fault,
I would deny it; but you see my finger
Hath not the ring upon it; it is gone.

PORTIA

Even so void is your false heart of truth;
By heaven, I will ne'er come in your bed
Until I see the ring.

NERISSA

    Nor I in yours

    Till I again see mine.

BASSANIO

    Sweet Portia,

    If you did know to whom I gave the ring,

    If you did know for whom I gave the ring,

    And would conceive for what I gave the ring,

    And how unwillingly I left the ring,

    When nought would be accepted but the ring,

    You would abate the strength of your displeasure.

PORTIA

    If you had known the virtue of the ring,

    Or half her worthiness that gave the ring,

    Or your own honour to contain the ring,

    You would not then have parted with the ring.

    What man is there so much unreasonable,

    If you had pleas'd to have defended it

    With any terms of zeal, wanted the modesty

    To urge the thing held as a ceremony?

    Nerissa teaches me what to believe:

    I'll die for't but some woman had the ring.

BASSANIO

    No, by my honour, madam, by my soul,

    No woman had it, but a civil doctor,

    Which did refuse three thousand ducats of me,

    And begg'd the ring; the which I did deny him,

    And suffer'd him to go displeas'd away;

    Even he that had held up the very life

    Of my dear friend. What should I say, sweet lady?

    I was enforc'd to send it after him;

    I was beset with shame and courtesy;

    My honour would not let ingratitude

    So much besmear it. Pardon me, good lady;

    For, by these blessed candles of the night,

    Had you been there, I think you would have begg'd

    The ring of me to give the worthy doctor.

PORTIA

    Let not that doctor e'er come near my house;
    Since he hath got the jewel that I loved,
    And that which you did swear to keep for me,
    I will become as liberal as you;
    I'll not deny him anything I have,
    No, not my body, nor my husband's bed.
    Know him I shall, I am well sure of it.
    Lie not a night from home; watch me like Argus;
    If you do not, if I be left alone,
    Now, by mine honour which is yet mine own,
    I'll have that doctor for mine bedfellow.

NERISSA

    And I his clerk; therefore be well advis'd
    How you do leave me to mine own protection.

GRATIANO

    Well, do you so: let not me take him then;
    For, if I do, I'll mar the young clerk's pen.

ANTONIO

    I am the unhappy subject of these quarrels.

PORTIA

    Sir, grieve not you; you are welcome notwithstanding.

BASSANIO

    Portia, forgive me this enforced wrong;
    And in the hearing of these many friends
    I swear to thee, even by thine own fair eyes,
    Wherein I see myself—

PORTIA

    Mark you but that!
    In both my eyes he doubly sees himself,
    In each eye one; swear by your double self,
    And there's an oath of credit.

BASSANIO

    Nay, but hear me:
    Pardon this fault, and by my soul I swear
    I never more will break an oath with thee.

ANTONIO

I once did lend my body for his wealth,
Which, but for him that had your husband's ring,
Had quite miscarried; I dare be bound again,
My soul upon the forfeit, that your lord
Will never more break faith advisedly.

PORTIA

Then you shall be his surety. Give him this,
And bid him keep it better than the other.

ANTONIO

Here, Lord Bassanio, swear to keep this ring.

BASSANIO

By heaven! it is the same I gave the doctor!

PORTIA

I had it of him: pardon me, Bassanio,
For, by this ring, the doctor lay with me.

NERISSA

And pardon me, my gentle Gratiano,
For that same scrubbed boy, the doctor's clerk,
In lieu of this, last night did lie with me.

GRATIANO

Why, this is like the mending of high ways
In summer, where the ways are fair enough.
What! are we cuckolds ere we have deserv'd it?

PORTIA

Speak not so grossly. You are all amaz'd:
Here is a letter; read it at your leisure;
It comes from Padua, from Bellario:
There you shall find that Portia was the doctor,
Nerissa there, her clerk: Lorenzo here
Shall witness I set forth as soon as you,
And even but now return'd; I have not yet
Enter'd my house. Antonio, you are welcome;
And I have better news in store for you
Than you expect: unseal this letter soon,
There you shall find three of your argosies
Are richly come to harbour suddenly.

You shall not know by what strange accident
I chanced on this letter.

ANTONIO

I am dumb.

BASSANIO

Were you the doctor, and I knew you not?

GRATIANO

Were you the clerk that is to make me cuckold?

NERISSA

Ay, but the clerk that never means to do it,
Unless he live until he be a man.

BASSANIO

Sweet doctor, you shall be my bedfellow:
When I am absent, then lie with my wife.

ANTONIO

Sweet lady, you have given me life and living;
For here I read for certain that my ships
Are safely come to road.

PORTIA

How now, Lorenzo!
My clerk hath some good comforts too for you.

NERISSA

Ay, and I'll give them him without a fee.
There do I give to you and Jessica,
From the rich Jew, a special deed of gift,
After his death, of all he dies possess'd of.

LORENZO

Fair ladies, you drop manna in the way
Of starved people.

PORTIA

It is almost morning,
And yet I am sure you are not satisfied
Of these events at full. Let us go in;
And charge us there upon inter'gatories,
And we will answer all things faithfully.

GRATIANO

Let it be so: he first inter'gatory

That my Nerissa shall be sworn on is,
Whe'r till the next night she had rather stay,
Or go to bed now, being two hours to day:
But were the day come, I should wish it dark,
Till I were couching with the doctor's clerk.
Well, while I live, I'll fear no other thing
So sore as keeping safe Nerissa's ring.

Exeunt

The Comedy of Errors

"Am I in earth, in heaven, or in hell?
Sleeping or waking? mad or well-advised?
Known unto these, and to myself disguised!"

The Comedy of Errors

Characters of the Play[*]

SOLINUS[†], Duke of Ephesus
ÆGEON, a merchant of Syracuse
ÆMILIA, wife to Ægeon, an abbess at Ephesus
ANTIPHOLUS[‡] of Ephesus   } twin brothers, and sons to
ANTIPHOLUS of Syracuse   } Ægeon and Æmilia
DROMIO of Ephesus   } twin brothers, and attendants on
DROMIO of Syracuse   } the two Antipholuses
ADRIANA, wife to Antipholus of Ephesus
LUCIANA, her sister
BALTHAZAR, a merchant
ANGELO, a goldsmith
FIRST MERCHANT, friend to Antipholus of Syracuse
SECOND MERCHANT, to whom Angelo is a debtor
PINCH, a schoolmaster
LUCE, servant to Adriana
A Courtesan
Gaoler, Officers, and other Attendants

---

* DRAMATIS PERSONÆ first given by Rowe.

† SOLINUS] See note (I).

‡ ANTIPHOLUS] See note (I).

SCENE: Ephesus

ACT

I

SCENE I.
A HALL IN THE DUKE'S PALACE.

Enter Duke, Ægeon, *Gaoler,*
Officers, and other Attendants

Ægeon

Proceed, Solinus, to procure my fall,
And by the doom of death end woes and all.

Duke

Merchant of Syracusa, plead no more;
I am not partial to infringe our laws.
The enmity and discord which of late
Sprung from the rancorous outrage of your Duke
To merchants, our well-dealing countrymen,
Who, wanting guilders to redeem their lives,
Have seal'd his rigorous statutes with their bloods,
Excludes all pity from our threatening looks.
For, since the mortal and intestine jars
'Twixt thy seditious countrymen and us,
It hath in solemn synods been decreed,
Both by the Syracusians and ourselves,
To admit no traffic to our adverse towns.

Nay, more,
If any born at Ephesus be seen
At any Syracusian marts and fairs;
Again, if any Syracusian born
Come to the bay of Ephesus, he dies,
His goods confiscate to the Duke's dispose;
Unless a thousand marks be levied,
To quit the penalty and to ransom him.
Thy substance, valued at the highest rate,
Cannot amount unto a hundred marks;
Therefore by law thou art condemn'd to die.

ÆGEON

Yet this my comfort: when your words are done,
My woes end likewise with the evening sun.

DUKE

Well, Syracusian, say, in brief, the cause
Why thou departed'st from thy native home,
And for what cause thou camest to Ephesus.

ÆGEON

A heavier task could not have been imposed
Than I to speak my griefs unspeakable.
Yet, that the world may witness that my end
Was wrought by nature, not by vile offence,
I'll utter what my sorrow gives me leave.
In Syracusa was I born; and wed
Unto a woman, happy but for me,
And by me, had not our hap been bad.
With her I lived in joy; our wealth increased
By prosperous voyages I often made
To Epidamnum; till my factor's death,
And the great care of goods at random left,
Drew me from kind embracements of my spouse,
From whom my absence was not six months old,
Before herself, almost at fainting under
The pleasing punishment that women bear,
Had made provision for her following me,
And soon and safe arrived where I was.

There had she not been long but she became
A joyful mother of two goodly sons;
And, which was strange, the one so like the other
As could not be distinguish'd but by names.
That very hour, and in the self-same inn,
A meaner woman was delivered
Of such a burden, male twins, both alike.
Those, for their parents were exceeding poor,
I bought, and brought up to attend my sons.
My wife, not meanly proud of two such boys,
Made daily motions for our home return.
Unwilling I agreed; alas! too soon
We came aboard.
A league from Epidamnum had we sail'd,
Before the always-wind-obeying deep
Gave any tragic instance of our harm.
But longer did we not retain much hope;
For what obscured light the heavens did grant
Did but convey unto our fearful minds
A doubtful warrant of immediate death;
Which though myself would gladly have embraced,
Yet the incessant weepings of my wife,
Weeping before for what she saw must come,
And piteous plainings of the pretty babes,
That mourn'd for fashion, ignorant what to fear,
Forced me to seek delays for them and me.
And this it was, for other means was none,
The sailors sought for safety by our boat,
And left the ship, then sinking-ripe, to us.
My wife, more careful for the latter-born,
Had fasten'd him unto a small spare mast,
Such as seafaring men provide for storms;
To him one of the other twins was bound,
Whilst I had been like heedful of the other.
The children thus disposed, my wife and I,
Fixing our eyes on whom our care was fix'd,
Fasten'd ourselves at either end the mast;

And floating straight, obedient to the stream,
Was carried towards Corinth, as we thought.
At length the sun, gazing upon the earth,
Dispersed those vapours that offended us;
And, by the benefit of his wished light,
The seas wax'd calm, and we discovered
Two ships from far making amain to us,
Of Corinth that, of Epidaurus this.
But ere they came—O, let me say no more!
Gather the sequel by that went before.

DUKE

Nay, forward, old man; do not break off so;
For we may pity, though not pardon thee.

ÆGEON

O, had the gods done so, I had not now
Worthily term'd them merciless to us!
For, ere the ships could meet by twice five leagues,
We were encounter'd by a mighty rock;
Which being violently borne upon,
Our helpful ship was splitted in the midst;
So that, in this unjust divorce of us,
Fortune had left to both of us alike
What to delight in, what to sorrow for.
Her part, poor soul! seeming as burdened
With lesser weight, but not with lesser woe,
Was carried with more speed before the wind;
And in our sight they three were taken up
By fishermen of Corinth, as we thought.
At length, another ship had seized on us;
And, knowing whom it was their hap to save,
Gave healthful welcome to their shipwreck'd guests;
And would have reft the fishers of their prey,
Had not their bark been very slow of sail;
And therefore homeward did they bend their course.
Thus have you heard me sever'd from my bliss;
That by misfortunes was my life prolong'd,
To tell sad stories of my own mishaps.

DUKE
>   And, for the sake of them thou sorrowest for,
>   Do me the favour to dilate at full
>   What hath befall'n of them and thee till now.

ÆGEON
>   My youngest boy, and yet my eldest care,
>   At eighteen years became inquisitive
>   After his brother, and importuned me
>   That his attendant—so his case was like,
>   Reft of his brother, but retain'd his name—
>   Might bear him company in the quest of him;
>   Whom whilst I labour'd of a love to see,
>   I hazarded the loss of whom I loved.
>   Five summers have I spent in furthest Greece,
>   Roaming clean through the bounds of Asia,
>   And, coasting homeward, came to Ephesus;
>   Hopeless to find, yet loath to leave unsought
>   Or that, or any place that harbours men.
>   But here must end the story of my life;
>   And happy were I in my timely death,
>   Could all my travels warrant me they live.

DUKE
>   Hapless Ægeon, whom the fates have mark'd
>   To bear the extremity of dire mishap!
>   Now, trust me, were it not against our laws,
>   Against my crown, my oath, my dignity,
>   Which princes, would they, may not disannul,
>   My soul should sue as advocate for thee.
>   But, though thou art adjudged to the death,
>   And passed sentence may not be recall'd
>   But to our honour's great disparagement,
>   Yet will I favour thee in what I can.
>   Therefore, merchant, I'll limit thee this day
>   To seek thy help by beneficial help.
>   Try all the friends thou hast in Ephesus;
>   Beg thou, or borrow, to make up the sum,

And live; if no, then thou art doom'd to die.
Gaoler, take him to thy custody.

GAOLER

I will, my lord.

ÆGEON

Hopeless and helpless doth Ægeon wend,
But to procrastinate his lifeless end.

Exeunt

SCENE II.
THE MART.

Enter ANTIPHOLUS OF SYRACUSE,
DROMIO OF SYRACUSE, *and* FIRST MERCHANT

FIRST MERCHANT

Therefore give out you are of Epidamnum,
Lest that your goods too soon be confiscate.
This very day a Syracusian merchant
Is apprehended for arrival here;
And, not being able to buy out his life,
According to the statute of the town,
Dies ere the weary sun set in the west.
There is your money that I had to keep.

ANTIPHOLUS OF SYRACUSE

Go bear it to the Centaur, where we host,
And stay there, Dromio, till I come to thee.
Within this hour it will be dinner-time.
Till that, I'll view the manners of the town,
Peruse the traders, gaze upon the buildings,
And then return, and sleep within mine inn;
For with long travel I am stiff and weary.
Get thee away.

DROMIO OF SYRACUSE

Many a man would take you at your word,
And go indeed, having so good a mean.

Exit

ANTIPHOLUS OF SYRACUSE

A trusty villain, sir; that very oft,

When I am dull with care and melancholy,
Lightens my humour with his merry jests.
What, will you walk with me about the town,
And then go to my inn, and dine with me?

FIRST MERCHANT
I am invited, sir, to certain merchants,
Of whom I hope to make much benefit;
I crave your pardon. Soon at five o'clock,
Please you, I'll meet with you upon the mart,
And afterward consort you till bed-time.
My present business calls me from you now.

ANTIPHOLUS OF SYRACUSE
Farewell till then. I will go lose myself,
And wander up and down to view the city.

FIRST MERCHANT
Sir, I commend you to your own content.

Exit

ANTIPHOLUS OF SYRACUSE
He that commends me to mine own content
Commends me to the thing I cannot get.
I to the world am like a drop of water,
That in the ocean seeks another drop;
Who, falling there to find his fellow forth,
Unseen, inquisitive, confounds himself.
So I, to find a mother and a brother,
In quest of them, unhappy, lose myself.

Enter DROMIO OF EPHESUS
Here comes the almanac of my true date.
What now? How chance thou art return'd so soon?

DROMIO OF EPHESUS
Return'd so soon! rather approach'd too late.
The capon burns, the pig falls from the spit;
The clock hath strucken twelve upon the bell;
My mistress made it one upon my cheek.
She is so hot, because the meat is cold;
The meat is cold, because you come not home;
You come not home, because you have no stomach;

You have no stomach, having broke your fast;
But we, that know what 'tis to fast and pray,
Are penitent for your default to-day.

ANTIPHOLUS OF SYRACUSE

Stop in your wind, sir. Tell me this, I pray:
Where have you left the money that I gave you?

DROMIO OF EPHESUS

O, sixpence, that I had o' Wednesday last
To pay the saddler for my mistress' crupper?
The saddler had it, sir; I kept it not.

ANTIPHOLUS OF SYRACUSE

I am not in a sportive humour now.
Tell me, and dally not, where is the money?
We being strangers here, how darest thou trust
So great a charge from thine own custody?

DROMIO OF EPHESUS

I pray you, jest, sir, as you sit at dinner.
I from my mistress come to you in post;
If I return, I shall be post indeed,
For she will score your fault upon my pate.
Methinks your maw, like mine, should be your clock,
And strike you home without a messenger.

ANTIPHOLUS OF SYRACUSE

Come, Dromio, come, these jests are out of season;
Reserve them till a merrier hour than this.
Where is the gold I gave in charge to thee?

DROMIO OF EPHESUS

To me, sir? Why, you gave no gold to me.

ANTIPHOLUS OF SYRACUSE

Come on, sir knave, have done your foolishness,
And tell me how thou hast disposed thy charge.

DROMIO OF EPHESUS

My charge was but to fetch you from the mart
Home to your house, the Phœnix, sir, to dinner.
My mistress and her sister stays for you.

ANTIPHOLUS OF SYRACUSE

Now, as I am a Christian, answer me,

In what safe place you have bestow'd my money;
Or I shall break that merry sconce of yours,
That stands on tricks when I am undisposed.
Where is the thousand marks thou hadst of me?

DROMIO OF EPHESUS
I have some marks of yours upon my pate,
Some of my mistress' marks upon my shoulders;
But not a thousand marks between you both.
If I should pay your worship those again,
Perchance you will not bear them patiently.

ANTIPHOLUS OF SYRACUSE
Thy mistress' marks? What mistress, slave, hast thou?

DROMIO OF EPHESUS
Your worship's wife, my mistress at the Phœnix;
She that doth fast till you come home to dinner,
And prays that you will hie you home to dinner.

ANTIPHOLUS OF SYRACUSE
What, wilt thou flout me thus unto my face,
Being forbid? There, take you that, sir knave.

He beats Dromio

DROMIO OF EPHESUS
What mean you, sir? For God's sake, hold your hands!
Nay, an you will not, sir, I'll take my heels.

Exit

ANTIPHOLUS OF SYRACUSE
Upon my life, by some device or other
The villain is o'er-raught of all my money.
They say this town is full of cozenage;
As, nimble jugglers that deceive the eye,
Dark-working sorcerers that change the mind,
Soul-killing witches that deform the body,
Disguised cheaters, prating mountebanks,
And many such-like liberties of sin.
If it prove so, I will be gone the sooner.
I'll to the Centaur, to go seek this slave.
I greatly fear my money is not safe.

Exit

ACT

II

SCENE I.
THE HOUSE OF ANTIPHOLUS OF EPHESUS.

Enter ADRIANA *and* LUCIANA

ADRIANA
Neither my husband nor the slave return'd,
That in such haste I sent to seek his master!
Sure, Luciana, it is two o'clock.

LUCIANA
Perhaps some merchant hath invited him,
And from the mart he's somewhere gone to dinner.
Good sister, let us dine, and never fret.
A man is master of his liberty.
Time is their master; and when they see time,
They'll go or come. If so, be patient, sister.

ADRIANA
Why should their liberty than ours be more?

LUCIANA
Because their business still lies out o' door.

ADRIANA
Look, when I serve him so, he takes it ill.

LUCIANA

    O, know he is the bridle of your will.

ADRIANA

    There's none but asses will be bridled so.

LUCIANA

    Why, headstrong liberty is lash'd with woe.

    There's nothing situate under heaven's eye

    But hath his bound, in earth, in sea, in sky.

    The beasts, the fishes, and the winged fowls,

    Are their males' subjects and at their controls.

    Men, more divine, the masters of all these,

    Lords of the wide world and wild watery seas,

    Indued with intellectual sense and souls,

    Of more pre-eminence than fish and fowls,

    Are masters to their females, and their lords.

    Then let your will attend on their accords.

ADRIANA

    This servitude makes you to keep unwed.

LUCIANA

    Not this, but troubles of the marriage-bed.

ADRIANA

    But, were you wedded, you would bear some sway.

LUCIANA

    Ere I learn love, I'll practise to obey.

ADRIANA

    How if your husband start some otherwhere?

LUCIANA

    Till he come home again, I would forbear.

ADRIANA

    Patience unmoved! No marvel though she pause;

    They can be meek that have no other cause.

    A wretched soul, bruised with adversity,

    We bid be quiet when we hear it cry;

    But were we burden'd with like weight of pain,

    As much, or more, we should ourselves complain.

    So thou, that hast no unkind mate to grieve thee,

With urging helpless patience wouldst relieve me;
But, if thou live to see like right bereft,
This fool-begg'd patience in thee will be left.

LUCIANA

Well, I will marry one day, but to try.
Here comes your man; now is your husband nigh.

Enter DROMIO OF EPHESUS

ADRIANA

Say, is your tardy master now at hand?

DROMIO OF EPHESUS

Nay, he's at two hands with me, and that my two ears can
witness.

ADRIANA

Say, didst thou speak with him? Know'st thou his mind?

DROMIO OF EPHESUS

Ay, ay, he told his mind upon mine ear.
Beshrew his hand, I scarce could understand it.

LUCIANA

Spake he so doubtfully, thou couldst not feel his meaning?

DROMIO OF EPHESUS

Nay, he struck so plainly, I could too well feel his blows; and
withal so doubtfully, that I could scarce understand them.

ADRIANA

But say, I prithee, is he coming home?
It seems he hath great care to please his wife.

DROMIO OF EPHESUS

Why, mistress, sure my master is horn-mad.

ADRIANA

Horn-mad, thou villain!

DROMIO OF EPHESUS

I mean not cuckold-mad;
But, sure, he is stark mad.
When I desired him to come home to dinner,
He ask'd me for a thousand marks in gold.
''Tis dinner-time,' quoth I; 'My gold!' quoth he.
'Your meat doth burn,' quoth I; 'My gold!' quoth he.
'Will you come home?' quoth I; 'My gold!' quoth he,

'Where is the thousand marks I gave thee, villain?'
'The pig,' quoth I, 'is burn'd;' 'My gold!' quoth he.
'My mistress, sir,' quoth I; 'Hang up thy mistress!
I know not thy mistress; out on thy mistress!'

LUCIANA

Quoth who?

DROMIO OF EPHESUS

Quoth my master.
'I know,' quoth he, 'no house, no wife, no mistress.'
So that my errand, due unto my tongue,
I thank him, I bare home upon my shoulders;
For, in conclusion, he did beat me there.

ADRIANA

Go back again, thou slave, and fetch him home.

DROMIO OF EPHESUS

Go back again, and be new-beaten home?
For God's sake, send some other messenger.

ADRIANA

Back, slave, or I will break thy pate across.

DROMIO OF EPHESUS

And he will bless that cross with other beating,
Between you I shall have a holy head.

ADRIANA

Hence, prating peasant! fetch thy master home.

She beats Dromio

DROMIO OF EPHESUS

Am I so round with you as you with me,
That like a football you do spurn me thus?
You spurn me hence, and he will spurn me hither.
If I last in this service, you must case me in leather.

Exit

LUCIANA

Fie, how impatience lowereth in your face!

ADRIANA

His company must do his minions grace,
Whilst I at home starve for a merry look.
Hath homely age the alluring beauty took

From my poor cheek? Then he hath wasted it.
Are my discourses dull? barren my wit?
If voluble and sharp discourse be marr'd,
Unkindness blunts it more than marble hard.
Do their gay vestments his affections bait?
That's not my fault; he's master of my state.
What ruins are in me that can be found,
By him not ruin'd? Then is he the ground
Of my defeatures. My decayed fair
A sunny look of his would soon repair.
But, too unruly deer, he breaks the pale,
And feeds from home; poor I am but his stale.

LUCIANA
Self-harming jealousy! fie, beat it hence!

ADRIANA
Unfeeling fools can with such wrongs dispense.
I know his eye doth homage otherwhere;
Or else what lets it but he would be here?
Sister, you know he promised me a chain;
Would that alone, alone he would detain,
So he would keep fair quarter with his bed!
I see the jewel best enamelled
Will lose his beauty; yet the gold bides still,
That others touch, and often touching will
Wear gold, and no man that hath a name,
By falsehood and corruption doth it shame.
Since that my beauty cannot please his eye,
I'll weep what's left away, and weeping die.

LUCIANA
How many fond fools serve mad jealousy!

Exeunt

SCENE II.
A PUBLIC PLACE.

Enter ANTIPHOLUS OF SYRACUSE

ANTIPHOLUS OF SYRACUSE

    The gold I gave to Dromio is laid up
    Safe at the Centaur; and the heedful slave
    Is wander'd forth, in care to seek me out
    By computation and mine host's report.
    I could not speak with Dromio since at first
    I sent him from the mart. See, here he comes.

Enter DROMIO OF SYRACUSE

    How now, sir! Is your merry humour alter'd?
    As you love strokes, so jest with me again.
    You know no Centaur? You receiv'd no gold?
    Your mistress sent to have me home to dinner?
    My house was at the Phœnix? Wast thou mad,
    That thus so madly thou didst answer me?

DROMIO OF SYRACUSE

    What answer, sir? When spake I such a word?

ANTIPHOLUS OF SYRACUSE

    Even now, even here, not half an hour since.

DROMIO OF SYRACUSE

    I did not see you since you sent me hence,
    Home to the Centaur, with the gold you gave me.

ANTIPHOLUS OF SYRACUSE

    Villain, thou didst deny the gold's receipt,
    And told'st me of a mistress and a dinner;
    For which, I hope, thou felt'st I was displeased.

DROMIO OF SYRACUSE

    I am glad to see you in this merry vein.
    What means this jest? I pray you, master, tell me.

ANTIPHOLUS OF SYRACUSE

    Yea, dost thou jeer and flout me in the teeth?
    Think'st thou I jest? Hold, take thou that, and that.

Beating him

DROMIO OF SYRACUSE

    Hold, sir, for God's sake! now your jest is earnest.
    Upon what bargain do you give it me?

ANTIPHOLUS OF SYRACUSE

    Because that I familiarly sometimes
    Do use you for my fool, and chat with you,
    Your sauciness will jest upon my love,
    And make a common of my serious hours.
    When the sun shines let foolish gnats make sport,
    But creep in crannies when he hides his beams.
    If you will jest with me, know my aspect,
    And fashion your demeanour to my looks,
    Or I will beat this method in your sconce.

DROMIO OF SYRACUSE

    Sconce call you it? So you would leave battering, I had rather
    have it a head. An you use these blows long, I must get a sconce
    for my head, and insconce it too; or else I shall seek my wit in my
    shoulders. But, I pray, sir, why am I beaten?

ANTIPHOLUS OF SYRACUSE

    Dost thou not know?

DROMIO OF SYRACUSE

    Nothing, sir, but that I am beaten.

ANTIPHOLUS OF SYRACUSE

    Shall I tell you why?

DROMIO OF SYRACUSE

    Ay, sir, and wherefore; for they say every why hath a wherefore.

ANTIPHOLUS OF SYRACUSE

    Why, first—for flouting me; and then, wherefore—
    For urging it the second time to me.

DROMIO OF SYRACUSE

    Was there ever any man thus beaten out of season,
    When in the why and the wherefore is neither rhyme nor reason?
    Well, sir, I thank you.

ANTIPHOLUS OF SYRACUSE

    Thank me, sir! for what?

DROMIO OF SYRACUSE

Marry, sir, for this something that you gave me for nothing.

ANTIPHOLUS OF SYRACUSE

I'll make you amends next, to give you nothing for something. But say, sir, is it dinner-time?

DROMIO OF SYRACUSE

No, sir. I think the meat wants that I have.

ANTIPHOLUS OF SYRACUSE

In good time, sir; what's that?

DROMIO OF SYRACUSE

Basting.

ANTIPHOLUS OF SYRACUSE

Well, sir, then 'twill be dry.

DROMIO OF SYRACUSE

If it be, sir, I pray you, eat none of it.

ANTIPHOLUS OF SYRACUSE

Your reason?

DROMIO OF SYRACUSE

Lest it make you choleric, and purchase me another dry basting.

ANTIPHOLUS OF SYRACUSE

Well, sir, learn to jest in good time. There's a time for all things.

DROMIO OF SYRACUSE

I durst have denied that, before you were so choleric.

ANTIPHOLUS OF SYRACUSE

By what rule, sir?

DROMIO OF SYRACUSE

Marry, sir, by a rule as plain as the plain bald pate of Father Time himself.

ANTIPHOLUS OF SYRACUSE

Let's hear it.

DROMIO OF SYRACUSE

There's no time for a man to recover his hair that grows bald by nature.

ANTIPHOLUS OF SYRACUSE

May he not do it by fine and recovery?

DROMIO OF SYRACUSE
Yes, to pay a fine for a periwig, and recover the lost hair of another man.

ANTIPHOLUS OF SYRACUSE
Why is Time such a niggard of hair, being, as it is, so plentiful an excrement?

DROMIO OF SYRACUSE
Because it is a blessing that he bestows on beasts, and what he hath scanted men in hair, he hath given them in wit.

ANTIPHOLUS OF SYRACUSE
Why, but there's many a man hath more hair than wit.

DROMIO OF SYRACUSE
Not a man of those but he hath the wit to lose his hair.

ANTIPHOLUS OF SYRACUSE
Why, thou didst conclude hairy men plain dealers without wit.

DROMIO OF SYRACUSE
The plainer dealer, the sooner lost. Yet he loseth it in a kind of jollity.

ANTIPHOLUS OF SYRACUSE
For what reason?

DROMIO OF SYRACUSE
For two; and sound ones too.

ANTIPHOLUS OF SYRACUSE
Nay, not sound, I pray you.

DROMIO OF SYRACUSE
Sure ones, then.

ANTIPHOLUS OF SYRACUSE
Nay, not sure, in a thing falsing.

DROMIO OF SYRACUSE
Certain ones, then.

ANTIPHOLUS OF SYRACUSE
Name them.

DROMIO OF SYRACUSE
The one, to save the money that he spends in trimming; the other, that at dinner they should not drop in his porridge.

ANTIPHOLUS OF SYRACUSE

    You would all this time have proved there is no time for all
    things.

DROMIO OF SYRACUSE

    Marry, and did, sir; namely, no time to recover hair lost by nature.

ANTIPHOLUS OF SYRACUSE

    But your reason was not substantial, why there is no time to
    recover.

DROMIO OF SYRACUSE

    Thus I mend it: Time himself is bald, and therefore to the world's
    end will have bald followers.

ANTIPHOLUS OF SYRACUSE

    I knew 'twould be a bald conclusion.
    But, soft! who wafts us yonder?

                      Enter ADRIANA *and* LUCIANA

ADRIANA

    Ay, ay, Antipholus, look strange and frown.
    Some other mistress hath thy sweet aspects;
    I am not Adriana nor thy wife.
    The time was once when thou unurged wouldst vow
    That never words were music to thine ear,
    That never object pleasing in thine eye,
    That never touch well welcome to thy hand,
    That never meat sweet-savour'd in thy taste,
    Unless I spake, or look'd, or touch'd, or carved to thee.
    How comes it now, my husband, O, how comes it,
    That thou art then estranged from thyself?
    Thyself I call it, being strange to me,
    That, undividable, incorporate,
    Am better than thy dear self's better part.
    Ah, do not tear away thyself from me!
    For know, my love, as easy mayst thou fall
    A drop of water in the breaking gulf,
    And take unmingled thence that drop again,
    Without addition or diminishing,

As take from me thyself, and not me too.
How dearly would it touch thee to the quick,
Shouldst thou but hear I were licentious,
And that this body, consecrate to thee,
By ruffian lust should be contaminate!
Wouldst thou not spit at me and spurn at me,
And hurl the name of husband in my face,
And tear the stain'd skin off my harlot brow,
And from my false hand cut the wedding ring,
And break it with a deep-divorcing vow?
I know thou canst; and therefore see thou do it.
I am possess'd with an adulterate blot;
My blood is mingled with the crime of lust;
For if we two be one, and thou play false,
I do digest the poison of thy flesh,
Being strumpeted by thy contagion.
Keep, then, fair league and truce with thy true bed;
I live distain'd, thou undishonoured.

ANTIPHOLUS OF SYRACUSE

Plead you to me, fair dame? I know you not.
In Ephesus I am but two hours old,
As strange unto your town as to your talk;
Who, every word by all my wit being scann'd,
Wants wit in all one word to understand.

LUCIANA

Fie, brother! how the world is changed with you!
When were you wont to use my sister thus?
She sent for you by Dromio home to dinner.

ANTIPHOLUS OF SYRACUSE

By Dromio?

DROMIO OF SYRACUSE

By me?

ADRIANA

By thee; and this thou didst return from him,
That he did buffet thee, and, in his blows,
Denied my house for his, me for his wife.

ANTIPHOLUS OF SYRACUSE

Did you converse, sir, with this gentlewoman?
What is the course and drift of your compact?

DROMIO OF SYRACUSE

I, sir? I never saw her till this time.

ANTIPHOLUS OF SYRACUSE

Villain, thou liest; for even her very words
Didst thou deliver to me on the mart.

DROMIO OF SYRACUSE

I never spake with her in all my life.

ANTIPHOLUS OF SYRACUSE

How can she thus, then, call us by our names,
Unless it be by inspiration.

ADRIANA

How ill agrees it with your gravity
To counterfeit thus grossly with your slave,
Abetting him to thwart me in my mood!
Be it my wrong you are from me exempt,
But wrong not that wrong with a more contempt.
Come, I will fasten on this sleeve of thine.
Thou art an elm, my husband, I a vine,
Whose weakness, married to thy stronger state,
Makes me with thy strength to communicate.
If aught possess thee from me, it is dross,
Usurping ivy, brier, or idle moss;
Who, all for want of pruning, with intrusion
Infect thy sap, and live on thy confusion.

ANTIPHOLUS OF SYRACUSE

To me she speaks; she moves me for her theme.
What, was I married to her in my dream?
Or sleep I now, and think I hear all this?
What error drives our eyes and ears amiss?
Until I know this sure uncertainty,
I'll entertain the offer'd fallacy.

LUCIANA

Dromio, go bid the servants spread for dinner.

DROMIO OF SYRACUSE

    O, for my beads! I cross me for a sinner.

    This is the fairy land;—O spite of spites!

    We talk with goblins, owls, and sprites.

    If we obey them not, this will ensue,

    They'll suck our breath, or pinch us black and blue.

LUCIANA

    Why pratest thou to thyself, and answer'st not?

    Dromio, thou drone, thou snail, thou slug, thou sot!

DROMIO OF SYRACUSE

    I am transformed, master, am I not?

ANTIPHOLUS OF SYRACUSE

    I think thou art in mind, and so am I.

DROMIO OF SYRACUSE

    Nay, master, both in mind and in my shape.

ANTIPHOLUS OF SYRACUSE

    Thou hast thine own form.

DROMIO OF SYRACUSE

    No, I am an ape.

LUCIANA

    If thou art chang'd to aught, 'tis to an ass.

DROMIO OF SYRACUSE

    'Tis true; she rides me, and I long for grass.

    'Tis so, I am an ass; else it could never be

    But I should know her as well as she knows me.

ADRIANA

    Come, come, no longer will I be a fool,

    To put the finger in the eye and weep,

    Whilst man and master laughs my woes to scorn.

    Come, sir, to dinner. Dromio, keep the gate.

    Husband, I'll dine above with you to-day,

    And shrive you of a thousand idle pranks.

    Sirrah, if any ask you for your master,

    Say he dines forth, and let no creature enter.

    Come, sister. Dromio, play the porter well.

ANTIPHOLUS OF SYRACUSE

    Am I in earth, in heaven, or in hell?

Sleeping or waking? mad or well-advised?
Known unto these, and to myself disguised!
I'll say as they say, and persever so,
And in this mist at all adventures go.

DROMIO OF SYRACUSE
Master, shall I be porter at the gate?

ADRIANA
Ay; and let none enter, lest I break your pate.

LUCIANA
Come, come, Antipholus, we dine too late.

Exeunt

ACT

III

❦

SCENE I.
BEFORE THE HOUSE OF
ANTIPHOLUS OF EPHESUS.

Enter ANTIPHOLUS OF EPHESUS,
DROMIO OF EPHESUS, ANGELO, *and* BALTHAZAR

ANTIPHOLUS OF EPHESUS

    Good Signior Angelo, you must excuse us all;
    My wife is shrewish when I keep not hours.
    Say that I linger'd with you at your shop
    To see the making of her carcanet,
    And that to-morrow you will bring it home.
    But here's a villain that would face me down
    He met me on the mart, and that I beat him,
    And charged him with a thousand marks in gold,
    And that I did deny my wife and house.
    Thou drunkard, thou, what didst thou mean by this?

DROMIO OF EPHESUS

    Say what you will, sir, but I know what I know;
    That you beat me at the mart, I have your hand to show.
    If the skin were parchment, and the blows you gave were ink,
    Your own handwriting would tell you what I think.

ANTIPHOLUS OF EPHESUS
  I think thou art an ass.
DROMIO OF EPHESUS
  Marry, so it doth appear
  By the wrongs I suffer, and the blows I bear.
  I should kick, being kick'd; and, being at that pass,
  You would keep from my heels, and beware of an ass.
ANTIPHOLUS OF EPHESUS
  You're sad, Signior Balthazar. Pray God our cheer
  May answer my good will and your good welcome here.
BALTHASAR
  I hold your dainties cheap, sir, and your welcome dear.
ANTIPHOLUS OF EPHESUS
  O, Signior Balthazar, either at flesh or fish,
  A table full of welcome makes scarce one dainty dish.
BALTHASAR
  Good meat, sir, is common; that every churl affords.
ANTIPHOLUS OF EPHESUS
  And welcome more common; for that's nothing but words.
BALTHASAR
  Small cheer and great welcome makes a merry feast.
ANTIPHOLUS OF EPHESUS
  Ay to a niggardly host and more sparing guest.
  But though my cates be mean, take them in good part;
  Better cheer may you have, but not with better heart.
  But, soft! my door is lock'd. Go bid them let us in.
DROMIO OF EPHESUS
  Maud, Bridget, Marian, Cicely, Gillian, Ginn!
DROMIO OF SYRACUSE [*Within*]
  Mome, malthorse, capon, coxcomb, idiot, patch!
  Either get thee from the door, or sit down at the hatch.
  Dost thou conjure for wenches, that thou call'st for such store,
  When one is one too many? Go get thee from the door,
DROMIO OF EPHESUS
  What patch is made our porter? My master stays in the street.
DROMIO OF SYRACUSE [*Within*]
  Let him walk from whence he came, lest he catch cold on's feet.

ANTIPHOLUS OF EPHESUS

Who talks within there? Ho, open the door!

DROMIO OF SYRACUSE [*Within*]

Right, sir; I'll tell you when, an you'll tell me wherefore.

ANTIPHOLUS OF EPHESUS

Wherefore? For my dinner. I have not dined to-day.

DROMIO OF SYRACUSE [*Within*]

Nor to-day here you must not; come again when you may.

ANTIPHOLUS OF EPHESUS

What art thou that keepest me out from the house I owe?

DROMIO OF SYRACUSE [*Within*]

The porter for this time, sir, and my name is Dromio.

DROMIO OF EPHESUS

O villain, thou hast stolen both mine office and my name!

The one ne'er got me credit, the other mickle blame.

If thou hadst been Dromio to-day in my place,

Thou wouldst have changed thy face for a name, or thy name
for an ass.

LUCE [*Within*]

What a coil is there, Dromio? Who are those at the gate?

DROMIO OF EPHESUS

Let my master in, Luce.

LUCE [*Within*]

Faith, no; he comes too late;

And so tell your master.

DROMIO OF EPHESUS

O Lord, I must laugh!

Have at you with a proverb: shall I set in my staff?

LUCE [*Within*]

Have at you with another; that's—When? Can you tell?

DROMIO OF SYRACUSE [*Within*]

If thy name be call'd Luce, Luce, thou hast answer'd him well.

ANTIPHOLUS OF EPHESUS

Do you hear, you minion? you'll let us in, I hope?

LUCE [*Within*]

I thought to have ask'd you.

DROMIO OF SYRACUSE [*Within*]
 And you said no.

DROMIO OF EPHESUS
 So, come, help. Well struck! There was blow for blow.

ANTIPHOLUS OF EPHESUS
 Thou baggage, let me in.

LUCE [*Within*]
 Can you tell for whose sake?

DROMIO OF EPHESUS
 Master, knock the door hard.

LUCE [*Within*]
 Let him knock till it ache.

ANTIPHOLUS OF EPHESUS
 You'll cry for this, minion, if I beat the door down.

LUCE [*Within*]
 What needs all that, and a pair of stocks in the town?

ADRIANA [*Within*]
 Who is that at the door that keeps all this noise?

DROMIO OF SYRACUSE [*Within*]
 By my troth, your town is troubled with unruly boys.

ANTIPHOLUS OF EPHESUS
 Are you, there, wife? You might have come before.

ADRIANA [*Within*]
 Your wife, sir knave! go get you from the door.

Exit with LUCE

DROMIO OF EPHESUS
 If you went in pain, master, this 'knave' would go sore.

ANGELO
 Here is neither cheer, sir, nor welcome. We would fain have
 either.

BALTHASAR
 In debating which was best, we shall part with neither.

DROMIO OF EPHESUS
 They stand at the door, master; bid them welcome hither.

ANTIPHOLUS OF EPHESUS
 There is something in the wind, that we cannot get in.

DROMIO OF EPHESUS

    You would say so, master, if your garments were thin.

    Your cake here is warm within; you stand here in the cold.

    It would make a man mad as a buck, to be so bought and sold.

ANTIPHOLUS OF EPHESUS

    Go fetch me something. I'll break ope the gate.

DROMIO OF SYRACUSE [*Within*]

    Break any breaking here, and I'll break your knave's pate.

DROMIO OF EPHESUS

    A man may break a word with you, sir; and words are but wind;

    Ay, and break it in your face, so he break it not behind.

DROMIO OF SYRACUSE [*Within*]

    It seems thou want'st breaking. Out upon thee, hind!

DROMIO OF EPHESUS

    Here's too much 'out upon thee!' I pray thee, let me in.

DROMIO OF SYRACUSE [*Within*]

    Ay, when fowls have no feathers, and fish have no fin.

ANTIPHOLUS OF EPHESUS

    Well, I'll break in. Go borrow me a crow.

DROMIO OF EPHESUS

    A crow without feather? Master, mean you so?

    For a fish without a fin, there's a fowl without a feather.

    If a crow help us in, sirrah, we'll pluck a crow together.

ANTIPHOLUS OF EPHESUS

    Go get thee gone; fetch me an iron crow.

BALTHASAR

    Have patience, sir; O, let it not be so!

    Herein you war against your reputation,

    And draw within the compass of suspect

    Th' unviolated honour of your wife.

    Once this—your long experience of her wisdom,

    Her sober virtue, years, and modesty,

    Plead on her part some cause to you unknown;

    And doubt not, sir, but she will well excuse

    Why at this time the doors are made against you.

    Be ruled by me. Depart in patience,

And let us to the Tiger all to dinner;
And about evening come yourself alone
To know the reason of this strange restraint.
If by strong hand you offer to break in
Now in the stirring passage of the day,
A vulgar comment will be made of it,
And that supposed by the common rout
Against your yet ungalled estimation,
That may with foul intrusion enter in,
And dwell upon your grave when you are dead;
For slander lives upon succession,
For ever housed where it gets possession.

ANTIPHOLUS OF EPHESUS
You have prevail'd. I will depart in quiet,
And, in despite of mirth, mean to be merry.
I know a wench of excellent discourse,
Pretty and witty; wild, and yet, too, gentle.
There will we dine. This woman that I mean,
My wife—but, I protest, without desert—
Hath oftentimes upbraided me withal.
To her will we to dinner. [*To* ANGELO] Get you home,
And fetch the chain; by this I know 'tis made.
Bring it, I pray you, to the Porpentine;
For there's the house. That chain will I bestow—
Be it for nothing but to spite my wife—
Upon mine hostess there. Good sir, make haste.
Since mine own doors refuse to entertain me,
I'll knock elsewhere, to see if they'll disdain me.

ANGELO
I'll meet you at that place some hour hence.

ANTIPHOLUS OF EPHESUS
Do so. This jest shall cost me some expense.

Exeunt

SCENE II.
THE SAME.

Enter LUCIANA *and* ANTIPHOLUS OF SYRACUSE

LUCIANA

    And may it be that you have quite forgot
    A husband's office? Shall, Antipholus,
    Even in the spring of love, thy love-springs rot?
    Shall love, in building, grow so ruinous?
    If you did wed my sister for her wealth,
    Then for her wealth's sake use her with more kindness;
    Or if you like elsewhere, do it by stealth;
    Muffle your false love with some show of blindness.
    Let not my sister read it in your eye;
    Be not thy tongue thy own shame's orator;
    Look sweet, speak fair, become disloyalty;
    Apparel vice like virtue's harbinger;
    Bear a fair presence, though your heart be tainted;
    Teach sin the carriage of a holy saint;
    Be secret-false: what need she be acquainted?
    What simple thief brags of his own attaint?
    'Tis double wrong, to truant with your bed,
    And let her read it in thy looks at board.
    Shame hath a bastard fame, well managed;
    Ill deeds are doubled with an evil word.
    Alas, poor women! make us but believe,
    Being compact of credit, that you love us;
    Though others have the arm, show us the sleeve;
    We in your motion turn, and you may move us.
    Then, gentle brother, get you in again;
    Comfort my sister, cheer her, call her wife.
    'Tis holy sport, to be a little vain,
    When the sweet breath of flattery conquers strife.

ANTIPHOLUS OF SYRACUSE

    Sweet mistress—what your name is else, I know not,
    Nor by what wonder you do hit of mine—
    Less in your knowledge and your grace you show not

Than our earth's wonder; more than earth divine.
Teach me, dear creature, how to think and speak;
Lay open to my earthy-gross conceit,
Smother'd in errors, feeble, shallow, weak,
The folded meaning of your words' deceit.
Against my soul's pure truth why labour you
To make it wander in an unknown field?
Are you a god? Would you create me new?
Transform me, then, and to your power I'll yield.
But if that I am I, then well I know
Your weeping sister is no wife of mine,
Nor to her bed no homage do I owe.
Far more, far more to you do I decline.
O, train me not, sweet mermaid, with thy note,
To drown me in thy sister flood of tears.
Sing, siren, for thyself, and I will dote.
Spread o'er the silver waves thy golden hairs,
And as a bed I'll take them, and there lie;
And, in that glorious supposition, think
He gains by death that hath such means to die.
Let Love, being light, be drowned if she sink!

LUCIANA
What, are you mad, that you do reason so?

ANTIPHOLUS OF SYRACUSE
Not mad, but mated; how, I do not know.

LUCIANA
It is a fault that springeth from your eye.

ANTIPHOLUS OF SYRACUSE
For gazing on your beams, fair sun, being by.

LUCIANA
Gaze where you should, and that will clear your sight.

ANTIPHOLUS OF SYRACUSE
As good to wink, sweet love, as look on night.

LUCIANA
Why call you me love? Call my sister so.

ANTIPHOLUS OF SYRACUSE
Thy sister's sister.

LUCIANA

That's my sister.

ANTIPHOLUS OF SYRACUSE

No;

It is thyself, mine own self's better part,

Mine eye's clear eye, my dear heart's dearer heart,

My food, my fortune, and my sweet hope's aim,

My sole earth's heaven, and my heaven's claim.

LUCIANA

All this my sister is, or else should be.

ANTIPHOLUS OF SYRACUSE

Call thyself sister, sweet, for I am thee.

Thee will I love, and with thee lead my life.

Thou hast no husband yet, nor I no wife.

Give me thy hand.

LUCIANA

O, soft, sir! hold you still.

I'll fetch my sister, to get her good will.

Exit

Enter DROMIO OF SYRACUSE

ANTIPHOLUS OF SYRACUSE

Why, how now, Dromio! where runn'st thou so fast?

DROMIO OF SYRACUSE

Do you know me, sir? Am I Dromio? Am I your man? Am I myself?

ANTIPHOLUS OF SYRACUSE

Thou art Dromio, thou art my man, thou art thyself.

DROMIO OF SYRACUSE

I am an ass, I am a woman's man, and besides myself.

ANTIPHOLUS OF SYRACUSE

What woman's man? And how besides thyself?

DROMIO OF SYRACUSE

Marry, sir, besides myself, I am due to a woman; one that claims
me, one that haunts me, one that will have me.

ANTIPHOLUS OF SYRACUSE

What claim lays she to thee?

DROMIO OF SYRACUSE

Marry, sir, such claim as you would lay to your horse; and she would have me as a beast: not that, I being a beast, she would have me; but that she, being a very beastly creature, lays claim to me.

ANTIPHOLUS OF SYRACUSE

What is she?

DROMIO OF SYRACUSE

A very reverent body; ay, such a one as a man may not speak of, without he say Sir-reverence. I have but lean luck in the match, and yet is she a wondrous fat marriage.

ANTIPHOLUS OF SYRACUSE

How dost thou mean a fat marriage?

DROMIO OF SYRACUSE

Marry, sir, she's the kitchen-wench, and all grease; and I know not what use to put her to, but to make a lamp of her, and run from her by her own light. I warrant, her rags, and the tallow in them, will burn a Poland winter. If she lives till doomsday, she'll burn a week longer than the whole world.

ANTIPHOLUS OF SYRACUSE

What complexion is she of?

DROMIO OF SYRACUSE

Swart, like my shoe, but her face nothing like so clean kept. For why she sweats; a man may go overshoes in the grime of it.

ANTIPHOLUS OF SYRACUSE

That's a fault that water will mend.

DROMIO OF SYRACUSE

No, sir, 'tis in grain; Noah's flood could not do it.

ANTIPHOLUS OF SYRACUSE

What's her name?

DROMIO OF SYRACUSE

Nell, sir; but her name and three quarters, that's an ell and three quarters, will not measure her from hip to hip.

ANTIPHOLUS OF SYRACUSE

Then she bears some breadth?

DROMIO OF SYRACUSE

No longer from head to foot than from hip to hip. She is spherical, like a globe; I could find out countries in her.

ANTIPHOLUS OF SYRACUSE

In what part of her body stands Ireland?

DROMIO OF SYRACUSE

Marry, sir, in her buttocks. I found it out by the bogs.

ANTIPHOLUS OF SYRACUSE

Where Scotland?

DROMIO OF SYRACUSE

I found it by the barrenness; hard in the palm of the hand.

ANTIPHOLUS OF SYRACUSE

Where France?

DROMIO OF SYRACUSE

In her forehead; armed and reverted, making war against her heir.

ANTIPHOLUS OF SYRACUSE

Where England?

DROMIO OF SYRACUSE

I looked for the chalky cliffs, but I could find no whiteness in them; but I guess it stood in her chin, by the salt rheum that ran between France and it.

ANTIPHOLUS OF SYRACUSE

Where Spain?

DROMIO OF SYRACUSE

Faith, I saw it not; but I felt it hot in her breath.

ANTIPHOLUS OF SYRACUSE

Where America, the Indies?

DROMIO OF SYRACUSE

Oh, sir, upon her nose, all o'er embellished with rubies, carbuncles, sapphires, declining their rich aspect to the hot breath of Spain; who sent whole armadoes of caracks to be ballast at her nose.

ANTIPHOLUS OF SYRACUSE

Where stood Belgia, the Netherlands?

DROMIO OF SYRACUSE

Oh, sir, I did not look so low. To conclude, this drudge, or diviner, laid claim to me; called me Dromio; swore I was assured to her; told me what privy marks I had about me, as, the mark of my shoulder, the mole in my neck, the great wart on my left arm, that I, amazed, ran from her as a witch.

And, I think, if my breast had not been made of faith, and my
heart of steel,
She had transform'd me to a curtal dog, and made me turn i' the
wheel.

ANTIPHOLUS OF SYRACUSE

Go hie thee presently, post to the road.
An if the wind blow any way from shore,
I will not harbour in this town to-night.
If any bark put forth, come to the mart,
Where I will walk till thou return to me.
If every one knows us, and we know none,
'Tis time, I think, to trudge, pack, and be gone.

DROMIO OF SYRACUSE

As from a bear a man would run for life,
So fly I from her that would be my wife.

Exit

ANTIPHOLUS OF SYRACUSE

There's none but witches do inhabit here;
And therefore 'tis high time that I were hence.
She that doth call me husband, even my soul
Doth for a wife abhor. But her fair sister,
Possess'd with such a gentle sovereign grace,
Of such enchanting presence and discourse,
Hath almost made me traitor to myself.
But, lest myself be guilty to self-wrong,
I'll stop mine ears against the mermaid's song.

Enter ANGELO *with the chain*

ANGELO

Master Antipholus—

ANTIPHOLUS OF SYRACUSE

Ay, that's my name.

ANGELO

I know it well, sir. Lo, here is the chain.
I thought to have ta'en you at the Porpentine.
The chain unfinish'd made me stay thus long.

ANTIPHOLUS OF SYRACUSE

What is your will that I shall do with this?

ANGELO

    What please yourself, sir. I have made it for you.

ANTIPHOLUS OF SYRACUSE

    Made it for me, sir! I bespoke it not.

ANGELO

    Not once, nor twice, but twenty times you have.

    Go home with it, and please your wife withal;

    And soon at supper-time I'll visit you,

    And then receive my money for the chain.

ANTIPHOLUS OF SYRACUSE

    I pray you, sir, receive the money now,

    For fear you ne'er see chain nor money more.

ANGELO

    You are a merry man, sir. Fare you well.

Exit

ANTIPHOLUS OF SYRACUSE

    What I should think of this, I cannot tell.

    But this I think, there's no man is so vain

    That would refuse so fair an offer'd chain.

    I see a man here needs not live by shifts,

    When in the streets he meets such golden gifts.

    I'll to the mart, and there for Dromio stay;

    If any ship put out, then straight away.

Exit

ACT

IV

Scene I.
A PUBLIC PLACE.

Enter Second Merchant, Angelo, *and an Officer*

Second Merchant

 You know since Pentecost the sum is due,
 And since I have not much importuned you;
 Nor now I had not, but that I am bound
 To Persia, and want guilders for my voyage.
 Therefore make present satisfaction,
 Or I'll attach you by this officer.

Angelo

 Even just the sum that I do owe to you
 Is growing to me by Antipholus;
 And in the instant that I met with you
 He had of me a chain. At five o'clock
 I shall receive the money for the same.
 Pleaseth you walk with me down to his house,
 I will discharge my bond, and thank you too.

   Enter Antipholus of Ephesus *and*
   Dromio of Ephesus *from the courtesan's*

OFFICER

    That labour may you save. See where he comes.

ANTIPHOLUS OF EPHESUS

    While I go to the goldsmith's house, go thou

    And buy a rope's end; that will I bestow

    Among my wife and her confederates,

    For locking me out of my doors by day.

    But, soft! I see the goldsmith. Get thee gone;

    Buy thou a rope, and bring it home to me.

DROMIO OF EPHESUS

    I buy a thousand pound a year, I buy a rope.

Exit

ANTIPHOLUS OF EPHESUS

    A man is well holp up that trusts to you.

    I promised your presence and the chain;

    But neither chain nor goldsmith came to me.

    Belike you thought our love would last too long,

    If it were chain'd together, and therefore came not.

ANGELO

    Saving your merry humour, here's the note

    How much your chain weighs to the utmost carat,

    The fineness of the gold, and chargeful fashion,

    Which doth amount to three odd ducats more

    Than I stand debted to this gentleman.

    I pray you, see him presently discharged,

    For he is bound to sea, and stays but for it.

ANTIPHOLUS OF EPHESUS

    I am not furnish'd with the present money;

    Besides, I have some business in the town.

    Good signior, take the stranger to my house,

    And with you take the chain, and bid my wife

    Disburse the sum on the receipt thereof.

    Perchance I will be there as soon as you.

ANGELO

    Then you will bring the chain to her yourself?

ANTIPHOLUS OF EPHESUS

    No; bear it with you, lest I come not time enough.

ANGELO

    Well, sir, I will. Have you the chain about you?

ANTIPHOLUS OF EPHESUS

    An if I have not, sir, I hope you have;

    Or else you may return without your money.

ANGELO

    Nay, come, I pray you, sir, give me the chain.

    Both wind and tide stays for this gentleman,

    And I, to blame, have held him here too long.

ANTIPHOLUS OF EPHESUS

    Good Lord! You use this dalliance to excuse

    Your breach of promise to the Porpentine.

    I should have chid you for not bringing it,

    But, like a shrew, you first begin to brawl.

SECOND MERCHANT

    The hour steals on; I pray you, sir, dispatch.

ANGELO

    You hear how he importunes me; the chain!

ANTIPHOLUS OF EPHESUS

    Why, give it to my wife, and fetch your money.

ANGELO

    Come, come, you know I gave it you even now.

    Either send the chain, or send me by some token.

ANTIPHOLUS OF EPHESUS

    Fie, now you run this humour out of breath.

    Come, where's the chain? I pray you, let me see it.

SECOND MERCHANT

    My business cannot brook this dalliance.

    Good sir, say whether you'll answer me or no.

    If not, I'll leave him to the officer.

ANTIPHOLUS OF EPHESUS

    I answer you! what should I answer you?

ANGELO

    The money that you owe me for the chain.

ANTIPHOLUS OF EPHESUS

    I owe you none till I receive the chain.

ANGELO
    You know I gave it you half an hour since.
ANTIPHOLUS OF EPHESUS
    You gave me none. You wrong me much to say so.
ANGELO
    You wrong me more, sir, in denying it.
    Consider how it stands upon my credit.
SECOND MERCHANT
    Well, officer, arrest him at my suit.
OFFICER
    I do; and charge you in the Duke's name to obey me.
ANGELO
    This touches me in reputation.
    Either consent to pay this sum for me,
    Or I attach you by this officer.
ANTIPHOLUS OF EPHESUS
    Consent to pay thee that I never had!
    Arrest me, foolish fellow, if thou darest.
ANGELO
    Here is thy fee; arrest him, officer.
    I would not spare my brother in this case,
    If he should scorn me so apparently.
OFFICER
    I do arrest you, sir. You hear the suit.
ANTIPHOLUS OF EPHESUS
    I do obey thee till I give thee bail.
    But, sirrah, you shall buy this sport as dear
    As all the metal in your shop will answer.
ANGELO
    Sir, sir, I shall have law in Ephesus,
    To your notorious shame; I doubt it not.
                Enter DROMIO OF SYRACUSE, *from the bay*
DROMIO OF SYRACUSE
    Master, there is a bark of Epidamnum
    That stays but till her owner comes aboard,
    And then, sir, she bears away. Our fraughtage, sir,
    I have convey'd aboard; and I have bought

The oil, the balsamum, and aqua-vitæ.
The ship is in her trim; the merry wind
Blows fair from land. They stay for nought at all
But for their owner, master, and yourself.

ANTIPHOLUS OF EPHESUS
How now! A madman! Why, thou peevish sheep,
What ship of Epidamnum stays for me?

DROMIO OF SYRACUSE
A ship you sent me to, to hire waftage.

ANTIPHOLUS OF EPHESUS
Thou drunken slave, I sent thee for a rope,
And told thee to what purpose and what end.

DROMIO OF SYRACUSE
You sent me for a rope's end as soon.
You sent me to the bay, sir, for a bark.

ANTIPHOLUS OF EPHESUS
I will debate this matter at more leisure,
And teach your ears to list me with more heed.
To Adriana, villain, hie thee straight.
Give her this key, and tell her, in the desk
That's cover'd o'er with Turkish tapestry
There is a purse of ducats; let her send it.
Tell her I am arrested in the street,
And that shall bail me. Hie thee, slave, be gone!
On, officer, to prison till it come.

Exeunt SECOND MERCHANT, ANGELO,
Officer, and ANTIPHOLUS OF EPHESUS

DROMIO OF SYRACUSE
To Adriana! that is where we dined,
Where Dowsabel did claim me for her husband.
She is too big, I hope, for me to compass.
Thither I must, although against my will,
For servants must their masters' minds fulfil.

Exit

SCENE II.
THE HOUSE OF ANTIPHOLUS OF EPHESUS.

Enter ADRIANA *and* LUCIANA

ADRIANA

    Ah, Luciana, did he tempt thee so?
    Mightst thou perceive austerely in his eye
    That he did plead in earnest, yea or no?
    Look'd he or red or pale, or sad or merrily?
    What observation madest thou, in this case,
    Of his heart's meteors tilting in his face?

LUCIANA

    First he denied you had in him no right.

ADRIANA

    He meant he did me none; the more my spite.

LUCIANA

    Then swore he that he was a stranger here.

ADRIANA

    And true he swore, though yet forsworn he were.

LUCIANA

    Then pleaded I for you.

ADRIANA

    And what said he?

LUCIANA

    That love I begg'd for you he begg'd of me.

ADRIANA

    With what persuasion did he tempt thy love?

LUCIANA

    With words that in an honest suit might move.
    First he did praise my beauty, then my speech.

ADRIANA

    Didst speak him fair?

LUCIANA

    Have patience, I beseech.

ADRIANA

    I cannot, nor I will not, hold me still;
    My tongue, though not my heart, shall have his will.

He is deformed, crooked, old, and sere,
Ill-faced, worse bodied, shapeless everywhere;
Vicious, ungentle, foolish, blunt, unkind;
Stigmatical in making, worse in mind.

LUCIANA

Who would be jealous, then, of such a one?
No evil lost is wail'd when it is gone.

ADRIANA

Ah, but I think him better than I say,
And yet would herein others' eyes were worse.
Far from her nest the lapwing cries away.
My heart prays for him, though my tongue do curse.

Enter DROMIO OF SYRACUSE

DROMIO OF SYRACUSE

Here! go; the desk, the purse! sweet, now, make haste.

LUCIANA

How hast thou lost thy breath?

DROMIO OF SYRACUSE

By running fast.

ADRIANA

Where is thy master, Dromio? Is he well?

DROMIO OF SYRACUSE

No, he's in Tartar limbo, worse than hell.
A devil in an everlasting garment hath him;
One whose hard heart is button'd up with steel;
A fiend, a fury, pitiless and rough;
A wolf, nay, worse; a fellow all in buff;
A back-friend, a shoulder-clapper, one that countermands
The passages of alleys, creeks, and narrow lands;
A hound that runs counter, and yet draws dry-foot well;
One that, before the Judgment, carries poor souls to hell.

ADRIANA

Why, man, what is the matter?

DROMIO OF SYRACUSE

I do not know the matter, he is 'rested on the case.

ADRIANA

What, is he arrested? Tell me at whose suit.

DROMIO OF SYRACUSE

    I know not at whose suit he is arrested well;

    But he's in a suit of buff which 'rested him, that can I tell.

    Will you send him, mistress, redemption, the money in his desk?

ADRIANA

    Go fetch it, sister. [*Exit* LUCIANA] This I wonder at,

    That he, unknown to me, should be in debt.

    Tell me, was he arrested on a band?

DROMIO OF SYRACUSE

    Not on a band, but on a stronger thing;

    A chain, a chain! Do you not hear it ring?

ADRIANA

    What, the chain?

DROMIO OF SYRACUSE

    No, no, the bell. 'Tis time that I were gone.

    It was two ere I left him, and now the clock strikes one.

ADRIANA

    The hours come back—that did I never hear.

DROMIO OF SYRACUSE

    O, yes; if any hour meet a sergeant, 'a turns back for very fear.

ADRIANA

    As if Time were in debt! How fondly dost thou reason!

DROMIO OF SYRACUSE

    Time is a very bankrupt, and owes more than he's worth to
    season.

    Nay, he's a thief too. Have you not heard men say,

    That Time comes stealing on by night and day?

    If Time be in debt and theft, and a sergeant in the way,

    Hath he not reason to turn back an hour in a day?

            Re-enter LUCIANA *with a purse*

ADRIANA

    Go, Dromio; there's the money, bear it straight;

    And bring thy master home immediately.

    Come, sister, I am press'd down with conceit—

    Conceit, my comfort and my injury.

                           Exeunt

SCENE III.
A PUBLIC PLACE.

Enter ANTIPHOLUS OF SYRACUSE

ANTIPHOLUS OF SYRACUSE

There's not a man I meet but doth salute me
As if I were their well-acquainted friend;
And every one doth call me by my name.
Some tender money to me; some invite me;
Some other give me thanks for kindnesses;
Some offer me commodities to buy;
Even now a tailor call'd me in his shop,
And show'd me silks that he had bought for me,
And therewithal took measure of my body.
Sure, these are but imaginary wiles,
And Lapland sorcerers inhabit here.

Enter DROMIO OF SYRACUSE

DROMIO OF SYRACUSE

Master, here's the gold you sent me for.—
What, have you got the picture of old Adam new-apparelled?

ANTIPHOLUS OF SYRACUSE

What gold is this? What Adam dost thou mean?

DROMIO OF SYRACUSE

Not that Adam that kept the Paradise, but that Adam that keeps
the prison. He that goes in the calf's skin that was killed for the
Prodigal; he that came behind you, sir, like an evil angel, and bid
you forsake your liberty.

ANTIPHOLUS OF SYRACUSE

I understand thee not.

DROMIO OF SYRACUSE

No? Why, 'tis a plain case: he that went, like a base-viol, in a case
of leather; the man, sir, that, when gentlemen are tired, gives
them a sob, and 'rests them; he, sir, that takes pity on decayed
men, and gives them suits of durance; he that sets up his rest to
do more exploits with his mace than a morris-pike.

ANTIPHOLUS OF SYRACUSE

What, thou meanest an officer?

DROMIO OF SYRACUSE

Ay, sir, the sergeant of the band; he that brings any man to answer it that breaks his band; one that thinks a man always going to bed, and says, 'God give you good rest!'

ANTIPHOLUS OF SYRACUSE

Well, sir, there rest in your foolery. Is there any ship puts forth to-night? May we be gone?

DROMIO OF SYRACUSE

Why, sir, I brought you word an hour since, that the bark *Expedition* put forth to-night; and then were you hindered by the sergeant, to tarry for the hoy *Delay*. Here are the angels that you sent for to deliver you.

ANTIPHOLUS OF SYRACUSE

The fellow is distract, and so am I;

And here we wander in illusions.

Some blessed power deliver us from hence!

Enter a COURTESAN

COURTESAN

Well met, well met, Master Antipholus.

I see, sir, you have found the goldsmith now.

Is that the chain you promised me to-day?

ANTIPHOLUS OF SYRACUSE

Satan, avoid! I charge thee, tempt me not.

DROMIO OF SYRACUSE

Master, is this Mistress Satan?

ANTIPHOLUS OF SYRACUSE

It is the devil.

DROMIO OF SYRACUSE

Nay, she is worse, she is the devil's dam; and here she comes in the habit of a light wench; and thereof comes that the wenches say, 'God damn me;' that's as much to say, 'God make me a light wench.' It is written, they appear to men like angels of light. Light is an effect of fire, and fire will burn; ergo, light wenches will burn. Come not near her.

COURTESAN

Your man and you are marvellous merry, sir.

Will you go with me? We'll mend our dinner here?

DROMIO OF SYRACUSE
Master, if you do, expect spoon-meat; or bespeak a long spoon.
ANTIPHOLUS OF SYRACUSE
Why, Dromio?
DROMIO OF SYRACUSE
Marry, he must have a long spoon that must eat with the devil.
ANTIPHOLUS OF SYRACUSE
Avoid then, fiend! what tell'st thou me of supping?
Thou art, as you are all, a sorceress.
I conjure thee to leave me and be gone.
COURTESAN
Give me the ring of mine you had at dinner,
Or, for my diamond, the chain you promised,
And I'll be gone, sir, and not trouble you.
DROMIO OF SYRACUSE
Some devils ask but the parings of one's nail,
A rush, a hair, a drop of blood, a pin,
A nut, a cherry-stone;
But she, more covetous, would have a chain.
Master, be wise; an if you give it her,
The devil will shake her chain, and fright us with it.
COURTESAN
I pray you, sir, my ring, or else the chain!
I hope you do not mean to cheat me so.
ANTIPHOLUS OF SYRACUSE
Avaunt, thou witch!—Come, Dromio, let us go.
DROMIO OF SYRACUSE
'Fly pride,' says the peacock. Mistress, that you know.
Exeunt ANTIPHOLUS OF SYRACUSE
and DROMIO OF SYRACUSE
COURTESAN
Now, out of doubt Antipholus is mad,
Else would he never so demean himself.
A ring he hath of mine worth forty ducats,
And for the same he promised me a chain.
Both one and other he denies me now.
The reason that I gather he is mad,

Besides this present instance of his rage,
Is a mad tale he told to-day at dinner,
Of his own doors being shut against his entrance.
Belike his wife, acquainted with his fits,
On purpose shut the doors against his way.
My way is now to his home to his house,
And tell his wife that, being lunatic,
He rush'd into my house, and took perforce
My ring away. This course I fittest choose;
For forty ducats is too much to lose.

Exit

SCENE IV.
A STREET.

Enter ANTIPHOLUS OF EPHESUS *and the Officer*

ANTIPHOLUS OF EPHESUS
Fear me not, man; I will not break away.
I'll give thee, ere I leave thee, so much money,
To warrant thee, as I am 'rested for.
My wife is in a wayward mood to-day,
And will not lightly trust the messenger.
That I should be attach'd in Ephesus,
I tell you, 'twill sound harshly in her ears.

Enter DROMIO OF EPHESUS *with a rope's end*

Here comes my man; I think he brings the money.
How now, sir! have you that I sent you for?

DROMIO OF EPHESUS
Here's that, I warrant you, will pay them all.

ANTIPHOLUS OF EPHESUS
But where's the money?

DROMIO OF EPHESUS
Why, sir, I gave the money for the rope.

ANTIPHOLUS OF EPHESUS
Five hundred ducats, villain, for a rope?

DROMIO OF EPHESUS
I'll serve you, sir, five hundred at the rate.

ANTIPHOLUS OF EPHESUS

To what end did I bid thee hie thee home?

DROMIO OF EPHESUS

To a rope's end, sir; and to that end am I returned.

ANTIPHOLUS OF EPHESUS

And to that end, sir, I will welcome you.

Beating him

OFFICER

Good sir, be patient.

DROMIO OF EPHESUS

Nay, 'tis for me to be patient; I am in adversity.

OFFICER

Good, now, hold thy tongue.

DROMIO OF EPHESUS

Nay, rather persuade him to hold his hands.

ANTIPHOLUS OF EPHESUS

Thou whoreson, senseless villain!

DROMIO OF EPHESUS

I would I were senseless, sir, that I might not feel your blows.

ANTIPHOLUS OF EPHESUS

Thou art sensible in nothing but blows, and so is an ass.

DROMIO OF EPHESUS

I am an ass, indeed; you may prove it by my long ears. I have served him from the hour of my nativity to this instant, and have nothing at his hands for my service but blows. When I am cold, he heats me with beating; when I am warm, he cools me with beating. I am waked with it when I sleep; raised with it when I sit; driven out of doors with it when I go from home; welcomed home with it when I return; nay, I bear it on my shoulders, as a beggar wont her brat; and, I think, when he hath lamed me, I shall beg with it from door to door.

ANTIPHOLUS OF EPHESUS

Come, go along; my wife is coming yonder.

Enter ADRIANA, LUCIANA, *the* COURTESAN, *and* PINCH

DROMIO OF EPHESUS

Mistress, 'respice finem,' respect your end; or rather, the prophecy like the parrot, 'beware the rope's end.'

ANTIPHOLUS OF EPHESUS
>Wilt thou still talk?

Beating him

COURTESAN
>How say you now? Is not your husband mad?

ADRIANA
>His incivility confirms no less.
>Good Doctor Pinch, you are a conjurer;
>Establish him in his true sense again,
>And I will please you what you will demand.

LUCIANA
>Alas, how fiery and how sharp he looks!

COURTESAN
>Mark how he trembles in his ecstasy!

PINCH
>Give me your hand, and let me feel your pulse.

ANTIPHOLUS OF EPHESUS
>There is my hand, and let it feel your ear.

Striking him

PINCH
>I charge thee, Satan, housed within this man,
>To yield possession to my holy prayers,
>And to thy state of darkness his thee straight.
>I conjure thee by all the saints in heaven!

ANTIPHOLUS OF EPHESUS
>Peace, doting wizard, peace! I am not mad.

ADRIANA
>O, that thou wert not, poor distressed soul!

ANTIPHOLUS OF EPHESUS
>You minion, you, are these your customers?
>Did this companion with the saffron face
>Revel and feast it at my house to-day,
>Whilst upon me the guilty doors were shut,
>And I denied to enter in my house?

ADRIANA
>O husband, God doth know you dined at home;

Where would you had remain'd until this time,
Free from these slanders and this open shame!

ANTIPHOLUS OF EPHESUS

Dined at home! Thou villain, what sayest thou?

DROMIO OF EPHESUS

Sir, sooth to say, you did not dine at home.

ANTIPHOLUS OF EPHESUS

Were not my doors lock'd up, and I shut out?

DROMIO OF EPHESUS

Perdie, your doors were lock'd, and you shut out.

ANTIPHOLUS OF EPHESUS

And did not she herself revile me there?

DROMIO OF EPHESUS

Sans fable, she herself reviled you there.

ANTIPHOLUS OF EPHESUS

Did not her kitchen-maid rail, taunt, and scorn me?

DROMIO OF EPHESUS

Certes, she did; the kitchen-vestal scorn'd you.

ANTIPHOLUS OF EPHESUS

And did not I in rage depart from thence?

DROMIO OF EPHESUS

In verity you did; my bones bear witness,
That since have felt the vigour of his rage.

ADRIANA

Is't good to soothe him in these contraries?

PINCH

It is no shame. The fellow finds his vein,
And, yielding to him, humours well his frenzy.

ANTIPHOLUS OF EPHESUS

Thou hast suborn'd the goldsmith to arrest me.

ADRIANA

Alas, I sent you money to redeem you,
By Dromio here, who came in haste for it.

DROMIO OF EPHESUS

Money by me! heart and good-will you might;
But surely, master, not a rag of money.

ANTIPHOLUS OF EPHESUS

    Went'st not thou to her for a purse of ducats?

ADRIANA

    He came to me, and I deliver'd it.

LUCIANA

    And I am witness with her that she did.

DROMIO OF EPHESUS

    God and the rope-maker bear me witness

    That I was sent for nothing but a rope!

PINCH

    Mistress, both man and master is possess'd;

    I know it by their pale and deadly looks.

    They must be bound, and laid in some dark room.

ANTIPHOLUS OF EPHESUS

    Say, wherefore didst them lock me forth to-day?

    And why dost thou deny the bag of gold?

ADRIANA

    I did not, gentle husband, lock thee forth.

DROMIO OF EPHESUS

    And, gentle master, I received no gold;

    But I confess, sir, that we were lock'd out.

ADRIANA

    Dissembling villain, them speak'st false in both.

ANTIPHOLUS OF EPHESUS

    Dissembling harlot, them art false in all,

    And art confederate with a damned pack

    To make a loathsome abject scorn of me.

    But with these nails I'll pluck out these false eyes,

    That would behold in me this shameful sport.

              Enter three or four, and offer to bind him.

                        He strives.

ADRIANA

    O, bind him, bind him! let him not come near me.

PINCH

    More company! The fiend is strong within him.

LUCIANA

    Ay me, poor man, how pale and wan he looks!

ANTIPHOLUS OF EPHESUS

What, will you murder me? Thou gaoler, thou,
I am thy prisoner: wilt thou suffer them
To make a rescue?

OFFICER

Masters, let him go.
He is my prisoner, and you shall not have him.

PINCH

Go bind this man, for he is frantic too.

They offer to bind DROMIO OF EPHESUS

ADRIANA

What wilt thou do, thou peevish officer?
Hast thou delight to see a wretched man
Do outrage and displeasure to himself?

OFFICER

He is my prisoner. If I let him go,
The debt he owes will be required of me.

ADRIANA

I will discharge thee ere I go from thee.
Bear me forthwith unto his creditor,
And, knowing how the debt grows, I will pay it.
Good master doctor, see him safe convey'd
Home to my house. O most unhappy day!

ANTIPHOLUS OF EPHESUS

O most unhappy strumpet!

DROMIO OF EPHESUS

Master, I am here entered in bond for you.

ANTIPHOLUS OF EPHESUS

Out on thee, villain! wherefore dost thou mad me?

DROMIO OF EPHESUS

Will you be bound for nothing? Be mad, good master: cry, 'the devil!'

LUCIANA

God help, poor souls, how idly do they talk!

ADRIANA

Go bear him hence. Sister, go you with me.

Say now; whose suit is he arrested at?

OFFICER

One Angelo, a goldsmith. Do you know him?

ADRIANA

I know the man. What is the sum he owes?

OFFICER

Two hundred ducats.

ADRIANA

Say, how grows it due?

OFFICER

Due for a chain your husband had of him.

ADRIANA

He did bespeak a chain for me, but had it not.

COURTESAN

When as your husband, all in rage, to-day
Came to my house, and took away my ring,
The ring I saw upon his finger now,
Straight after did I meet him with a chain.

ADRIANA

It may be so, but I did never see it.
Come, gaoler, bring me where the goldsmith is.
I long to know the truth hereof at large.

Enter ANTIPHOLUS OF SYRACUSE *with*
his rapier drawn, and DROMIO OF SYRACUSE

LUCIANA

God, for thy mercy! they are loose again.

ADRIANA

And come with naked swords.
Let's call more help to have them bound again.

OFFICER

Away! they'll kill us.

Exeunt all but ANTIPHOLUS OF SYRACUSE
and DROMIO OF SYRACUSE

ANTIPHOLUS OF SYRACUSE

I see these witches are afraid of swords.

DROMIO OF SYRACUSE

She that would be your wife now ran from you.

ANTIPHOLUS OF SYRACUSE

Come to the Centaur; fetch our stuff from thence.

I long that we were safe and sound aboard.

DROMIO OF SYRACUSE

Faith, stay here this night; they will surely do us no harm. You saw they speak us fair, give us gold. Methinks they are such a gentle nation, that, but for the mountain of mad flesh that claims marriage of me, I could find in my heart to stay here still, and turn witch.

ANTIPHOLUS OF SYRACUSE

I will not stay to-night for all the town;

Therefore away, to get our stuff aboard.

Exeunt

ACT

V

SCENE I.
A STREET BEFORE A PRIORY.

Enter SECOND MERCHANT *and* ANGELO

ANGELO

    I am sorry, sir, that I have hinder'd you;
    But, I protest, he had the chain of me,
    Though most dishonestly he doth deny it.

SECOND MERCHANT

    How is the man esteem'd here in the city?

ANGELO

    Of very reverent reputation, sir,
    Of credit infinite, highly beloved,
    Second to none that lives here in the city.
    His word might bear my wealth at any time.

SECOND MERCHANT

    Speak softly. Yonder, as I think, he walks.

        Enter ANTIPHOLUS OF SYRACUSE *and*
            DROMIO OF SYRACUSE

ANGELO

    'Tis so; and that self chain about his neck,
    Which he forswore most monstrously to have.

Good sir, draw near to me, I'll speak to him;
Signior Antipholus, I wonder much
That you would put me to this shame and trouble;
And, not without some scandal to yourself,
With circumstance and oaths so to deny
This chain which now you wear so openly.
Beside the charge, the shame, imprisonment,
You have done wrong to this my honest friend;
Who, but for staying on our controversy,
Had hoisted sail and put to sea to-day.
This chain you had of me; can you deny it?

ANTIPHOLUS OF SYRACUSE

I think I had; I never did deny it.

SECOND MERCHANT

Yes, that you did, sir, and forswore it too.

ANTIPHOLUS OF SYRACUSE

Who heard me to deny it or forswear it?

SECOND MERCHANT

These ears of mine, thou know'st, did hear thee.
Fie on thee, wretch! 'tis pity that thou livest
To walk where any honest men resort.

ANTIPHOLUS OF SYRACUSE

Thou art a villain to impeach me thus.
I'll prove mine honour and mine honesty
Against thee presently, if thou darest stand.

SECOND MERCHANT

I dare, and do defy thee for a villain. *They draw.*

Enter ADRIANA, LUCIANA, *the* COURTESAN, *and others*

ADRIANA

Hold, hurt him not, for God's sake! he is mad.
Some get within him, take his sword away.
Bind Dromio too, and bear them to my house.

DROMIO OF SYRACUSE

Run, master, run; for God's sake, take a house!
This is some priory. In, or we are spoil'd!

Exeunt ANTIPHOLUS OF SYRACUSE
and DROMIO OF SYRACUSE *to the Priory*

Enter the LADY ABBESS

ABBESS
Be quiet, people. Wherefore throng you hither?
ADRIANA
To fetch my poor distracted husband hence.
Let us come in, that we may bind him fast,
And bear him home for his recovery.
ANGELO
I knew he was not in his perfect wits.
SECOND MERCHANT
I am sorry now that I did draw on him.
ABBESS
How long hath this possession held the man?
ADRIANA
This week he hath been heavy, sour, sad,
And much different from the man he was;
But till this afternoon his passion
Ne'er brake into extremity of rage.
ABBESS
Hath he not lost much wealth by wreck of sea?
Buried some dear friend? Hath not else his eye
Stray'd his affection in unlawful love?
A sin prevailing much in youthful men,
Who give their eyes the liberty of gazing.
Which of these sorrows is he subject to?
ADRIANA
To none of these, except it be the last;
Namely, some love that drew him oft from home.
ABBESS
You should for that have reprehended him.
ADRIANA
Why, so I did.
ABBESS
Ay, but not rough enough.
ADRIANA
As roughly as my modesty would let me.

ABBESS

Haply, in private.

ADRIANA

And in assemblies too.

ABBESS

Ay, but not enough.

ADRIANA

It was the copy of our conference.
In bed, he slept not for my urging it;
At board, he fed not for my urging it;
Alone, it was the subject of my theme;
In company I often glanced it;
Still did I tell him it was vile and bad.

ABBESS

And thereof came it that the man was mad.
The venom clamours of a jealous woman,
Poisons more deadly than a mad dog's tooth.
It seems his sleeps were hinder'd by thy railing,
And thereof comes it that his head is light.
Thou say'st his meat was sauced with thy upbraidings.
Unquiet meals make ill digestions;
Thereof the raging fire of fever bred;
And what's a fever but a fit of madness?
Thou say'st his sports were hinder'd by thy brawls.
Sweet recreation barr'd, what doth ensue
But moody and dull melancholy,
Kinsman to grim and comfortless despair;
And at her heels a huge infectious troop
Of pale distemperatures and foes to life?
In food, in sport, and life-preserving rest
To be disturb'd, would mad or man or beast.
The consequence is, then, thy jealous fits
Have scared thy husband from the use of wits.

LUCIANA

She never reprehended him but mildly,
When he demean'd himself rough, rude, and wildly.
Why bear you these rebukes, and answer not?

ADRIANA

    She did betray me to my own reproof.

    Good people, enter, and lay hold on him.

ABBESS

    No, not a creature enters in my house.

ADRIANA

    Then let your servants bring my husband forth.

ABBESS

    Neither. He took this place for sanctuary,

    And it shall privilege him from your hands

    Till I have brought him to his wits again,

    Or lose my labour in assaying it.

ADRIANA

    I will attend my husband, be his nurse,

    Diet his sickness, for it is my office,

    And will have no attorney but myself;

    And therefore let me have him home with me.

ABBESS

    Be patient; for I will not let him stir

    Till I have used the approved means I have,

    With wholesome syrups, drugs and holy prayers,

    To make of him a formal man again.

    It is a branch and parcel of mine oath,

    A charitable duty of my order.

    Therefore depart, and leave him here with me.

ADRIANA

    I will not hence, and leave my husband here.

    And ill it doth beseem your holiness

    To separate the husband and the wife.

ABBESS

    Be quiet, and depart. Thou shalt not have him.

Exit

LUCIANA

    Complain unto the Duke of this indignity.

ADRIANA

    Come, go. I will fall prostrate at his feet,

    And never rise until my tears and prayers

Have won his Grace to come in person hither,
And take perforce my husband from the abbess.

SECOND MERCHANT
By this, I think, the dial points at five.
Anon, I'm sure, the Duke himself in person
Comes this way to the melancholy vale,
The place of death and sorry execution,
Behind the ditches of the abbey here.

ANGELO
Upon what cause?

SECOND MERCHANT
To see a reverend Syracusian merchant,
Who put unluckily into this bay
Against the laws and statutes of this town,
Beheaded publicly for his offence.

ANGELO
See where they come. We will behold his death.

LUCIANA
Kneel to the Duke before he pass the abbey.

Enter DUKE, *attended;* ÆGEON *bareheaded,*
with the Headsman and other Officers

DUKE
Yet once again proclaim it publicly,
If any friend will pay the sum for him,
He shall not die; so much we tender him.

ADRIANA
Justice, most sacred Duke, against the abbess!

DUKE
She is a virtuous and a reverend lady.
It cannot be that she hath done thee wrong.

ADRIANA
May it please your Grace, Antipholus my husband,
Whom I made lord of me and all I had,
At your important letters, this ill day
A most outrageous fit of madness took him;
That desperately he hurried through the street,
With him his bondman, all as mad as he,

Doing displeasure to the citizens
By rushing in their houses, bearing thence
Rings, jewels, any thing his rage did like.
Once did I get him bound, and sent him home,
Whilst to take order for the wrongs I went,
That here and there his fury had committed.
Anon, I wot not by what strong escape,
He broke from those that had the guard of him;
And with his mad attendant and himself,
Each one with ireful passion, with drawn swords,
Met us again, and, madly bent on us,
Chased us away; till, raising of more aid,
We came again to bind them. Then they fled
Into this abbey, whither we pursued them;
And here the abbess shuts the gates on us,
And will not suffer us to fetch him out,
Nor send him forth, that we may bear him hence.
Therefore, most gracious Duke, with thy command
Let him be brought forth, and borne hence for help.

DUKE

Long since thy husband served me in my wars;
And I to thee engaged a prince's word,
When thou didst make him master of thy bed,
To do him all the grace and good I could.
Go, some of you, knock at the abbey-gate,
And bid the lady abbess come to me.
I will determine this before I stir.

Enter a Servant

SERVANT

O mistress, mistress, shift and save yourself!
My master and his man are both broke loose,
Beaten the maids a-row, and bound the doctor,
Whose beard they have singed off with brands of fire;
And ever, as it blazed, they threw on him
Great pails of puddled mire to quench the hair.
My master preaches patience to him, and the while
His man with scissors nicks him like a fool;

And sure, unless you send some present help,
Between them they will kill the conjurer.

ADRIANA

Peace, fool! thy master and his man are here;
And that is false thou dost report to us.

SERVANT

Mistress, upon my life, I tell you true;
I have not breathed almost since I did see it.
He cries for you, and vows, if he can take you,
To scorch your face and to disfigure you.

Cry within

Hark, hark! I hear him, mistress. Fly, be gone!

DUKE

Come, stand by me; fear nothing. Guard with halberds!

ADRIANA

Ay me, it is my husband! Witness you,
That he is borne about invisible.
Even now we housed him in the abbey here;
And now he's there, past thought of human reason.

Enter ANTIPHOLUS OF EPHESUS *and*
DROMIO OF EPHESUS

ANTIPHOLUS OF EPHESUS

Justice, most gracious Duke, O, grant me justice!
Even for the service that long since I did thee,
When I bestrid thee in the wars, and took
Deep scars to save thy life; even for the blood
That then I lost for thee, now grant me justice.

ÆGEON

Unless the fear of death doth make me dote,
I see my son Antipholus, and Dromio.

ANTIPHOLUS OF EPHESUS

Justice, sweet prince, against that woman there!
She whom thou gavest to me to be my wife,
That hath abused and dishonour'd me
Even in the strength and height of injury.
Beyond imagination is the wrong
That she this day hath shameless thrown on me.

DUKE

    Discover how, and thou shalt find me just.

ANTIPHOLUS OF EPHESUS

    This day, great Duke, she shut the doors upon me,

    While she with harlots feasted in my house.

DUKE

    A grievous fault! Say, woman, didst thou so?

ADRIANA

    No, my good lord. Myself, he and my sister

    To-day did dine together. So befal my soul

    As this is false he burdens me withal!

LUCIANA

    Ne'er may I look on day, nor sleep on night,

    But she tells to your Highness simple truth!

ANGELO

    O perjured woman! They are both forsworn.

    In this the madman justly chargeth them.

ANTIPHOLUS OF EPHESUS

    My liege, I am advised what I say;

    Neither disturbed with the effect of wine,

    Nor heady-rash, provoked with raging ire,

    Albeit my wrongs might make one wiser mad.

    This woman lock'd me out this day from dinner.

    That goldsmith there, were he not pack'd with her,

    Could witness it, for he was with me then;

    Who parted with me to go fetch a chain,

    Promising to bring it to the Porpentine,

    Where Balthazar and I did dine together.

    Our dinner done, and he not coming thither,

    I went to seek him. In the street I met him,

    And in his company that gentleman.

    There did this perjured goldsmith swear me down

    That I this day of him received the chain,

    Which, God he knows, I saw not. For the which

    He did arrest me with an officer.

    I did obey; and sent my peasant home

    For certain ducats. He with none return'd.

Then fairly I bespoke the officer
To go in person with me to my house.
By the way we met my wife, her sister, and a rabble more
Of vile confederates. Along with them
They brought one Pinch, a hungry lean-faced villain,
A mere anatomy, a mountebank,
A threadbare juggler, and a fortune-teller,
A needy, hollow-eyed, sharp-looking wretch,
A living-dead man. This pernicious slave,
Forsooth, took on him as a conjurer;
And, gazing in mine eyes, feeling my pulse,
And with no face, as 'twere, outfacing me,
Cries out, I was possess'd. Then all together
They fell upon me, bound me, bore me thence,
And in a dark and dankish vault at home
There left me and my man, both bound together;
Till, gnawing with my teeth my bonds in sunder,
I gain'd my freedom, and immediately
Ran hither to your Grace; whom I beseech
To give me ample satisfaction
For these deep shames and great indignities.

ANGELO
    My lord, in truth, thus far I witness with him,
    That he dined not at home, but was lock'd out.

DUKE
    But had he such a chain of thee or no?

ANGELO
    He had, my lord, and when he ran in here,
    These people saw the chain about his neck.

SECOND MERCHANT
    Besides, I will be sworn these ears of mine
    Heard you confess you had the chain of him,
    After you first forswore it on the mart,
    And thereupon I drew my sword on you;
    And then you fled into this abbey here,
    From whence, I think, you are come by miracle.

ANTIPHOLUS OF EPHESUS
   I never came within these abbey walls;
   Nor ever didst thou draw thy sword on me.
   I never saw the chain, so help me Heaven,
   And this is false you burden me withal!
DUKE
   Why, what an intricate impeach is this!
   I think you all have drunk of Circe's cup.
   If here you housed him, here he would have been;
   If he were mad, he would not plead so coldly.
   You say he dined at home; the goldsmith here
   Denies that saying. Sirrah, what say you?
DROMIO OF EPHESUS
   Sir, he dined with her there, at the Porpentine.
COURTESAN
   He did; and from my finger snatch'd that ring.
ANTIPHOLUS OF EPHESUS
   'Tis true, my liege; this ring I had of her.
DUKE
   Saw'st thou him enter at the abbey here?
COURTESAN
   As sure, my liege, as I do see your Grace.
DUKE
   Why, this is strange. Go call the abbess hither.
   I think you are all mated, or stark mad.

Exit one to the Abbess

ÆGEON
   Most mighty Duke, vouchsafe me speak a word.
   Haply I see a friend will save my life,
   And pay the sum that may deliver me.
DUKE
   Speak freely, Syracusian, what thou wilt.
ÆGEON
   Is not your name, sir, call'd Antipholus?
   And is not that your bondman, Dromio?
DROMIO OF EPHESUS
   Within this hour I was his bondman, sir,

But he, I thank him, gnaw'd in two my cords.
Now am I Dromio, and his man unbound.

ÆGEON

I am sure you both of you remember me.

DROMIO OF EPHESUS

Ourselves we do remember, sir, by you;
For lately we were bound, as you are now.
You are not Pinch's patient, are you, sir?

ÆGEON

Why look you strange on me? You know me well.

ANTIPHOLUS OF EPHESUS

I never saw you in my life till now.

ÆGEON

O, grief hath changed me since you saw me last,
And careful hours with time's deformed hand
Have written strange defeatures in my face.
But tell me yet, dost thou not know my voice?

ANTIPHOLUS OF EPHESUS

Neither.

ÆGEON

Dromio, nor thou?

DROMIO OF EPHESUS

No, trust me, sir, nor I.

ÆGEON

I am sure thou dost.

DROMIO OF EPHESUS

Ay, sir, but I am sure I do not; and whatsoever a man denies, you
are now bound to believe him.

ÆGEON

Not know my voice! O time's extremity,
Hast thou so crack'd and splitted my poor tongue
In seven short years, that here my only son
Knows not my feeble key of untuned cares?
Though now this grained face of mine be hid
In sap-consuming winter's drizzled snow,
And all the conduits of my blood froze up,
Yet hath my night of life some memory,

My wasting lamps some fading glimmer left,
My dull deaf ears a little use to hear.
All these old witnesses—I cannot err—
Tell me thou art my son Antipholus.

ANTIPHOLUS OF EPHESUS

I never saw my father in my life.

ÆGEON

But seven years since, in Syracusa, boy,
Thou know'st we parted. But perhaps, my son,
Thou shamest to acknowledge me in misery.

ANTIPHOLUS OF EPHESUS

The Duke and all that know me in the city
Can witness with me that it is not so.
I ne'er saw Syracusa in my life.

DUKE

I tell thee, Syracusian, twenty years
Have I been patron to Antipholus,
During which time he ne'er saw Syracusa.
I see thy age and dangers make thee dote.

Re-enter ABBESS, *with* ANTIPHOLUS OF
SYRACUSE *and* DROMIO OF SYRACUSE

ABBESS

Most mighty Duke, behold a man much wrong'd.

All gather to see them

ADRIANA

I see two husbands, or mine eyes deceive me.

DUKE

One of these men is Genius to the other;
And so of these. Which is the natural man,
And which the spirit? Who deciphers them?

DROMIO OF SYRACUSE

I, sir, am Dromio. Command him away.

DROMIO OF EPHESUS

I, sir, am Dromio. Pray, let me stay.

ANTIPHOLUS OF SYRACUSE

Ægeon art thou not? or else his ghost?

DROMIO OF SYRACUSE
    O, my old master! who hath bound him here?
ABBESS
    Whoever bound him, I will loose his bonds,
    And gain a husband by his liberty.
    Speak, old Ægeon, if thou be'st the man
    That hadst a wife once call'd Æmilia,
    That bore thee at a burden two fair sons.
    O, if thou be'st the same Ægeon, speak,
    And speak unto the same Æmilia!
ÆGEON
    If I dream not, thou art Æmilia.
    If thou art she, tell me where is that son
    That floated with thee on the fatal raft?
ABBESS
    By men of Epidamnum he and I
    And the twin Dromio, all were taken up;
    But by and by rude fishermen of Corinth
    By force took Dromio and my son from them,
    And me they left with those of Epidamnum.
    What then became of them I cannot tell;
    I to this fortune that you see me in.
DUKE
    Why, here begins his morning story right.
    These two Antipholuses, these two so like,
    And these two Dromios, one in semblance,
    Besides her urging of her wreck at sea—
    These are the parents to these children,
    Which accidentally are met together.
    Antipholus, thou camest from Corinth first?
ANTIPHOLUS OF SYRACUSE
    No, sir, not I; I came from Syracuse.
DUKE
    Stay, stand apart; I know not which is which.
ANTIPHOLUS OF EPHESUS
    I came from Corinth, my most gracious lord.

DROMIO OF EPHESUS

And I with him.

ANTIPHOLUS OF EPHESUS

Brought to this town by that most famous warrior.

Duke Menaphon, your most renowned uncle.

ADRIANA

Which of you two did dine with me to-day?

ANTIPHOLUS OF SYRACUSE

I, gentle mistress.

ADRIANA

And are not you my husband?

ANTIPHOLUS OF EPHESUS

No; I say nay to that.

ANTIPHOLUS OF SYRACUSE

And so do I; yet did she call me so,

And this fair gentlewoman, her sister here,

Did call me brother. [*To Lucia*] What I told you then,

I hope I shall have leisure to make good;

If this be not a dream I see and hear.

ANGELO

That is the chain, sir, which you had of me.

ANTIPHOLUS OF SYRACUSE

I think it be, sir; I deny it not.

ANTIPHOLUS OF EPHESUS

And you, sir, for this chain arrested me.

ANGELO

I think I did, sir; I deny it not.

ADRIANA

I sent you money, sir, to be your bail,

By Dromio; but I think he brought it not.

DROMIO OF EPHESUS

No, none by me.

ANTIPHOLUS OF SYRACUSE

This purse of ducats I received from you,

And Dromio my man did bring them me.

I see we still did meet each other's man;

And I was ta'en for him, and he for me;
And thereupon these ERRORS are arose.

ANTIPHOLUS OF EPHESUS

These ducats pawn I for my father here.

DUKE

It shall not need; thy father hath his life.

COURTESAN

Sir, I must have that diamond from you.

ANTIPHOLUS OF EPHESUS

There, take it; and much thanks for my good cheer.

ABBESS

Renowned Duke, vouchsafe to take the pains
To go with us into the abbey here,
And hear at large discoursed all our fortunes;
And all that are assembled in this place,
That by this sympathized one day's error
Have suffer'd wrong, go keep us company,
And we shall make full satisfaction.
Thirty-three years have I but gone in travail
Of you, my sons; and till this present hour
My heavy burthen ne'er delivered.
The Duke, my husband, and my children both,
And you the calendars of their nativity,
Go to a gossips' feast, and go with me;
After so long grief, such nativity!

DUKE

With all my heart, I'll gossip at this feast.

Exeunt all but ANTIPHOLUS OF SYRACUSE,
ANTIPHOLUS OF EPHESUS, DROMIO OF SYRACUSE,
and DROMIO OF EPHESUS

DROMIO OF SYRACUSE

Master, shall I fetch your stuff from ship-board?

ANTIPHOLUS OF EPHESUS

Dromio, what stuff of mine hast thou embark'd?

DROMIO OF SYRACUSE

Your goods that lay at host, sir, in the Centaur.

ANTIPHOLUS OF SYRACUSE

 He speaks to me—I am your master, Dromio!
 Come, go with us; we'll look to that anon.
 Embrace thy brother there; rejoice with him.

Exeunt ANTIPHOLUS OF SYRACUSE
and ANTIPHOLUS OF EPHESUS

DROMIO OF SYRACUSE

 There is a fat friend at your master's house,
 That kitchen'd me for you to-day at dinner.
 She now shall be my sister, not my wife.

DROMIO OF EPHESUS

 Methinks you are my glass, and not my brother.
 I see by you I am a sweet-faced youth.
 Will you walk in to see their gossiping?

DROMIO OF SYRACUSE

 Not I, sir; you are my elder.

DROMIO OF EPHESUS

 That's a question. How shall we try it?

DROMIO OF SYRACUSE

 We'll draw cuts for the senior. Till then lead thou first.

DROMIO OF EPHESUS

 Nay, then, thus:—
 We came into the world like brother and brother;
 And now let's go hand in hand, not one before another.

Exeunt

Twelfth Night

"Some are born great, some achieve greatness, and some have greatness thrown upon them."

Characters of the Play

ORSINO, Duke of Illyria
SEBASTIAN, brother to Viola
ANTONIO, a sea captain, friend to Sebastian
A Sea Captain, friend to Viola
VALENTINE and CURIO, gentlemen attending on the Duke
SIR TOBY BELCH, uncle to Olivia
SIR ANDREW AGUECHEEK
MALVOLIO, steward to Olivia
FABIAN and FESTE, a Clown, servants to Olivia
OLIVIA
VIOLA
MARIA, Olivia's woman
Lords, Priests, Sailors, Officers, Musicians, and other
Attendants

SCENE:
A city in Illyria, and the sea-coast near it

ACT

I

SCENE I.
DUKE ORSINO'S PALACE.

Enter DUKE ORSINO, CURIO,
and other Lords; Musicians attending

DUKE ORSINO

    If music be the food of love, play on;
    Give me excess of it, that, surfeiting,
    The appetite may sicken, and so die.
    That strain again! It had a dying fall:
    O, it came o'er my ear like the sweet sound,
    That breathes upon a bank of violets,
    Stealing and giving odour! Enough; no more:
    'Tis not so sweet now as it was before.
    O spirit of love! How quick and fresh art thou,
    That, notwithstanding thy capacity
    Receiveth as the sea, nought enters there,
    Of what validity and pitch soe'er,
    But falls into abatement and low price,
    Even in a minute: so full of shapes is fancy
    That it alone is high fantastical.

CURIO

Will you go hunt, my lord?

DUKE ORSINO

What, Curio?

CURIO

The hart.

DUKE ORSINO

Why, so I do, the noblest that I have:
O, when mine eyes did see Olivia first,
Methought she purged the air of pestilence!
That instant was I turn'd into a hart;
And my desires, like fell and cruel hounds,
E'er since pursue me.

Enter VALENTINE

How now! What news from her?

VALENTINE

So please my lord, I might not be admitted;
But from her handmaid do return this answer:
The element itself, till seven years' heat,
Shall not behold her face at ample view;
But, like a cloistress, she will veiled walk
And water once a day her chamber round
With eye-offending brine: all this to season
A brother's dead love, which she would keep fresh
And lasting in her sad remembrance.

DUKE ORSINO

O, she that hath a heart of that fine frame
To pay this debt of love but to a brother,
How will she love, when the rich golden shaft
Hath kill'd the flock of all affections else
That live in her; when liver, brain and heart,
These sovereign thrones, are all supplied, and fill'd
Her sweet perfections with one self king!
Away before me to sweet beds of flowers:
Love-thoughts lie rich when canopied with bowers.

Exeunt

SCENE II.
THE SEA-COAST.

Enter VIOLA, *a Captain, and Sailors*

VIOLA

What country, friends, is this?

CAPTAIN

This is Illyria, lady.

VIOLA

And what should I do in Illyria?
My brother he is in Elysium.
Perchance he is not drown'd: what think you, sailors?

CAPTAIN

It is perchance that you yourself were saved.

VIOLA

O my poor brother! And so perchance may he be.

CAPTAIN

True, madam: and, to comfort you with chance,
Assure yourself, after our ship did split,
When you and those poor number saved with you
Hung on our driving boat, I saw your brother,
Most provident in peril, bind himself,
Courage and hope both teaching him the practice,
To a strong mast that lived upon the sea;
Where, like Arion on the dolphin's back,
I saw him hold acquaintance with the waves
So long as I could see.

VIOLA

For saying so, there's gold:
Mine own escape unfoldeth to my hope,
Whereto thy speech serves for authority,
The like of him. Know'st thou this country?

CAPTAIN

Ay, madam, well; for I was bred and born
Not three hours' travel from this very place.

VIOLA

Who governs here?

CAPTAIN

A noble duke, in nature as in name.

VIOLA

What is the name?

CAPTAIN

Orsino.

VIOLA

Orsino! I have heard my father name him:
He was a bachelor then.

CAPTAIN

And so is now, or was so very late;
For but a month ago I went from hence,
And then 'twas fresh in murmur—as, you know,
What great ones do the less will prattle of—
That he did seek the love of fair Olivia.

VIOLA

What's she?

CAPTAIN

A virtuous maid, the daughter of a count
That died some twelvemonth since, then leaving her
In the protection of his son, her brother,
Who shortly also died: for whose dear love,
They say, she hath abjured the company
And sight of men.

VIOLA

O that I served that lady
And might not be delivered to the world,
Till I had made mine own occasion mellow,
What my estate is!

CAPTAIN

That were hard to compass;
Because she will admit no kind of suit,
No, not the duke's.

VIOLA

There is a fair behavior in thee, captain;
And though that nature with a beauteous wall

Doth oft close in pollution, yet of thee
I will believe thou hast a mind that suits
With this thy fair and outward character.
I prithee, and I'll pay thee bounteously,
Conceal me what I am, and be my aid
For such disguise as haply shall become
The form of my intent. I'll serve this duke:
Thou shall present me as an eunuch to him:
It may be worth thy pains; for I can sing
And speak to him in many sorts of music
That will allow me very worth his service.
What else may hap to time I will commit;
Only shape thou thy silence to my wit.

CAPTAIN

Be you his eunuch, and your mute I'll be:
When my tongue blabs, then let mine eyes not see.

VIOLA

I thank thee: lead me on.

Exeunt

SCENE III.
OLIVIA'S HOUSE.

Enter SIR TOBY BELCH *and* MARIA

SIR TOBY BELCH

What a plague means my niece, to take the death of her brother
thus? I am sure care's an enemy to life.

MARIA

By my troth, Sir Toby, you must come in earlier o' nights: your
cousin, my lady, takes great exceptions to your ill hours.

SIR TOBY BELCH

Why, let her except, before excepted.

MARIA

Ay, but you must confine yourself within the modest limits of
order.

SIR TOBY BELCH

Confine! I'll confine myself no finer than I am: these clothes are good enough to drink in; and so be these boots too: an they be not, let them hang themselves in their own straps.

MARIA

That quaffing and drinking will undo you: I heard my lady talk of it yesterday; and of a foolish knight that you brought in one night here to be her wooer.

SIR TOBY BELCH

Who, Sir Andrew Aguecheek?

MARIA

Ay, he.

SIR TOBY BELCH

He's as tall a man as any's in Illyria.

MARIA

What's that to the purpose?

SIR TOBY BELCH

Why, he has three thousand ducats a year.

MARIA

Ay, but he'll have but a year in all these ducats: he's a very fool and a prodigal.

SIR TOBY BELCH

Fie, that you'll say so! He plays o' the viol-de-gamboys, and speaks three or four languages word for word without book, and hath all the good gifts of nature.

MARIA

He hath indeed, almost natural: for besides that he's a fool, he's a great quarreller: and but that he hath the gift of a coward, to allay the gust he hath in quarrelling, 'tis thought among the prudent, he would quickly have the gift of a grave.

SIR TOBY BELCH

By this hand, they are scoundrels and subtractors that say so of him. Who are they?

MARIA

They that add, moreover, he's drunk nightly in your company.

SIR TOBY BELCH

With drinking healths to my niece: I'll drink to her as long as there is a passage in my throat and drink in Illyria: he's a coward and a coystrill that will not drink to my niece till his brains turn o' the toe like a parish-top. What, wench! *Castiliano vulgo*! For here comes Sir Andrew Agueface.

Enter SIR ANDREW

SIR ANDREW

Sir Toby Belch! How now, Sir Toby Belch!

SIR TOBY BELCH

Sweet Sir Andrew!

SIR ANDREW

Bless you, fair shrew.

MARIA

And you too, sir.

SIR TOBY BELCH

Accost, Sir Andrew, accost.

SIR ANDREW

What's that?

SIR TOBY BELCH

My niece's chambermaid.

SIR ANDREW

Good Mistress Accost, I desire better acquaintance.

MARIA

My name is Mary, sir.

SIR ANDREW

Good Mistress Mary Accost—

SIR TOBY BELCH

You mistake, knight; 'accost' is front her, board her, woo her, assail her.

SIR ANDREW

By my troth, I would not undertake her in this company. Is that the meaning of 'accost'?

MARIA

Fare you well, gentlemen.

SIR TOBY BELCH

An thou let part so, Sir Andrew, would thou mightst never draw sword again.

SIR ANDREW

An you part so, mistress, I would I might never draw sword again. Fair lady, do you think you have fools in hand?

MARIA

Sir, I have not you by the hand.

SIR ANDREW

Marry, but you shall have; and here's my hand.

MARIA

Now, sir, 'thought is free:' I pray you, bring your hand to the buttery-bar and let it drink.

SIR ANDREW

Wherefore, sweet-heart? What's your metaphor?

MARIA

It's dry, sir.

SIR ANDREW

Why, I think so: I am not such an ass but I can keep my hand dry. But what's your jest?

MARIA

A dry jest, sir.

SIR ANDREW

Are you full of them?

MARIA

Ay, sir, I have them at my fingers' ends: marry, now I let go your hand, I am barren.

Exit MARIA

SIR TOBY BELCH

O knight thou lackest a cup of canary: when did I see thee so put down?

SIR ANDREW

Never in your life, I think; unless you see canary put me down. Methinks sometimes I have no more wit than a Christian or an ordinary man has: but I am a great eater of beef and I believe that does harm to my wit.

SIR TOBY BELCH

No question.

SIR ANDREW

An I thought that, I'ld forswear it. I'll ride home to-morrow, Sir Toby.

SIR TOBY BELCH

Pourquoi, my dear knight?

SIR ANDREW

What is '*Pourquoi*'? Do or not do? I would I had bestowed that time in the tongues that I have in fencing, dancing and bear-baiting: O, had I but followed the arts!

SIR TOBY BELCH

Then hadst thou had an excellent head of hair.

SIR ANDREW

Why, would that have mended my hair?

SIR TOBY BELCH

Past question; for thou seest it will not curl by nature.

SIR ANDREW

But it becomes me well enough, does't not?

SIR TOBY BELCH

Excellent; it hangs like flax on a distaff; and I hope to see a housewife take thee between her legs and spin it off.

SIR ANDREW

Faith, I'll home to-morrow, Sir Toby: your niece will not be seen; or if she be, it's four to one she'll none of me: the count himself here hard by woos her.

SIR TOBY BELCH

She'll none o' the count: she'll not match above her degree, neither in estate, years, nor wit; I have heard her swear't. Tut, there's life in't, man.

SIR ANDREW

I'll stay a month longer. I am a fellow o' the strangest mind i' the world; I delight in masques and revels sometimes altogether.

SIR TOBY BELCH

Art thou good at these kickshawses, knight?

SIR ANDREW

As any man in Illyria, whatsoever he be, under the degree of my betters; and yet I will not compare with an old man.

SIR TOBY BELCH

What is thy excellence in a galliard, knight?

SIR ANDREW

Faith, I can cut a caper.

SIR TOBY BELCH

And I can cut the mutton to't.

SIR ANDREW

And I think I have the back-trick simply as strong as any man in Illyria.

SIR TOBY BELCH

Wherefore are these things hid? Wherefore have these gifts a curtain before 'em? Are they like to take dust, like Mistress Mall's picture? Why dost thou not go to church in a galliard and come home in a coranto? My very walk should be a jig; I would not so much as make water but in a sink-a-pace. What dost thou mean? Is it a world to hide virtues in? I did think, by the excellent constitution of thy leg, it was formed under the star of a galliard.

SIR ANDREW

Ay, 'tis strong, and it does indifferent well in a flame-coloured stock. Shall we set about some revels?

SIR TOBY BELCH

What shall we do else? Were we not born under Taurus?

SIR ANDREW

Taurus! That's sides and heart.

SIR TOBY BELCH

No, sir; it is legs and thighs. Let me see the caper; ha, higher: ha, ha, excellent!

Exeunt

SCENE IV.
DUKE ORSINO'S PALACE.

Enter VALENTINE *and* VIOLA *in Man's Attire*

VALENTINE

If the duke continue these favours towards you, Cesario, you are like to be much advanced: he hath known you but three days, and already you are no stranger.

VIOLA

You either fear his humour or my negligence, that you call in question the continuance of his love: is he inconstant, sir, in his favours?

VALENTINE

    No, believe me.

VIOLA

    I thank you. Here comes the count.

        Enter DUKE ORSINO, CURIO, *and Attendants*

DUKE ORSINO

    Who saw Cesario, ho?

VIOLA

    On your attendance, my lord; here.

DUKE ORSINO

    Stand you a while aloof, Cesario,

    Thou know'st no less but all; I have unclasp'd

    To thee the book even of my secret soul:

    Therefore, good youth, address thy gait unto her;

    Be not denied access, stand at her doors,

    And tell them, there thy fixed foot shall grow

    Till thou have audience.

VIOLA

    Sure, my noble lord,

    If she be so abandon'd to her sorrow

    As it is spoke, she never will admit me.

DUKE ORSINO

    Be clamorous and leap all civil bounds

    Rather than make unprofited return.

VIOLA

    Say I do speak with her, my lord, what then?

DUKE ORSINO

    O, then unfold the passion of my love,

    Surprise her with discourse of my dear faith:

    It shall become thee well to act my woes;

    She will attend it better in thy youth

    Than in a nuncio's of more grave aspect.

VIOLA

    I think not so, my lord.

DUKE ORSINO

    Dear lad, believe it;

For they shall yet belie thy happy years,
That say thou art a man: Diana's lip
Is not more smooth and rubious; thy small pipe
Is as the maiden's organ, shrill and sound,
And all is semblative a woman's part.
I know thy constellation is right apt
For this affair. Some four or five attend him;
All, if you will; for I myself am best
When least in company. Prosper well in this,
And thou shalt live as freely as thy lord,
To call his fortunes thine.

VIOLA

I'll do my best
To woo your lady: [*Aside*] yet, a barful strife!
Whoe'er I woo, myself would be his wife.

Exeunt

SCENE V.
OLIVIA'S HOUSE.

Enter MARIA *and* CLOWN

MARIA

Nay, either tell me where thou hast been, or I will not open my
lips so wide as a bristle may enter in way of thy excuse: my lady
will hang thee for thy absence.

CLOWN

Let her hang me: he that is well hanged in this world needs to
fear no colours.

MARIA

Make that good.

CLOWN

He shall see none to fear.

MARIA

A good lenten answer. I can tell thee where that saying was
born, of 'I fear no colours.'

CLOWN

Where, good Mistress Mary?

MARIA

In the wars; and that may you be bold to say in your foolery.

CLOWN

Well, God give them wisdom that have it; and those that are fools, let them use their talents.

MARIA

Yet you will be hanged for being so long absent; or, to be turned away, is not that as good as a hanging to you?

CLOWN

Many a good hanging prevents a bad marriage; and, for turning away, let summer bear it out.

MARIA

You are resolute, then?

CLOWN

Not so, neither; but I am resolved on two points.

MARIA

That if one break, the other will hold; or, if both break, your gaskins fall.

CLOWN

Apt, in good faith; very apt. Well, go thy way; if Sir Toby would leave drinking, thou wert as witty a piece of Eve's flesh as any in Illyria.

MARIA

Peace, you rogue, no more o' that. Here comes my lady: make your excuse wisely, you were best.

Exit

CLOWN

Wit, an't be thy will, put me into good fooling! Those wits, that think they have thee, do very oft prove fools; and I, that am sure I lack thee, may pass for a wise man. For what says Quinapalus? 'Better a witty fool, than a foolish wit.'

Enter OLIVIA *with* MALVOLIO

God bless thee, lady!

OLIVIA

Take the fool away.

CLOWN

Do you not hear, fellows? Take away the lady.

OLIVIA

Go to, you're a dry fool; I'll no more of you: besides, you grow dishonest.

CLOWN

Two faults, madonna, that drink and good counsel will amend: for give the dry fool drink, then is the fool not dry: bid the dishonest man mend himself; if he mend, he is no longer dishonest; if he cannot, let the botcher mend him. Any thing that's mended is but patched: virtue that transgresses is but patched with sin; and sin that amends is but patched with virtue. If that this simple syllogism will serve, so; if it will not, what remedy? As there is no true cuckold but calamity, so beauty's a flower. The lady bade take away the fool; therefore, I say again, take her away.

OLIVIA

Sir, I bade them take away you.

CLOWN

Misprision in the highest degree! Lady, *cucullus non facit monachum*; that's as much to say as I wear not motley in my brain. Good madonna, give me leave to prove you a fool.

OLIVIA

Can you do it?

CLOWN

Dexterously, good madonna.

OLIVIA

Make your proof.

CLOWN

I must catechise you for it, madonna: good my mouse of virtue, answer me.

OLIVIA

Well, sir, for want of other idleness, I'll bide your proof.

CLOWN

Good madonna, why mournest thou?

OLIVIA

Good fool, for my brother's death.

CLOWN

I think his soul is in hell, madonna.

OLIVIA

I know his soul is in heaven, fool.

CLOWN

The more fool, madonna, to mourn for your brother's soul being in heaven. Take away the fool, gentlemen.

OLIVIA

What think you of this fool, Malvolio? Doth he not mend?

MALVOLIO

Yes, and shall do till the pangs of death shake him: infirmity, that decays the wise, doth ever make the better fool.

CLOWN

God send you, sir, a speedy infirmity, for the better increasing your folly! Sir Toby will be sworn that I am no fox; but he will not pass his word for two pence that you are no fool.

OLIVIA

How say you to that, Malvolio?

MALVOLIO

I marvel your ladyship takes delight in such a barren rascal: I saw him put down the other day with an ordinary fool that has no more brain than a stone. Look you now, he's out of his guard already; unless you laugh and minister occasion to him, he is gagged. I protest, I take these wise men, that crow so at these set kind of fools, no better than the fools' zanies.

OLIVIA

Oh, you are sick of self-love, Malvolio, and taste with a distempered appetite. To be generous, guiltless and of free disposition, is to take those things for bird-bolts that you deem cannon-bullets: there is no slander in an allowed fool, though he do nothing but rail; nor no railing in a known discreet man, though he do nothing but reprove.

CLOWN

Now Mercury indue thee with leasing, for thou speakest well of fools!

Re-enter MARIA

MARIA

Madam, there is at the gate a young gentleman much desires to speak with you.

OLIVIA

From the Count Orsino, is it?

MARIA

I know not, madam: 'tis a fair young man, and well attended.

OLIVIA

Who of my people hold him in delay?

MARIA

Sir Toby, madam, your kinsman.

OLIVIA

Fetch him off, I pray you; he speaks nothing but madman: fie on him!

Exit MARIA

Go you, Malvolio: if it be a suit from the count, I am sick, or not at home; what you will, to dismiss it.

Exit MALVOLIO

Now you see, sir, how your fooling grows old, and people dislike it.

CLOWN

Thou hast spoke for us, madonna, as if thy eldest son should be a fool; whose skull Jove cram with brains! For—here he comes—one of thy kin has a most weak *pia mater*.

Enter SIR TOBY BELCH

OLIVIA

By mine honour, half drunk. What is he at the gate, cousin?

SIR TOBY BELCH

A gentleman.

OLIVIA

A gentleman! What gentleman?

SIR TOBY BELCH

'Tis a gentle man here—a plague o' these pickle-herring! How now, sot!

CLOWN

Good Sir Toby!

OLIVIA

Cousin, cousin, how have you come so early by this lethargy?

SIR TOBY BELCH

Lechery! I defy lechery. There's one at the gate.

OLIVIA

Ay, marry, what is he?

SIR TOBY BELCH

Let him be the devil, an he will, I care not: give me faith, say I. Well, it's all one.

Exit

OLIVIA

What's a drunken man like, fool?

CLOWN

Like a drowned man, a fool and a mad man: one draught above heat makes him a fool; the second mads him; and a third drowns him.

OLIVIA

Go thou and seek the crowner, and let him sit o' my coz; for he's in the third degree of drink, he's drowned: go, look after him.

CLOWN

He is but mad yet, madonna; and the fool shall look to the madman.

Exit

Re-enter MALVOLIO

MALVOLIO

Madam, yond young fellow swears he will speak with you. I told him you were sick; he takes on him to understand so much, and therefore comes to speak with you. I told him you were asleep; he seems to have a foreknowledge of that too, and therefore comes to speak with you. What is to be said to him, lady? He's fortified against any denial.

OLIVIA

Tell him he shall not speak with me.

MALVOLIO

Has been told so; and he says, he'll stand at your door like a sheriff's post, and be the supporter to a bench, but he'll speak with you.

OLIVIA

What kind o' man is he?

MALVOLIO

Why, of mankind.

OLIVIA

What manner of man?

MALVOLIO

Of very ill manner; he'll speak with you, will you or no.

OLIVIA

Of what personage and years is he?

MALVOLIO

Not yet old enough for a man, nor young enough for a boy; as a squash is before 'tis a peascod, or a cooling when 'tis almost an apple: 'tis with him in standing water, between boy and man. He is very well-favoured and he speaks very shrewishly; one would think his mother's milk were scarce out of him.

OLIVIA

Let him approach: call in my gentlewoman.

MALVOLIO

Gentlewoman, my lady calls.

Exit

Re-enter MARIA

OLIVIA

Give me my veil: come, throw it o'er my face. We'll once more hear Orsino's embassy.

Enter VIOLA, *and Attendants*

VIOLA

The honourable lady of the house, which is she?

OLIVIA

Speak to me; I shall answer for her. Your will?

VIOLA

Most radiant, exquisite and unmatchable beauty—I pray you, tell me if this be the lady of the house, for I never saw her: I would be loath to cast away my speech, for besides that it is excellently well penned, I have taken great pains to con it. Good beauties, let me sustain no scorn; I am very comptible, even to the least sinister usage.

OLIVIA

Whence came you, sir?

VIOLA

I can say little more than I have studied, and that question's out of my part. Good gentle one, give me modest assurance if you be the lady of the house, that I may proceed in my speech.

OLIVIA

Are you a comedian?

VIOLA

No, my profound heart: and yet, by the very fangs of malice I swear, I am not that I play. Are you the lady of the house?

OLIVIA

If I do not usurp myself, I am.

VIOLA

Most certain, if you are she, you do usurp yourself; for what is yours to bestow is not yours to reserve. But this is from my commission: I will on with my speech in your praise, and then show you the heart of my message.

OLIVIA

Come to what is important in't: I forgive you the praise.

VIOLA

Alas, I took great pains to study it, and 'tis poetical.

OLIVIA

It is the more like to be feigned: I pray you, keep it in. I heard you were saucy at my gates, and allowed your approach rather to wonder at you than to hear you. If you be not mad, be gone; if you have reason, be brief: 'tis not that time of moon with me to make one in so skipping a dialogue.

MARIA

Will you hoist sail, sir? Here lies your way.

VIOLA

No, good swabber; I am to hull here a little longer. Some mollification for your giant, sweet lady. Tell me your mind: I am a messenger.

OLIVIA

Sure, you have some hideous matter to deliver, when the courtesy of it is so fearful. Speak your office.

VIOLA

It alone concerns your ear. I bring no overture of war, no taxation of homage: I hold the olive in my hand; my words are as fun of peace as matter.

OLIVIA

Yet you began rudely. What are you? What would you?

VIOLA

The rudeness that hath appeared in me have I learned from my entertainment. What I am, and what I would, are as secret as maidenhead; to your ears, divinity, to any other's, profanation.

OLIVIA

Give us the place alone: we will hear this divinity.

Exeunt MARIA *and Attendants*

Now, sir, what is your text?

VIOLA

Most sweet lady—

OLIVIA

A comfortable doctrine, and much may be said of it. Where lies your text?

VIOLA

In Orsino's bosom.

OLIVIA

In his bosom! In what chapter of his bosom?

VIOLA

To answer by the method, in the first of his heart.

OLIVIA

O, I have read it: it is heresy. Have you no more to say?

VIOLA

Good madam, let me see your face.

OLIVIA

Have you any commission from your lord to negotiate with my face? You are now out of your text: but we will draw the curtain and show you the picture. Look you, sir, such a one I was this present: is't not well done?

Unveiling

VIOLA

Excellently done, if God did all.

OLIVIA

'Tis in grain, sir; 'twill endure wind and weather.

VIOLA

'Tis beauty truly blent, whose red and white

Nature's own sweet and cunning hand laid on:
Lady, you are the cruell'st she alive,
If you will lead these graces to the grave
And leave the world no copy.

OLIVIA

O, sir, I will not be so hard-hearted; I will give out divers
schedules of my beauty: it shall be inventoried, and every particle
and utensil labelled to my will: as, item, two lips, indifferent red;
item, two grey eyes, with lids to them; item, one neck, one chin,
and so forth. Were you sent hither to praise me?

VIOLA

I see you what you are, you are too proud;
But, if you were the devil, you are fair.
My lord and master loves you: O, such love
Could be but recompensed, though you were crown'd
The nonpareil of beauty!

OLIVIA

How does he love me?

VIOLA

With adorations, fertile tears,
With groans that thunder love, with sighs of fire.

OLIVIA

Your lord does know my mind; I cannot love him:
Yet I suppose him virtuous, know him noble,
Of great estate, of fresh and stainless youth;
In voices well divulged, free, learn'd and valiant;
And in dimension and the shape of nature
A gracious person: but yet I cannot love him;
He might have took his answer long ago.

VIOLA

If I did love you in my master's flame,
With such a suffering, such a deadly life,
In your denial I would find no sense;
I would not understand it.

OLIVIA

Why, what would you?

VIOLA

> Make me a willow cabin at your gate,
> And call upon my soul within the house;
> Write loyal cantons of contemned love
> And sing them loud even in the dead of night;
> Halloo your name to the reverberate hills
> And make the babbling gossip of the air
> Cry out 'Olivia!' O, You should not rest
> Between the elements of air and earth,
> But you should pity me!

OLIVIA

> You might do much. What is your parentage?

VIOLA

> Above my fortunes, yet my state is well:
> I am a gentleman.

OLIVIA

> Get you to your lord;
> I cannot love him: let him send no more;
> Unless, perchance, you come to me again,
> To tell me how he takes it. Fare you well:
> I thank you for your pains: spend this for me.

VIOLA

> I am no fee'd post, lady; keep your purse:
> My master, not myself, lacks recompense.
> Love make his heart of flint that you shall love;
> And let your fervor, like my master's, be
> Placed in contempt! Farewell, fair cruelty.

Exit

OLIVIA

> 'What is your parentage?'
> 'Above my fortunes, yet my state is well:
> I am a gentleman.' I'll be sworn thou art;
> Thy tongue, thy face, thy limbs, actions and spirit,
> Do give thee five-fold blazon: not too fast: soft, soft!
> Unless the master were the man. How now!
> Even so quickly may one catch the plague?
> Methinks I feel this youth's perfections

With an invisible and subtle stealth
To creep in at mine eyes. Well, let it be.
What ho, Malvolio!

Re-enter MALVOLIO

MALVOLIO

Here, madam, at your service.

OLIVIA

Run after that same peevish messenger,
The county's man: he left this ring behind him,
Would I or not: tell him I'll none of it.
Desire him not to flatter with his lord,
Nor hold him up with hopes; I am not for him:
If that the youth will come this way to-morrow,
I'll give him reasons for't: hie thee, Malvolio.

MALVOLIO

Madam, I will.

Exit

OLIVIA

I do I know not what, and fear to find
Mine eye too great a flatterer for my mind.
Fate, show thy force: ourselves we do not owe;
What is decreed must be, and be this so.

Exit

ACT

II

SCENE I.
THE SEA-COAST.

Enter ANTONIO *and* SEBASTIAN

ANTONIO

Will you stay no longer? Nor will you not that I go with you?

SEBASTIAN

By your patience, no. My stars shine darkly over me: the malignancy of my fate might perhaps distemper yours; therefore I shall crave of you your leave that I may bear my evils alone: it were a bad recompense for your love, to lay any of them on you.

ANTONIO

Let me yet know of you whither you are bound.

SEBASTIAN

No, sooth, sir: my determinate voyage is mere extravagancy. But I perceive in you so excellent a touch of modesty, that you will not extort from me what I am willing to keep in; therefore it charges me in manners the rather to express myself. You must know of me then, Antonio, my name is Sebastian, which I called Roderigo. My father was that

Sebastian of Messaline, whom I know you have heard of. He left behind him myself and a sister, both born in an hour: if the heavens had been pleased, would we had so ended! But you, sir, altered that; for some hour before you took me from the breach of the sea was my sister drowned.

ANTONIO

Alas the day!

SEBASTIAN

A lady, sir, though it was said she much resembled me, was yet of many accounted beautiful: but, though I could not with such estimable wonder overfar believe that, yet thus far I will boldly publish her; she bore a mind that envy could not but call fair. She is drowned already, sir, with salt water, though I seem to drown her remembrance again with more.

ANTONIO

Pardon me, sir, your bad entertainment.

SEBASTIAN

O good Antonio, forgive me your trouble.

ANTONIO

If you will not murder me for my love, let me be your servant.

SEBASTIAN

If you will not undo what you have done, that is, kill him whom you have recovered, desire it not. Fare ye well at once: my bosom is full of kindness, and I am yet so near the manners of my mother, that upon the least occasion more mine eyes will tell tales of me. I am bound to the Count Orsino's court: farewell.

Exit

ANTONIO

The gentleness of all the gods go with thee!
I have many enemies in Orsino's court,
Else would I very shortly see thee there.
But, come what may, I do adore thee so,
That danger shall seem sport, and I will go.

Exit

SCENE II.
A STREET.

Enter VIOLA, MALVOLIO *following*

MALVOLIO

Were not you even now with the Countess Olivia?

VIOLA

Even now, sir; on a moderate pace I have since arrived but hither.

MALVOLIO

She returns this ring to you, sir: you might have saved me my pains, to have taken it away yourself. She adds, moreover, that you should put your lord into a desperate assurance she will none of him: and one thing more, that you be never so hardy to come again in his affairs, unless it be to report your lord's taking of this. Receive it so.

VIOLA

She took the ring of me: I'll none of it.

MALVOLIO

Come, sir, you peevishly threw it to her; and her will is, it should be so returned: if it be worth stooping for, there it lies in your eye; if not, be it his that finds it.

Exit

VIOLA

I left no ring with her: what means this lady?
Fortune forbid my outside have not charm'd her!
She made good view of me; indeed, so much,
That sure methought her eyes had lost her tongue,
For she did speak in starts distractedly.
She loves me, sure; the cunning of her passion
Invites me in this churlish messenger.
None of my lord's ring! Why, he sent her none.
I am the man: if it be so, as 'tis,
Poor lady, she were better love a dream.
Disguise, I see, thou art a wickedness,
Wherein the pregnant enemy does much.
How easy is it for the proper-false
In women's waxen hearts to set their forms!

Alas, our frailty is the cause, not we!
For such as we are made of, such we be.
How will this fadge? My master loves her dearly;
And I, poor monster, fond as much on him;
And she, mistaken, seems to dote on me.
What will become of this? As I am man,
My state is desperate for my master's love;
As I am woman—now alas the day!—
What thriftless sighs shall poor Olivia breathe!
O time! Thou must untangle this, not I;
It is too hard a knot for me to untie!

Exit

SCENE III.
OLIVIA'S HOUSE.

Enter SIR TOBY BELCH *and* SIR ANDREW

SIR TOBY BELCH

Approach, Sir Andrew: not to be abed after midnight is to be up betimes; and *'diluculo surgere,'* thou know'st—

SIR ANDREW

Nay, my troth, I know not: but I know, to be up late is to be up late.

SIR TOBY BELCH

A false conclusion: I hate it as an unfilled can. To be up after midnight and to go to bed then, is early: so that to go to bed after midnight is to go to bed betimes. Does not our life consist of the four elements?

SIR ANDREW

Faith, so they say; but I think it rather consists of eating and drinking.

SIR TOBY BELCH

Thou'rt a scholar; let us therefore eat and drink. Marian, I say! A stoup of wine!

Enter CLOWN

SIR ANDREW

Here comes the fool, i' faith.

CLOWN

How now, my hearts! Did you never see the picture of 'we three'?

SIR TOBY BELCH

Welcome, ass. Now let's have a catch.

SIR ANDREW

By my troth, the fool has an excellent breast. I had rather than forty shillings I had such a leg, and so sweet a breath to sing, as the fool has. In sooth, thou wast in very gracious fooling last night, when thou spokest of Pigrogromitus, of the Vapians passing the equinoctial of Queubus: 'twas very good, i' faith. I sent thee sixpence for thy leman: hadst it?

CLOWN

I did impeticos thy gratillity; for Malvolio's nose is no whipstock: my lady has a white hand, and the Myrmidons are no bottle-ale houses.

SIR ANDREW

Excellent! Why, this is the best fooling, when all is done. Now, a song.

SIR TOBY BELCH

Come on; there is sixpence for you: let's have a song.

SIR ANDREW

There's a testril of me too: if one knight give a—

CLOWN

Would you have a love-song, or a song of good life?

SIR TOBY BELCH

A love-song, a love-song.

SIR ANDREW

Ay, ay: I care not for good life.

CLOWN

[Sings] O mistress mine, where are you roaming?
O, stay and hear; your true love's coming,
That can sing both high and low:
Trip no further, pretty sweeting;
Journeys end in lovers meeting,
Every wise man's son doth know.

SIR ANDREW

Excellent good, i' faith.

SIR TOBY BELCH

Good, good.

CLOWN

[*Sings*] *What is love? 'Tis not hereafter;*
Present mirth hath present laughter;
What's to come is still unsure:
In delay there lies no plenty;
Then come kiss me, sweet and twenty,
Youth's a stuff will not endure.

SIR ANDREW

A mellifluous voice, as I am true knight.

SIR TOBY BELCH

A contagious breath.

SIR ANDREW

Very sweet and contagious, i' faith.

SIR TOBY BELCH

To hear by the nose, it is dulcet in contagion. But shall we make the welkin dance indeed? Shall we rouse the night-owl in a catch that will draw three souls out of one weaver? Shall we do that?

SIR ANDREW

An you love me, let's do't: I am dog at a catch.

CLOWN

By'r lady, sir, and some dogs will catch well.

SIR ANDREW

Most certain. Let our catch be, '*Thou knave.*'

CLOWN

'*Hold thy peace, thou knave,*' knight? I shall be constrained in't to call thee knave, knight.

SIR ANDREW

'Tis not the first time I have constrained one to call me knave. Begin, fool: it begins '*Hold thy peace.*'

CLOWN

I shall never begin if I hold my peace.

SIR ANDREW

Good, i' faith. Come, begin.

Catch sung
Enter MARIA

MARIA
    What a caterwauling do you keep here! If my lady have not
    called up her steward Malvolio and bid him turn you out of
    doors, never trust me.
SIR TOBY BELCH
    My lady's a Cataian, we are politicians, Malvolio's a Peg-a-
    Ramsey, and '*Three merry men be we.*' Am not I consanguineous?
    Am I not of her blood? Tillyvally. Lady!
    [*Sings*] '*There dwelt a man in Babylon, lady, lady!*'
CLOWN
    Beshrew me, the knight's in admirable fooling.
SIR ANDREW
    Ay, he does well enough if he be disposed, and so do I too: he
    does it with a better grace, but I do it more natural.
SIR TOBY BELCH
    [*Sings*] '*O, the twelfth day of December,*'—
MARIA
    For the love o' God, peace!

                                    Enter MALVOLIO
MALVOLIO
    My masters, are you mad? Or what are you? Have ye no wit,
    manners, nor honesty, but to gabble like tinkers at this time of
    night? Do ye make an alehouse of my lady's house, that ye squeak
    out your coziers' catches without any mitigation or remorse of
    voice? Is there no respect of place, persons, nor time in you?
SIR TOBY BELCH
    We did keep time, sir, in our catches. Sneck up!
MALVOLIO
    Sir Toby, I must be round with you. My lady bade me tell you,
    that, though she harbours you as her kinsman, she's nothing
    allied to your disorders. If you can separate yourself and your
    misdemeanors, you are welcome to the house; if not, an it would
    please you to take leave of her, she is very willing to bid you
    farewell.
SIR TOBY BELCH
    'Farewell, dear heart, since I must needs be gone.'

MARIA

    Nay, good Sir Toby.

CLOWN

    'His eyes do show his days are almost done.'

MALVOLIO

    Is't even so?

SIR TOBY BELCH

    'But I will never die.'

CLOWN

    Sir Toby, there you lie.

MALVOLIO

    This is much credit to you.

SIR TOBY BELCH

    'Shall I bid him go?'

CLOWN

    'What an if you do?'

SIR TOBY BELCH

    'Shall I bid him go, and spare not?'

CLOWN

    'O no, no, no, no, you dare not.'

SIR TOBY BELCH

    Out o' tune, sir: ye lie. Art any more than a steward? Dost thou
    think, because thou art virtuous, there shall be no more cakes
    and ale?

CLOWN

    Yes, by Saint Anne, and ginger shall be hot i' the mouth too.

SIR TOBY BELCH

    Thou'rt i' the right. Go, sir, rub your chain with crumbs. A stoup
    of wine, Maria!

MALVOLIO

    Mistress Mary, if you prized my lady's favour at any thing more
    than contempt, you would not give means for this uncivil rule:
    she shall know of it, by this hand.

Exit

MARIA

    Go shake your ears.

SIR ANDREW

'Twere as good a deed as to drink when a man's a-hungry, to challenge him the field, and then to break promise with him and make a fool of him.

SIR TOBY BELCH

Do't, knight: I'll write thee a challenge: or I'll deliver thy indignation to him by word of mouth.

MARIA

Sweet Sir Toby, be patient for tonight: since the youth of the count's was today with thy lady, she is much out of quiet. For Monsieur Malvolio, let me alone with him: if I do not gull him into a nayword, and make him a common recreation, do not think I have wit enough to lie straight in my bed: I know I can do it.

SIR TOBY BELCH

Possess us, possess us; tell us something of him.

MARIA

Marry, sir, sometimes he is a kind of puritan.

SIR ANDREW

O, if I thought that I'ld beat him like a dog!

SIR TOBY BELCH

What, for being a puritan? Thy exquisite reason, dear knight?

SIR ANDREW

I have no exquisite reason for't, but I have reason good enough.

MARIA

The devil a puritan that he is, or any thing constantly, but a time-pleaser; an affectioned ass, that cons state without book and utters it by great swarths: the best persuaded of himself, so crammed, as he thinks, with excellencies, that it is his grounds of faith that all that look on him love him; and on that vice in him will my revenge find notable cause to work.

SIR TOBY BELCH

What wilt thou do?

MARIA

I will drop in his way some obscure epistles of love; wherein, by the colour of his beard, the shape of his leg, the manner of his gait, the expressure of his eye, forehead, and complexion, he shall find himself most feelingly personated. I can write very like my lady your niece: on a forgotten matter we can hardly make distinction of our hands.

SIR TOBY BELCH

Excellent! I smell a device.

SIR ANDREW

I have't in my nose too.

SIR TOBY BELCH

He shall think, by the letters that thou wilt drop, that they come from my niece, and that she's in love with him.

MARIA

My purpose is, indeed, a horse of that colour.

SIR ANDREW

And your horse now would make him an ass.

MARIA

Ass, I doubt not.

SIR ANDREW

O, 'twill be admirable!

MARIA

Sport royal, I warrant you: I know my physic will work with him. I will plant you two, and let the fool make a third, where he shall find the letter: observe his construction of it. For this night, to bed, and dream on the event. Farewell.

Exit

SIR TOBY BELCH

Good night, Penthesilea.

SIR ANDREW

Before me, she's a good wench.

SIR TOBY BELCH

She's a beagle, true-bred, and one that adores me: what o' that?

SIR ANDREW

I was adored once too.

SIR TOBY BELCH

Let's to bed, knight. Thou hadst need send for more money.

SIR ANDREW

If I cannot recover your niece, I am a foul way out.

SIR TOBY BELCH

    Send for money, knight: if thou hast her not i' the end, call me cut.

SIR ANDREW

    If I do not, never trust me, take it how you will.

SIR TOBY BELCH

    Come, come, I'll go burn some sack; 'tis too late to go to bed now: come, knight; come, knight.

Exeunt

SCENE IV.
DUKE ORSINO'S PALACE.

Enter DUKE ORSINO, VIOLA, CURIO, *and Others*

DUKE ORSINO

    Give me some music. Now, good morrow, friends.
    Now, good Cesario, but that piece of song,
    That old and antique song we heard last night:
    Methought it did relieve my passion much,
    More than light airs and recollected terms
    Of these most brisk and giddy-paced times:
    Come, but one verse.

CURIO

    He is not here, so please your lordship that should sing it.

DUKE ORSINO

    Who was it?

CURIO

    Feste, the jester, my lord; a fool that the lady Olivia's father took much delight in. He is about the house.

DUKE ORSINO

    Seek him out, and play the tune the while.

Exit CURIO. *Music plays*

    Come hither, boy: if ever thou shalt love,
    In the sweet pangs of it remember me;
    For such as I am all true lovers are,
    Unstaid and skittish in all motions else,
    Save in the constant image of the creature
    That is beloved. How dost thou like this tune?

VIOLA

    It gives a very echo to the seat
    Where Love is throned.

DUKE ORSINO

    Thou dost speak masterly:
    My life upon't, young though thou art, thine eye
    Hath stay'd upon some favour that it loves:
    Hath it not, boy?

VIOLA

    A little, by your favour.

DUKE ORSINO

    What kind of woman is't?

VIOLA

    Of your complexion.

DUKE ORSINO

    She is not worth thee, then. What years, i' faith?

VIOLA

    About your years, my lord.

DUKE ORSINO

    Too old by heaven: let still the woman take
    An elder than herself: so wears she to him,
    So sways she level in her husband's heart:
    For, boy, however we do praise ourselves,
    Our fancies are more giddy and unfirm,
    More longing, wavering, sooner lost and worn,
    Than women's are.

VIOLA

    I think it well, my lord.

DUKE ORSINO

    Then let thy love be younger than thyself,
    Or thy affection cannot hold the bent;
    For women are as roses, whose fair flower
    Being once display'd, doth fall that very hour.

VIOLA

    And so they are: alas, that they are so;
    To die, even when they to perfection grow!

                   Re-enter CURIO *and* CLOWN

DUKE ORSINO

O, fellow, come, the song we had last night.
Mark it, Cesario, it is old and plain;
The spinsters and the knitters in the sun
And the free maids that weave their thread with bones
Do use to chant it: it is silly sooth,
And dallies with the innocence of love,
Like the old age.

CLOWN

Are you ready, sir?

DUKE ORSINO

Ay; prithee, sing.

Music
Song

CLOWN

Come away, come away, death,
And in sad cypress let me be laid;
Fly away, fly away breath;
I am slain by a fair cruel maid.
My shroud of white, stuck all with yew,
O, prepare it!
My part of death, no one so true
Did share it.

Not a flower, not a flower sweet
On my black coffin let there be strown;
Not a friend, not a friend greet
My poor corpse, where my bones shall be thrown:
A thousand thousand sighs to save,
Lay me, O, where
Sad true lover never find my grave,
To weep there!

DUKE ORSINO

There's for thy pains.

CLOWN

No pains, sir: I take pleasure in singing, sir.

DUKE ORSINO

    I'll pay thy pleasure then.

CLOWN

    Truly, sir, and pleasure will be paid, one time or another.

DUKE ORSINO

    Give me now leave to leave thee.

CLOWN

    Now, the melancholy god protect thee; and the tailor make thy doublet of changeable taffeta, for thy mind is a very opal. I would have men of such constancy put to sea, that their business might be every thing and their intent every where; for that's it that always makes a good voyage of nothing. Farewell.

Exit

DUKE ORSINO

    Let all the rest give place.

Curio and Attendants retire

    Once more, Cesario,
    Get thee to yond same sovereign cruelty:
    Tell her, my love, more noble than the world,
    Prizes not quantity of dirty lands;
    The parts that fortune hath bestow'd upon her,
    Tell her, I hold as giddily as fortune;
    But 'tis that miracle and queen of gems
    That nature pranks her in attracts my soul.

VIOLA

    But if she cannot love you, sir?

DUKE ORSINO

    I cannot be so answer'd.

VIOLA

    Sooth, but you must.
    Say that some lady, as perhaps there is,
    Hath for your love a great a pang of heart
    As you have for Olivia: you cannot love her;
    You tell her so; must she not then be answer'd?

DUKE ORSINO

    There is no woman's sides
    Can bide the beating of so strong a passion

As love doth give my heart; no woman's heart
So big, to hold so much; they lack retention
Alas, their love may be call'd appetite,
No motion of the liver, but the palate,
That suffer surfeit, cloyment and revolt;
But mine is all as hungry as the sea,
And can digest as much: make no compare
Between that love a woman can bear me
And that I owe Olivia.

VIOLA

Ay, but I know—

DUKE ORSINO

What dost thou know?

VIOLA

Too well what love women to men may owe:
In faith, they are as true of heart as we.
My father had a daughter loved a man,
As it might be, perhaps, were I a woman,
I should your lordship.

DUKE ORSINO

And what's her history?

VIOLA

A blank, my lord. She never told her love,
But let concealment, like a worm i' the bud,
Feed on her damask cheek: she pined in thought,
And with a green and yellow melancholy
She sat like Patience on a monument,
Smiling at grief. Was not this love indeed?
We men may say more, swear more: but indeed
Our shows are more than will; for still we prove
Much in our vows, but little in our love.

DUKE ORSINO

But died thy sister of her love, my boy?

VIOLA

I am all the daughters of my father's house,
And all the brothers too: and yet I know not.
Sir, shall I to this lady?

DUKE ORSINO

Ay, that's the theme.
To her in haste; give her this jewel; say,
My love can give no place, bide no denay.

Exeunt

SCENE V.
OLIVIA'S GARDEN.

Enter SIR TOBY BELCH, SIR ANDREW, *and* FABIAN

SIR TOBY BELCH

Come thy ways, Signior Fabian.

FABIAN

Nay, I'll come: if I lose a scruple of this sport, let me be boiled
to death with melancholy.

SIR TOBY BELCH

Wouldst thou not be glad to have the niggardly rascally sheep-
biter come by some notable shame?

FABIAN

I would exult, man: you know, he brought me out o' favour with
my lady about a bear-baiting here.

SIR TOBY BELCH

To anger him we'll have the bear again; and we will fool him
black and blue: shall we not, Sir Andrew?

SIR ANDREW

An we do not, it is pity of our lives.

SIR TOBY BELCH

Here comes the little villain.

Enter MARIA

How now, my metal of India!

MARIA

Get ye all three into the box-tree: Malvolio's coming down this
walk: he has been yonder i' the sun practising behavior to his own
shadow this half hour: observe him, for the love of mockery; for
I know this letter will make a contemplative idiot of him. Close,
in the name of jesting! Lie thou there, [*Throws down a letter*] for
here comes the trout that must be caught with tickling.

Exit

Enter MALVOLIO

MALVOLIO

'Tis but fortune; all is fortune. Maria once told me she did affect me: and I have heard herself come thus near, that, should she fancy, it should be one of my complexion. Besides, she uses me with a more exalted respect than any one else that follows her. What should I think on't?

SIR TOBY BELCH

Here's an overweening rogue!

FABIAN

O, peace! Contemplation makes a rare turkey-cock of him: how he jets under his advanced plumes!

SIR ANDREW

'Slight, I could so beat the rogue!

SIR TOBY BELCH

Peace, I say.

MALVOLIO

To be Count Malvolio!

SIR TOBY BELCH

Ah, rogue!

SIR ANDREW

Pistol him, pistol him.

SIR TOBY BELCH

Peace, peace!

MALVOLIO

There is example for't; the lady of the Strachy married the yeoman of the wardrobe.

SIR ANDREW

Fie on him, Jezebel!

FABIAN

O, peace! Now he's deeply in: look how imagination blows him.

MALVOLIO

Having been three months married to her, sitting in my state—

SIR TOBY BELCH

O, for a stone-bow, to hit him in the eye!

MALVOLIO

Calling my officers about me, in my branched velvet gown;
having come from a day-bed, where I have left Olivia sleeping—

SIR TOBY BELCH

Fire and brimstone!

FABIAN

O, peace, peace!

MALVOLIO

And then to have the humour of state; and after a demure travel
of regard, telling them I know my place as I would they should
do theirs, to for my kinsman Toby—

SIR TOBY BELCH

Bolts and shackles!

FABIAN

O peace, peace, peace! Now, now.

MALVOLIO

Seven of my people, with an obedient start, make out for him:
I frown the while; and perchance wind up watch, or play with
my—some rich jewel. Toby approaches; courtesies there to me—

SIR TOBY BELCH

Shall this fellow live?

FABIAN

Though our silence be drawn from us with cars, yet peace.

MALVOLIO

I extend my hand to him thus, quenching my familiar smile with
an austere regard of control—

SIR TOBY BELCH

And does not Toby take you a blow o' the lips then?

MALVOLIO

Saying, 'Cousin Toby, my fortunes having cast me on your niece
give me this prerogative of speech,'—

SIR TOBY BELCH

What, what?

MALVOLIO

'You must amend your drunkenness.'

SIR TOBY BELCH

Out, scab!

FABIAN

Nay, patience, or we break the sinews of our plot.

MALVOLIO

'Besides, you waste the treasure of your time with a foolish knight,'—

SIR ANDREW

That's me, I warrant you.

MALVOLIO

'One Sir Andrew,'—

SIR ANDREW

I knew 'twas I; for many do call me fool.

MALVOLIO

What employment have we here?

Taking up the letter

FABIAN

Now is the woodcock near the gin.

SIR TOBY BELCH

O, peace! And the spirit of humour intimate reading aloud to him!

MALVOLIO

By my life, this is my lady's hand these be her very *C's*, her *U's* and her *T's* and thus makes she her great *P's*. It is, in contempt of question, her hand.

SIR ANDREW

Her *C's*, her *U's* and her *T's*: why that?

MALVOLIO

[*Reads*] *'To the unknown beloved, this, and my good wishes:'*—her very phrases! By your leave, wax. Soft! And the impressure her Lucrece, with which she uses to seal: 'tis my lady. To whom should this be?

FABIAN

This wins him, liver and all.

MALVOLIO

[*Reads*] *Jove knows I love· But who?*
Lips, do not move;
No man must know.

'No man must know.' What follows? The numbers altered! 'No man must know:' if this should be thee, Malvolio?

SIR TOBY BELCH

Marry, hang thee, brock!

MALVOLIO

[*Reads*] *I may command where I adore;*
But silence, like a Lucrece knife,
With bloodless stroke my heart doth gore:
M, O, A, I, doth sway my life.

FABIAN

A fustian riddle!

SIR TOBY BELCH

Excellent wench, say I.

MALVOLIO

'M, O, A, I, doth sway my life.' Nay, but first, let me see, let me see, let me see.

FABIAN

What dish o' poison has she dressed him!

SIR TOBY BELCH

And with what wing the staniel cheques at it!

MALVOLIO

'*I may command where I adore.*' Why, she may command me: I serve her; she is my lady. Why, this is evident to any formal capacity; there is no obstruction in this: and the end—what should that alphabetical position portend? If I could make that resemble something in me—Softly! M, O, A, I—

SIR TOBY BELCH

O, ay, make up that: he is now at a cold scent.

FABIAN

Sowter will cry upon't for all this, though it be as rank as a fox.

MALVOLIO

M—Malvolio; M—why, that begins my name.

FABIAN

Did not I say he would work it out? The cur is excellent at faults.

MALVOLIO

M—but then there is no consonancy in the sequel; that suffers under probation A should follow but O does.

FABIAN

And O shall end, I hope.

SIR TOBY BELCH

Ay, or I'll cudgel him, and make him cry O!

MALVOLIO

And then *I* comes behind.

FABIAN

Ay, an you had any eye behind you, you might see more detraction at your heels than fortunes before you.

MALVOLIO

M, O, A, I; this simulation is not as the former: and yet, to crush this a little, it would bow to me, for every one of these letters are in my name. Soft! Here follows prose.

[*Reads*] '*If this fall into thy hand, revolve. In my stars I am above thee; but be not afraid of greatness: some are born great, some achieve greatness, and some have greatness thrust upon 'em. Thy Fates open their hands; let thy blood and spirit embrace them; and, to inure thyself to what thou art like to be, cast thy humble slough and appear fresh. Be opposite with a kinsman, surly with servants; let thy tongue tang arguments of state; put thyself into the trick of singularity: she thus advises thee that sighs for thee. Remember who commended thy yellow stockings, and wished to see thee ever cross-gartered: I say, remember. Go to, thou art made, if thou desirest to be so; if not, let me see thee a steward still, the fellow of servants, and not worthy to touch Fortune's fingers. Farewell. She that would alter services with thee,*

The Fortunate-Unhappy.'

Daylight and champaign discovers not more: this is open. I will be proud, I will read politic authors, I will baffle Sir Toby, I will wash off gross acquaintance, I will be point-devise the very man. I do not now fool myself, to let imagination jade me; for every reason excites to this, that my lady loves me. She did commend my yellow stockings of late, she did praise my leg being cross-gartered; and in this she manifests herself to my love, and with a kind of injunction drives me to these habits of her liking. I thank my stars I am happy. I will be strange, stout, in yellow stockings, and cross-gartered, even with the swiftness of putting on. Jove and my stars be praised! Here is yet a postscript.

[*Reads*] '*Thou canst not choose but know who I am. If thou entertainest my love, let it appear in thy smiling; thy smiles become thee well; therefore in my presence still smile, dear my sweet, I prithee.'*

Jove, I thank thee: I will smile; I will do everything that thou wilt have me.

Exit

FABIAN

I will not give my part of this sport for a pension of thousands to be paid from the Sophy.

SIR TOBY BELCH

I could marry this wench for this device.

SIR ANDREW

So could I too.

SIR TOBY BELCH

And ask no other dowry with her but such another jest.

SIR ANDREW

Nor I neither.

FABIAN

Here comes my noble gull-catcher.

Re-enter MARIA

SIR TOBY BELCH

Wilt thou set thy foot o' my neck?

SIR ANDREW

Or o' mine either?

SIR TOBY BELCH

Shall I play my freedom at tray-trip, and become thy bond-slave?

SIR ANDREW

I' faith, or I either?

SIR TOBY BELCH

Why, thou hast put him in such a dream, that when the image of it leaves him he must run mad.

MARIA

Nay, but say true; does it work upon him?

SIR TOBY BELCH

Like aqua-vitae with a midwife.

MARIA

If you will then see the fruits of the sport, mark his first approach before my lady: he will come to her in yellow stockings, and 'tis a colour she abhors, and cross-gartered, a fashion she detests; and he will smile upon her, which will now be so unsuitable to her disposition, being addicted to a melancholy as she is, that it cannot but turn him into a notable contempt. If you will see it, follow me.

SIR TOBY BELCH

To the gates of Tartar, thou most excellent devil of wit!

SIR ANDREW

I'll make one too.

Exeunt

ACT

III

SCENE I.
OLIVIA'S GARDEN.

Enter VIOLA, *and* CLOWN *with a tabour*

VIOLA

Save thee, friend, and thy music: dost thou live by thy
tabour?

CLOWN

No, sir, I live by the church.

VIOLA

Art thou a churchman?

CLOWN

No such matter, sir: I do live by the church; for I do live at
my house, and my house doth stand by the church.

VIOLA

So thou mayst say, the king lies by a beggar, if a beggar
dwell near him; or, the church stands by thy tabour, if thy
tabour stand by the church.

CLOWN

You have said, sir. To see this age! A sentence is but a
cheveril glove to a good wit: how quickly the wrong side
may be turned outward!

VIOLA

Nay, that's certain; they that dally nicely with words may quickly make them wanton.

CLOWN

I would, therefore, my sister had had no name, sir.

VIOLA

Why, man?

CLOWN

Why, sir, her name's a word; and to dally with that word might make my sister wanton. But indeed words are very rascals since bonds disgraced them.

VIOLA

Thy reason, man?

CLOWN

Troth, sir, I can yield you none without words; and words are grown so false, I am loath to prove reason with them.

VIOLA

I warrant thou art a merry fellow and carest for nothing.

CLOWN

Not so, sir, I do care for something; but in my conscience, sir, I do not care for you: if that be to care for nothing, sir, I would it would make you invisible.

VIOLA

Art not thou the Lady Olivia's fool?

CLOWN

No, indeed, sir; the Lady Olivia has no folly: she will keep no fool, sir, till she be married; and fools are as like husbands as pilchards are to herrings; the husband's the bigger: I am indeed not her fool, but her corrupter of words.

VIOLA

I saw thee late at the Count Orsino's.

CLOWN

Foolery, sir, does walk about the orb like the sun, it shines every where. I would be sorry, sir, but the fool should be as oft with your master as with my mistress: I think I saw your wisdom there.

VIOLA

Nay, an thou pass upon me, I'll no more with thee. Hold, there's expenses for thee.

CLOWN

Now Jove, in his next commodity of hair, send thee a beard!

VIOLA

By my troth, I'll tell thee, I am almost sick for one; [*Aside*] though I would not have it grow on my chin. Is thy lady within?

CLOWN

Would not a pair of these have bred, sir?

VIOLA

Yes, being kept together and put to use.

CLOWN

I would play Lord Pandarus of Phrygia, sir, to bring a Cressida to this Troilus.

VIOLA

I understand you, sir; 'tis well begged.

CLOWN

The matter, I hope, is not great, sir, begging but a beggar: Cressida was a beggar. My lady is within, sir. I will construe to them whence you come; who you are and what you would are out of my welkin, I might say 'element,' but the word is over-worn.

Exit

VIOLA

This fellow is wise enough to play the fool;
And to do that well craves a kind of wit:
He must observe their mood on whom he jests,
The quality of persons, and the time,
And, like the haggard, cheque at every feather
That comes before his eye. This is a practise
As full of labour as a wise man's art
For folly that he wisely shows is fit;
But wise men, folly-fall'n, quite taint their wit.

Enter SIR TOBY BELCH, *and* SIR ANDREW

SIR TOBY BELCH

Save you, gentleman.

VIOLA

> And you, sir.

SIR ANDREW

> *Dieu vous garde, monsieur.*

VIOLA

> *Et vous aussi; votre serviteur.*

SIR ANDREW

> I hope, sir, you are; and I am yours.

SIR TOBY BELCH

> Will you encounter the house? My niece is desirous you should enter, if your trade be to her.

VIOLA

> I am bound to your niece, sir; I mean, she is the list of my voyage.

SIR TOBY BELCH

> Taste your legs, sir; put them to motion.

VIOLA

> My legs do better understand me, sir, than I understand what you mean by bidding me taste my legs.

SIR TOBY BELCH

> I mean, to go, sir, to enter.

VIOLA

> I will answer you with gait and entrance. But we are prevented.

> > *Enter* OLIVIA *and* MARIA

> Most excellent accomplished lady, the heavens rain odours on you!

SIR ANDREW

> That youth's a rare courtier: 'Rain odours;' well.

VIOLA

> My matter hath no voice, to your own most pregnant and vouchsafed ear.

SIR ANDREW

> 'Odours,' 'pregnant' and 'vouchsafed:' I'll get 'em all three all ready.

OLIVIA

> Let the garden door be shut, and leave me to my earing.

> > *Exeunt* SIR TOBY BELCH, SIR ANDREW, *and* MARIA

> Give me your hand, sir.

VIOLA

    My duty, madam, and most humble service.

OLIVIA

    What is your name?

VIOLA

    Cesario is your servant's name, fair princess.

OLIVIA

    My servant, sir! 'Twas never merry world
    Since lowly feigning was call'd compliment:
    You're servant to the Count Orsino, youth.

VIOLA

    And he is yours, and his must needs be yours:
    Your servant's servant is your servant, madam.

OLIVIA

    For him, I think not on him: for his thoughts,
    Would they were blanks, rather than fill'd with me!

VIOLA

    Madam, I come to whet your gentle thoughts On his behalf.

OLIVIA

    O, by your leave, I pray you,
    I bade you never speak again of him:
    But, would you undertake another suit,
    I had rather hear you to solicit that
    Than music from the spheres.

VIOLA

    Dear lady—

OLIVIA

    Give me leave, beseech you. I did send,
    After the last enchantment you did here,
    A ring in chase of you: so did I abuse
    Myself, my servant and, I fear me, you:
    Under your hard construction must I sit,
    To force that on you, in a shameful cunning,
    Which you knew none of yours: what might you think?
    Have you not set mine honour at the stake
    And baited it with all the unmuzzled thoughts
    That tyrannous heart can think? To one of your receiving

Enough is shown: a cypress, not a bosom,
Hideth my heart. So, let me hear you speak.

VIOLA

I pity you.

OLIVIA

That's a degree to love.

VIOLA

No, not a grize; for 'tis a vulgar proof,
That very oft we pity enemies.

OLIVIA

Why, then, methinks 'tis time to smile again.
O, world, how apt the poor are to be proud!
If one should be a prey, how much the better
To fall before the lion than the wolf!

Clock strikes

The clock upbraids me with the waste of time.
Be not afraid, good youth, I will not have you:
And yet, when wit and youth is come to harvest,
Your wife is like to reap a proper man:
There lies your way, due west.

VIOLA

Then westward-ho!
Grace and good disposition Attend your ladyship!
You'll nothing, madam, to my lord by me?

OLIVIA

Stay: I prithee, tell me what thou thinkest of me.

VIOLA

That you do think you are not what you are.

OLIVIA

If I think so, I think the same of you.

VIOLA

Then think you right: I am not what I am.

OLIVIA

I would you were as I would have you be!

VIOLA

Would it be better, madam, than I am?
I wish it might, for now I am your fool.

OLIVIA
    O, what a deal of scorn looks beautiful
    In the contempt and anger of his lip!
    A murderous guilt shows not itself more soon
    Than love that would seem hid: love's night is noon.
    Cesario, by the roses of the spring,
    By maidhood, honour, truth and every thing,
    I love thee so, that, maugre all thy pride,
    Nor wit nor reason can my passion hide.
    Do not extort thy reasons from this clause,
    For that I woo, thou therefore hast no cause,
    But rather reason thus with reason fetter,
    Love sought is good, but given unsought better.

VIOLA
    By innocence I swear, and by my youth
    I have one heart, one bosom and one truth,
    And that no woman has; nor never none
    Shall mistress be of it, save I alone.
    And so adieu, good madam: never more
    Will I my master's tears to you deplore.

OLIVIA
    Yet come again; for thou perhaps mayst move
    That heart, which now abhors, to like his love.

Exeunt

SCENE II.
OLIVIA'S HOUSE.

Enter SIR TOBY BELCH,
SIR ANDREW, *and* FABIAN

SIR ANDREW
    No, faith, I'll not stay a jot longer.

SIR TOBY BELCH
    Thy reason, dear venom, give thy reason.

FABIAN
    You must needs yield your reason, Sir Andrew.

SIR ANDREW

Marry, I saw your niece do more favours to the count's serving-
man than ever she bestowed upon me; I saw't i' the orchard.

SIR TOBY BELCH

Did she see thee the while, old boy? Tell me that.

SIR ANDREW

As plain as I see you now.

FABIAN

This was a great argument of love in her toward you.

SIR ANDREW

'Slight, will you make an ass o' me?

FABIAN

I will prove it legitimate, sir, upon the oaths of judgment and
reason.

SIR TOBY BELCH

And they have been grand-jury-men since before Noah was a
sailor.

FABIAN

She did show favour to the youth in your sight only to exasperate
you, to awake your dormouse valour, to put fire in your heart
and brimstone in your liver. You should then have accosted
her; and with some excellent jests, fire-new from the mint, you
should have banged the youth into dumbness. This was looked
for at your hand, and this was balked: the double gilt of this
opportunity you let time wash off, and you are now sailed into
the north of my lady's opinion; where you will hang like an
icicle on a Dutchman's beard, unless you do redeem it by some
laudable attempt either of valour or policy.

SIR ANDREW

An't be any way, it must be with valour; for policy I hate: I had
as lief be a Brownist as a politician.

SIR TOBY BELCH

Why, then, build me thy fortunes upon the basis of valour.
Challenge me the count's youth to fight with him; hurt him in
eleven places: my niece shall take note of it; and assure thyself,
there is no love-broker in the world can more prevail in man's
commendation with woman than report of valour.

FABIAN

There is no way but this, Sir Andrew.

SIR ANDREW

Will either of you bear me a challenge to him?

SIR TOBY BELCH

Go, write it in a martial hand; be curst and brief; it is no matter
how witty, so it be eloquent and fun of invention: taunt him with
the licence of ink: if thou thou'st him some thrice, it shall not be
amiss; and as many lies as will lie in thy sheet of paper, although
the sheet were big enough for the bed of Ware in England, set
'em down: go, about it. Let there be gall enough in thy ink,
though thou write with a goose-pen, no matter: about it.

SIR ANDREW

Where shall I find you?

SIR TOBY BELCH

We'll call thee at the cubiculo: go.

Exit SIR ANDREW

FABIAN

This is a dear manikin to you, Sir Toby.

SIR TOBY BELCH

I have been dear to him, lad, some two thousand strong, or so.

FABIAN

We shall have a rare letter from him: but you'll not deliver't?

SIR TOBY BELCH

Never trust me, then; and by all means stir on the youth to an
answer. I think oxen and wainropes cannot hale them together.
For Andrew, if he were opened, and you find so much blood
in his liver as will clog the foot of a flea, I'll eat the rest of the
anatomy.

FABIAN

And his opposite, the youth, bears in his visage no great presage
of cruelty.

Enter MARIA

SIR TOBY BELCH

Look, where the youngest wren of nine comes.

MARIA

If you desire the spleen, and will laugh yourself into stitches,

follow me. Yond gull Malvolio is turned heathen, a very
renegado; for there is no Christian, that means to be saved by
believing rightly, can ever believe such impossible passages of
grossness. He's in yellow stockings.

SIR TOBY BELCH

And cross-gartered?

MARIA

Most villanously; like a pedant that keeps a school i' the church.
I have dogged him, like his murderer. He does obey every point
of the letter that I dropped to betray him: he does smile his face
into more lines than is in the new map with the augmentation
of the Indies: you have not seen such a thing as 'tis. I can hardly
forbear hurling things at him. I know my lady will strike him: if
she do, he'll smile and take't for a great favour.

SIR TOBY BELCH

Come, bring us, bring us where he is.

Exeunt

SCENE III.
A STREET.

Enter SEBASTIAN *and* ANTONIO

SEBASTIAN

I would not by my will have troubled you;
But, since you make your pleasure of your pains,
I will no further chide you.

ANTONIO

I could not stay behind you: my desire,
More sharp than filed steel, did spur me forth;
And not all love to see you, though so much
As might have drawn one to a longer voyage,
But jealousy what might befall your travel,
Being skilless in these parts; which to a stranger,
Unguided and unfriended, often prove
Rough and unhospitable: my willing love,
The rather by these arguments of fear,
Set forth in your pursuit.

SEBASTIAN

My kind Antonio,
I can no other answer make but thanks,
And thanks; and ever oft good turns
Are shuffled off with such uncurrent pay:
But, were my worth as is my conscience firm,
You should find better dealing. What's to do?
Shall we go see the reliques of this town?

ANTONIO

To-morrow, sir: best first go see your lodging.

SEBASTIAN

I am not weary, and 'tis long to night:
I pray you, let us satisfy our eyes
With the memorials and the things of fame
That do renown this city.

ANTONIO

Would you'ld pardon me;
I do not without danger walk these streets:
Once, in a sea-fight, 'gainst the count his galleys
I did some service; of such note indeed,
That were I ta'en here it would scarce be answer'd.

SEBASTIAN

Belike you slew great number of his people.

ANTONIO

The offence is not of such a bloody nature;
Albeit the quality of the time and quarrel
Might well have given us bloody argument.
It might have since been answer'd in repaying
What we took from them; which, for traffic's sake,
Most of our city did: only myself stood out;
For which, if I be lapsed in this place,
I shall pay dear.

SEBASTIAN

Do not then walk too open.

ANTONIO

It doth not fit me. Hold, sir, here's my purse.
In the south suburbs, at the Elephant,

Is best to lodge: I will bespeak our diet,
Whiles you beguile the time and feed your knowledge
With viewing of the town: there shall you have me.

SEBASTIAN

Why I your purse?

ANTONIO

Haply your eye shall light upon some toy
You have desire to purchase; and your store,
I think, is not for idle markets, sir.

SEBASTIAN

I'll be your purse-bearer and leave you
For an hour.

ANTONIO

To the Elephant.

SEBASTIAN

I do remember.

Exeunt

SCENE IV.
OLIVIA'S GARDEN.

Enter OLIVIA *and* MARIA

OLIVIA

I have sent after him: he says he'll come;
How shall I feast him? What bestow of him?
For youth is bought more oft than begg'd or borrow'd.
I speak too loud.
Where is Malvolio? He is sad and civil,
And suits well for a servant with my fortunes:
Where is Malvolio?

MARIA

He's coming, madam; but in very strange manner. He is, sure,
possessed, madam.

OLIVIA

Why, what's the matter? Does he rave?

MARIA

No. madam, he does nothing but smile: your ladyship were best

to have some guard about you, if he come; for, sure, the man is
tainted in's wits.

OLIVIA

Go call him hither.

Exit MARIA

I am as mad as he,
If sad and merry madness equal be.

Re-enter MARIA, *with* MALVOLIO

How now, Malvolio!

MALVOLIO

Sweet lady, ho, ho.

OLIVIA

Smilest thou? I sent for thee upon a sad occasion.

MALVOLIO

Sad, lady! I could be sad: this does make some obstruction in
the blood, this cross-gartering; but what of that? If it please the
eye of one, it is with me as the very true sonnet is, 'Please one,
and please all.'

OLIVIA

Why, how dost thou, man? What is the matter with thee?

MALVOLIO

Not black in my mind, though yellow in my legs. It did come to
his hands, and commands shall be executed: I think we do know
the sweet Roman hand.

OLIVIA

Wilt thou go to bed, Malvolio?

MALVOLIO

To bed! Ay, sweet-heart, and I'll come to thee.

OLIVIA

God comfort thee! Why dost thou smile so and kiss thy hand
so oft?

MARIA

How do you, Malvolio?

MALVOLIO

At your request! Yes; nightingales answer daws.

MARIA

Why appear you with this ridiculous boldness before my lady?

MALVOLIO

'Be not afraid of greatness:' 'twas well writ.

OLIVIA

What meanest thou by that, Malvolio?

MALVOLIO

'Some are born great,'—

OLIVIA

Ha!

MALVOLIO

'Some achieve greatness,'—

OLIVIA

What sayest thou?

MALVOLIO

'And some have greatness thrust upon them.'

OLIVIA

Heaven restore thee!

MALVOLIO

'Remember who commended thy yellow stockings.'

OLIVIA

Thy yellow stockings!

MALVOLIO

'And wished to see thee cross-gartered.'

OLIVIA

Cross-gartered!

MALVOLIO

'Go to thou art made, if thou desirest to be so;'—

OLIVIA

Am I made?

MALVOLIO

'If not, let me see thee a servant still.'

OLIVIA

Why, this is very midsummer madness.

Enter Servant

SERVANT

Madam, the young gentleman of the Count Orsino's is returned: I could hardly entreat him back: he attends your ladyship's pleasure.

OLIVIA

I'll come to him.

Exit Servant

Good Maria, let this fellow be looked to. Where's my cousin Toby? Let some of my people have a special care of him: I would not have him miscarry for the half of my dowry.

Exeunt OLIVIA *and* MARIA

MALVOLIO

O, ho! Do you come near me now? No worse man than Sir Toby to look to me! This concurs directly with the letter: she sends him on purpose, that I may appear stubborn to him; for she incites me to that in the letter. 'Cast thy humble slough,' says she; 'be opposite with a kinsman, surly with servants; let thy tongue tang with arguments of state; put thyself into the trick of singularity;' and consequently sets down the manner how; as, a sad face, a reverend carriage, a slow tongue, in the habit of some sir of note, and so forth. I have limed her; but it is Jove's doing, and Jove make me thankful! And when she went away now, 'Let this fellow be looked to:' fellow! Not Malvolio, nor after my degree, but fellow. Why, every thing adheres together, that no dram of a scruple, no scruple of a scruple, no obstacle, no incredulous or unsafe circumstance—What can be said? Nothing that can be can come between me and the full prospect of my hopes. Well, Jove, not I, is the doer of this, and he is to be thanked.

Re-enter MARIA, *with*
SIR TOBY BELCH *and* FABIAN

SIR TOBY BELCH

Which way is he, in the name of sanctity? If all the devils of hell be drawn in little, and Legion himself possessed him, yet I'll speak to him.

FABIAN

Here he is, here he is. How is't with you, sir? How is't with you, man?

MALVOLIO

Go off; I discard you: let me enjoy my private: go off.

MARIA

Lo, how hollow the fiend speaks within him! Did not I tell you?
Sir Toby, my lady prays you to have a care of him.

MALVOLIO

Ah, ha! Does she so?

SIR TOBY BELCH

Go to, go to; peace, peace; we must deal gently with him: let me
alone. How do you, Malvolio? How is't with you? What, man!
Defy the devil: consider, he's an enemy to mankind.

MALVOLIO

Do you know what you say?

MARIA

La you, an you speak ill of the devil, how he takes it at heart!
Pray God, he be not bewitched!

FABIAN

Carry his water to the wise woman.

MARIA

Marry, and it shall be done to-morrow morning, if I live. My
lady would not lose him for more than I'll say.

MALVOLIO

How now, mistress!

MARIA

O Lord!

SIR TOBY BELCH

Prithee, hold thy peace; this is not the way: do you not see you
move him? Let me alone with him.

FABIAN

No way but gentleness; gently, gently: the fiend is rough, and will
not be roughly used.

SIR TOBY BELCH

Why, how now, my bawcock! How dost thou, chuck?

MALVOLIO

Sir!

SIR TOBY BELCH

Ay, Biddy, come with me. What, man! 'Tis not for gravity to play
at cherry-pit with Satan: hang him, foul collier!

MARIA

Get him to say his prayers, good Sir Toby, get him to pray.

MALVOLIO

My prayers, minx!

MARIA

No, I warrant you, he will not hear of godliness.

MALVOLIO

Go, hang yourselves all! You are idle shallow things: I am not of your element: you shall know more hereafter.

Exit

SIR TOBY BELCH

Is't possible?

FABIAN

If this were played upon a stage now, I could condemn it as an improbable fiction.

SIR TOBY BELCH

His very genius hath taken the infection of the device, man.

MARIA

Nay, pursue him now, lest the device take air and taint.

FABIAN

Why, we shall make him mad indeed.

MARIA

The house will be the quieter.

SIR TOBY BELCH

Come, we'll have him in a dark room and bound. My niece is already in the belief that he's mad: we may carry it thus, for our pleasure and his penance, till our very pastime, tired out of breath, prompt us to have mercy on him: at which time we will bring the device to the bar and crown thee for a finder of madmen. But see, but see.

Enter SIR ANDREW

FABIAN

More matter for a May morning.

SIR ANDREW

Here's the challenge, read it: warrant there's vinegar and pepper in't.

FABIAN

Is't so saucy?

SIR ANDREW

Ay, is't, I warrant him: do but read.

SIR TOBY BELCH

Give me.

[*Reads*] '*Youth, whatsoever thou art, thou art but a scurvy fellow.*'

FABIAN

Good, and valiant.

SIR TOBY BELCH

[*Reads*] '*Wonder not, nor admire not in thy mind, why I do call thee so, for I will show thee no reason for't.*'

FABIAN

A good note; that keeps you from the blow of the law.

SIR TOBY BELCH

[*Reads*] '*Thou comest to the lady Olivia, and in my sight she uses thee kindly: but thou liest in thy throat; that is not the matter I challenge thee for.*'

FABIAN

Very brief, and to exceeding good sense—less.

SIR TOBY BELCH

[*Reads*] '*I will waylay thee going home; where if it be thy chance to kill me,*'—

FABIAN

Good.

SIR TOBY BELCH

[*Reads*] '*Thou killest me like a rogue and a villain.*'

FABIAN

Still you keep o' the windy side of the law: good.

SIR TOBY BELCH

[*Reads*] '*Fare thee well; and God have mercy upon one of our souls! He may have mercy upon mine; but my hope is better, and so look to thyself. Thy friend, as thou usest him, and thy sworn enemy,*

Andrew Aguecheek.'

If this letter move him not, his legs cannot: I'll give't him.

MARIA

You may have very fit occasion for't: he is now in some commerce with my lady, and will by and by depart.

SIR TOBY BELCH

Go, Sir Andrew: scout me for him at the corner the orchard like a bum-baily: so soon as ever thou seest him, draw; and, as thou drawest swear horrible; for it comes to pass oft that a terrible oath, with a swaggering accent sharply twanged off, gives manhood more approbation than ever proof itself would have earned him. Away!

SIR ANDREW

Nay, let me alone for swearing.

Exit

SIR TOBY BELCH

Now will not I deliver his letter: for the behavior of the young gentleman gives him out to be of good capacity and breeding; his employment between his lord and my niece confirms no less: therefore this letter, being so excellently ignorant, will breed no terror in the youth: he will find it comes from a clodpole. But, sir, I will deliver his challenge by word of mouth; set upon Aguecheek a notable report of valour; and drive the gentleman, as I know his youth will aptly receive it, into a most hideous opinion of his rage, skill, fury and impetuosity. This will so fright them both that they will kill one another by the look, like cockatrices.

Re-enter OLIVIA, *with* VIOLA

FABIAN

Here he comes with your niece: give them way till he take leave, and presently after him.

SIR TOBY BELCH

I will meditate the while upon some horrid message for a challenge.

Exeunt SIR TOBY BELCH,
FABIAN, *and* MARIA

OLIVIA

I have said too much unto a heart of stone
And laid mine honour too unchary out:
There's something in me that reproves my fault;
But such a headstrong potent fault it is,
That it but mocks reproof.

VIOLA

With the same 'havior that your passion bears
Goes on my master's grief.

OLIVIA

Here, wear this jewel for me, 'tis my picture;
Refuse it not; it hath no tongue to vex you;
And I beseech you come again to-morrow.
What shall you ask of me that I'll deny,
That honour saved may upon asking give?

VIOLA

Nothing but this; your true love for my master.

OLIVIA

How with mine honour may I give him that
Which I have given to you?

VIOLA

I will acquit you.

OLIVIA

Well, come again to-morrow: fare thee well:
A fiend like thee might bear my soul to hell.

Exit

Re-enter SIR TOBY BELCH *and* FABIAN

SIR TOBY BELCH

Gentleman, God save thee.

VIOLA

And you, sir.

SIR TOBY BELCH

That defence thou hast, betake thee to't: of what nature the
wrongs are thou hast done him, I know not; but thy intercepter,
full of despite, bloody as the hunter, attends thee at the orchard-
end: dismount thy tuck, be yare in thy preparation, for thy
assailant is quick, skilful and deadly.

VIOLA

You mistake, sir; I am sure no man hath any quarrel to me: my
remembrance is very free and clear from any image of offence
done to any man.

SIR TOBY BELCH

You'll find it otherwise, I assure you: therefore, if you hold your life at any price, betake you to your guard; for your opposite hath in him what youth, strength, skill and wrath can furnish man withal.

VIOLA

I pray you, sir, what is he?

SIR TOBY BELCH

He is knight, dubbed with unhatched rapier and on carpet consideration; but he is a devil in private brawl: souls and bodies hath he divorced three; and his incensement at this moment is so implacable, that satisfaction can be none but by pangs of death and sepulchre. Hob, nob, is his word; give't or take't.

VIOLA

I will return again into the house and desire some conduct of the lady. I am no fighter. I have heard of some kind of men that put quarrels purposely on others, to taste their valour: belike this is a man of that quirk.

SIR TOBY BELCH

Sir, no; his indignation derives itself out of a very competent injury: therefore, get you on and give him his desire. Back you shall not to the house, unless you undertake that with me which with as much safety you might answer him: therefore, on, or strip your sword stark naked; for meddle you must, that's certain, or forswear to wear iron about you.

VIOLA

This is as uncivil as strange. I beseech you, do me this courteous office, as to know of the knight what my offence to him is: it is something of my negligence, nothing of my purpose.

SIR TOBY BELCH

I will do so. Signior Fabian, stay you by this gentleman till my return.

Exit

VIOLA

Pray you, sir, do you know of this matter?

FABIAN

I know the knight is incensed against you, even to a mortal arbitrement; but nothing of the circumstance more.

VIOLA

I beseech you, what manner of man is he?

FABIAN

Nothing of that wonderful promise, to read him by his form, as you are like to find him in the proof of his valour. He is, indeed, sir, the most skilful, bloody and fatal opposite that you could possibly have found in any part of Illyria. Will you walk towards him? I will make your peace with him if I can.

VIOLA

I shall be much bound to you for't: I am one that had rather go with sir priest than sir knight: I care not who knows so much of my mettle.

Exeunt

Re-enter SIR TOBY BELCH, *with* SIR ANDREW

Sir Toby Belch

Why, man, he's a very devil; I have not seen such a firago. I had a pass with him, rapier, scabbard and all, and he gives me the stuck in with such a mortal motion, that it is inevitable; and on the answer, he pays you as surely as your feet hit the ground they step on. They say he has been fencer to the Sophy.

SIR ANDREW

Pox on't, I'll not meddle with him.

SIR TOBY BELCH

Ay, but he will not now be pacified: Fabian can scarce hold him yonder.

SIR ANDREW

Plague on't, an I thought he had been valiant and so cunning in fence, I'ld have seen him damned ere I'ld have challenged him. Let him let the matter slip, and I'll give him my horse, grey Capilet.

SIR TOBY BELCH

I'll make the motion: stand here, make a good show on't: this shall end without the perdition of souls. [*Aside*] Marry, I'll ride your horse as well as I ride you.

Re-enter FABIAN *and* VIOLA

[*To Fabian*] I have his horse to take up the quarrel: I have persuaded him the youth's a devil.

FABIAN

He is as horribly conceited of him; and pants and looks pale, as if a bear were at his heels.

SIR TOBY BELCH

[*To Viola*] There's no remedy, sir; he will fight with you for's oath sake: marry, he hath better bethought him of his quarrel, and he finds that now scarce to be worth talking of: therefore draw, for the supportance of his vow; he protests he will not hurt you.

VIOLA

[*Aside*] Pray God defend me! A little thing would make me tell them how much I lack of a man.

FABIAN

Give ground, if you see him furious.

SIR TOBY BELCH

Come, Sir Andrew, there's no remedy; the gentleman will, for his honour's sake, have one bout with you; he cannot by the duello avoid it: but he has promised me, as he is a gentleman and a soldier, he will not hurt you. Come on; to't.

SIR ANDREW

Pray God, he keep his oath!

VIOLA

I do assure you, 'tis against my will.

They draw

Enter ANTONIO

ANTONIO

Put up your sword. If this young gentleman
Have done offence, I take the fault on me:
If you offend him, I for him defy you.

SIR TOBY BELCH

You, sir! Why, what are you?

ANTONIO

One, sir, that for his love dares yet do more
Than you have heard him brag to you he will.

SIR TOBY BELCH

Nay, if you be an undertaker, I am for you.

They draw
Enter Officers

FABIAN

O good Sir Toby, hold! Here come the officers.

SIR TOBY BELCH

I'll be with you anon.

VIOLA

Pray, sir, put your sword up, if you please.

Sir Andrew

Marry, will I, sir; and, for that I promised you, I'll be as good as my word: he will bear you easily and reins well.

FIRST OFFICER

This is the man; do thy office.

SECOND OFFICER

Antonio, I arrest thee at the suit of Count Orsino.

ANTONIO

You do mistake me, sir.

FIRST OFFICER

No, sir, no jot; I know your favour well,
Though now you have no sea-cap on your head.
Take him away: he knows I know him well.

ANTONIO

I must obey.
[*To Viola*] This comes with seeking you:
But there's no remedy; I shall answer it.
What will you do, now my necessity
Makes me to ask you for my purse? It grieves me
Much more for what I cannot do for you
Than what befalls myself. You stand amazed;
But be of comfort.

SECOND OFFICER

Come, sir, away.

ANTONIO

I must entreat of you some of that money.

VIOLA
What money, sir?
For the fair kindness you have show'd me here,
And, part, being prompted by your present trouble,
Out of my lean and low ability
I'll lend you something: my having is not much;
I'll make division of my present with you:
Hold, there's half my coffer.

ANTONIO
Will you deny me now?
Is't possible that my deserts to you
Can lack persuasion? Do not tempt my misery,
Lest that it make me so unsound a man
As to upbraid you with those kindnesses
That I have done for you.

VIOLA
I know of none;
Nor know I you by voice or any feature:
I hate ingratitude more in a man
Than lying, vainness, babbling, drunkenness,
Or any taint of vice whose strong corruption
Inhabits our frail blood.

ANTONIO
O heavens themselves!

SECOND OFFICER
Come, sir, I pray you, go.

ANTONIO
Let me speak a little. This youth that you see here
I snatch'd one half out of the jaws of death,
Relieved him with such sanctity of love,
And to his image, which methought did promise
Most venerable worth, did I devotion.

FIRST OFFICER
What's that to us? The time goes by: away!

ANTONIO
But O how vile an idol proves this god

Thou hast, Sebastian, done good feature shame.
In nature there's no blemish but the mind;
None can be call'd deform'd but the unkind:
Virtue is beauty, but the beauteous evil
Are empty trunks o'erflourish'd by the devil.

FIRST OFFICER
The man grows mad: away with him! Come, come, sir.

ANTONIO
Lead me on.

Exit with Officers

VIOLA
Methinks his words do from such passion fly,
That he believes himself: so do not I.
Prove true, imagination, O, prove true,
That I, dear brother, be now ta'en for you!

SIR TOBY BELCH
Come hither, knight; come hither, Fabian: we'll whisper o'er a
couplet or two of most sage saws.

VIOLA
He named Sebastian: I my brother know
Yet living in my glass; even such and so
In favour was my brother, and he went
Still in this fashion, colour, ornament,
For him I imitate: O, if it prove,
Tempests are kind and salt waves fresh in love.

Exit

SIR TOBY BELCH
A very dishonest paltry boy, and more a coward than a hare: his
dishonesty appears in leaving his friend here in necessity and
denying him; and for his cowardship, ask Fabian.

FABIAN
A coward, a most devout coward, religious in it.

SIR ANDREW
'Slid, I'll after him again and beat him.

SIR TOBY BELCH
Do; cuff him soundly, but never draw thy sword.

SIR ANDREW
    An I do not—

Exit

FABIAN
    Come, let's see the event.
SIR TOBY BELCH
    I dare lay any money 'twill be nothing yet.

Exeunt

ACT
IV

SCENE I.
BEFORE OLIVIA'S HOUSE.

Enter SEBASTIAN *and* CLOWN

CLOWN

Will you make me believe that I am not sent for you?

SEBASTIAN

Go to, go to, thou art a foolish fellow: Let me be clear of thee.

CLOWN

Well held out, i' faith! No, I do not know you; nor I am not sent to you by my lady, to bid you come speak with her; nor your name is not Master Cesario; nor this is not my nose neither. Nothing that is so is so.

SEBASTIAN

I prithee, vent thy folly somewhere else: Thou know'st not me.

CLOWN

Vent my folly! He has heard that word of some great man and now applies it to a fool. Vent my folly! I am afraid this great lubber, the world, will prove a cockney. I prithee now, ungird thy strangeness and tell me what I shall vent to my lady: shall I vent to her that thou art coming?

SEBASTIAN

I prithee, foolish Greek, depart from me: There's money for thee: if you tarry longer, I shall give worse payment.

CLOWN

By my troth, thou hast an open hand. These wise men that give fools money get themselves a good report—after fourteen years' purchase.

Enter SIR ANDREW, SIR TOBY BELCH, *and* FABIAN

SIR ANDREW

Now, sir, have I met you again? There's for you.

SEBASTIAN

Why, there's for thee, and there, and there. Are all the people mad?

SIR TOBY BELCH

Hold, sir, or I'll throw your dagger o'er the house.

CLOWN

This will I tell my lady straight: I would not be in some of your coats for two pence.

Exit

SIR TOBY BELCH

Come on, sir; hold.

SIR ANDREW

Nay, let him alone: I'll go another way to work with him; I'll have an action of battery against him, if there be any law in Illyria: though I struck him first, yet it's no matter for that.

SEBASTIAN

Let go thy hand.

SIR TOBY BELCH

Come, sir, I will not let you go. Come, my young soldier, put up your iron: you are well fleshed; come on.

SEBASTIAN

I will be free from thee. What wouldst thou now? If thou darest tempt me further, draw thy sword.

SIR TOBY BELCH

What, what? Nay, then I must have an ounce or two of this malapert blood from you.

Enter OLIVIA

OLIVIA

    Hold, Toby; on thy life I charge thee, hold!

SIR TOBY BELCH

    Madam!

OLIVIA

    Will it be ever thus? Ungracious wretch,

    Fit for the mountains and the barbarous caves,

    Where manners ne'er were preach'd! Out of my sight!

    Be not offended, dear Cesario.

    Rudesby, be gone!

> *Exeunt* SIR TOBY BELCH,
> SIR ANDREW, *and* FABIAN

    I prithee, gentle friend,

    Let thy fair wisdom, not thy passion, sway

    In this uncivil and thou unjust extent

    Against thy peace. Go with me to my house,

    And hear thou there how many fruitless pranks

    This ruffian hath botch'd up, that thou thereby

    Mayst smile at this: thou shalt not choose but go:

    Do not deny. Beshrew his soul for me,

    He started one poor heart of mine in thee.

SEBASTIAN

    What relish is in this? How runs the stream?

    Or I am mad, or else this is a dream:

    Let fancy still my sense in Lethe steep;

    If it be thus to dream, still let me sleep!

OLIVIA

    Nay, come, I prithee; would thou'ldst be ruled by me!

SEBASTIAN

    Madam, I will.

OLIVIA

    O, say so, and so be!

> *Exeunt*

SCENE II.
OLIVIA'S HOUSE.

Enter MARIA *and* CLOWN

MARIA

Nay, I prithee, put on this gown and this beard; make him believe thou art Sir Topas the curate: do it quickly; I'll call Sir Toby the whilst.

Exit

CLOWN

Well, I'll put it on, and I will dissemble myself in't; and I would I were the first that ever dissembled in such a gown. I am not tall enough to become the function well, nor lean enough to be thought a good student; but to be said an honest man and a good housekeeper goes as fairly as to say a careful man and a great scholar. The competitors enter.

Enter SIR TOBY BELCH *and* MARIA

SIR TOBY BELCH

Jove bless thee, master Parson.

CLOWN

Bonos dies, Sir Toby: for, as the old hermit of Prague, that never saw pen and ink, very wittily said to a niece of King Gorboduc, 'That that is is;' so I, being Master Parson, am Master Parson; for, what is 'that' but 'that,' and 'is' but 'is'?

SIR TOBY BELCH

To him, Sir Topas.

CLOWN

What, ho, I say! Peace in this prison!

SIR TOBY BELCH

The knave counterfeits well; a good knave.

MALVOLIO

[*Within*] Who calls there?

CLOWN

Sir Topas the curate, who comes to visit Malvolio the lunatic.

MALVOLIO

Sir Topas, Sir Topas, good Sir Topas, go to my lady.

CLOWN

Out, hyperbolical fiend! How vexest thou this man! Talkest thou nothing but of ladies?

SIR TOBY BELCH

Well said, Master Parson.

MALVOLIO

Sir Topas, never was man thus wronged: good Sir Topas, do not think I am mad: they have laid me here in hideous darkness.

CLOWN

Fie, thou dishonest Satan! I call thee by the most modest terms; for I am one of those gentle ones that will use the devil himself with courtesy: sayest thou that house is dark?

MALVOLIO

As hell, Sir Topas.

CLOWN

Why it hath bay windows transparent as barricadoes, and the clearstores toward the south north are as lustrous as ebony; and yet complainest thou of obstruction?

MALVOLIO

I am not mad, Sir Topas: I say to you, this house is dark.

CLOWN

Madman, thou errest: I say, there is no darkness but ignorance; in which thou art more puzzled than the Egyptians in their fog.

MALVOLIO

I say, this house is as dark as ignorance, though ignorance were as dark as hell; and I say, there was never man thus abused. I am no more mad than you are: make the trial of it in any constant question.

CLOWN

What is the opinion of Pythagoras concerning wild fowl?

MALVOLIO

That the soul of our grandam might haply inhabit a bird.

CLOWN

What thinkest thou of his opinion?

MALVOLIO

I think nobly of the soul, and no way approve his opinion.

CLOWN

Fare thee well. Remain thou still in darkness: thou shalt hold the opinion of Pythagoras ere I will allow of thy wits, and fear to kill a woodcock, lest thou dispossess the soul of thy grandam. Fare thee well.

MALVOLIO

Sir Topas, Sir Topas!

SIR TOBY BELCH

My most exquisite Sir Topas!

CLOWN

Nay, I am for all waters.

MARIA

Thou mightst have done this without thy beard and gown: he sees thee not.

SIR TOBY BELCH

To him in thine own voice, and bring me word how thou findest him: I would we were well rid of this knavery. If he may be conveniently delivered, I would he were, for I am now so far in offence with my niece that I cannot pursue with any safety this sport to the upshot. Come by and by to my chamber.

Exeunt SIR TOBY BELCH *and* MARIA

CLOWN

[*Singing*] 'Hey, Robin, jolly Robin,
   Tell me how thy lady does.'

MALVOLIO

Fool!

CLOWN

'My lady is unkind, perdy.'

MALVOLIO

Fool!

CLOWN

'Alas, why is she so?'

MALVOLIO

Fool, I say!

CLOWN

'She loves another'—Who calls, ha?

MALVOLIO

Good fool, as ever thou wilt deserve well at my hand, help me to a candle, and pen, ink and paper: as I am a gentleman, I will live to be thankful to thee for't.

CLOWN

Master Malvolio?

MALVOLIO

Ay, good fool.

CLOWN

Alas, sir, how fell you besides your five wits?

MALVOLIO

Fool, there was never a man so notoriously abused: I am as well in my wits, fool, as thou art.

CLOWN

But as well? Then you are mad indeed, if you be no better in your wits than a fool.

MALVOLIO

They have here propertied me; keep me in darkness, send ministers to me, asses, and do all they can to face me out of my wits.

CLOWN

Advise you what you say; the minister is here. Malvolio, Malvolio, thy wits the heavens restore! Endeavour thyself to sleep, and leave thy vain bibble babble.

MALVOLIO

Sir Topas!

CLOWN

Maintain no words with him, good fellow. Who, I, sir? Not I, sir. God be wi' you, good Sir Topas. Merry, amen. I will, sir, I will.

MALVOLIO

Fool, fool, fool, I say!

CLOWN

Alas, sir, be patient. What say you sir? I am shent for speaking to you.

MALVOLIO

Good fool, help me to some light and some paper: I tell thee, I am as well in my wits as any man in Illyria.

CLOWN

Well-a-day that you were, sir

MALVOLIO

By this hand, I am. Good fool, some ink, paper and light; and convey what I will set down to my lady: it shall advantage thee more than ever the bearing of letter did.

CLOWN

I will help you to't. But tell me true, are you not mad indeed? Or do you but counterfeit?

MALVOLIO

Believe me, I am not; I tell thee true.

CLOWN

Nay, I'll ne'er believe a madman till I see his brains. I will fetch you light and paper and ink.

MALVOLIO

Fool, I'll requite it in the highest degree: I prithee, be gone.

CLOWN

[*Singing*] I am gone, sir,
And anon, sir,
I'll be with you again,
In a trice,
Like to the old Vice,
Your need to sustain;
Who, with dagger of lath,
In his rage and his wrath,
Cries, ah, ha! To the devil:
Like a mad lad, Pare thy nails, dad;
Adieu, good man devil.

Exit

SCENE III. OLIVIA'S GARDEN.

Enter SEBASTIAN

SEBASTIAN

This is the air; that is the glorious sun;
This pearl she gave me, I do feel't and see't;
And though 'tis wonder that enwraps me thus,

Yet 'tis not madness. Where's Antonio, then?
I could not find him at the Elephant:
Yet there he was; and there I found this credit,
That he did range the town to seek me out.
His counsel now might do me golden service;
For though my soul disputes well with my sense,
That this may be some error, but no madness,
Yet doth this accident and flood of fortune
So far exceed all instance, all discourse,
That I am ready to distrust mine eyes
And wrangle with my reason that persuades me
To any other trust but that I am mad
Or else the lady's mad; yet, if 'twere so,
She could not sway her house, command her followers,
Take and give back affairs and their dispatch
With such a smooth, discreet and stable bearing
As I perceive she does: there's something in't
That is deceiveable. But here the lady comes.

Enter OLIVIA *and Priest*

OLIVIA

Blame not this haste of mine. If you mean well,
Now go with me and with this holy man
Into the chantry by: there, before him,
And underneath that consecrated roof,
Plight me the full assurance of your faith;
That my most jealous and too doubtful soul
May live at peace. He shall conceal it
Whiles you are willing it shall come to note,
What time we will our celebration keep
According to my birth. What do you say?

SEBASTIAN

I'll follow this good man, and go with you;
And, having sworn truth, ever will be true.

OLIVIA

Then lead the way, good father; and heavens so shine,
That they may fairly note this act of mine!

Exeunt

ACT

V

SCENE I.
BEFORE OLIVIA'S HOUSE.

Enter CLOWN *and* FABIAN

FABIAN

    Now, as thou lovest me, let me see his letter.

CLOWN

    Good Master Fabian, grant me another request.

FABIAN

    Any thing.

CLOWN

    Do not desire to see this letter.

FABIAN

    This is, to give a dog, and in recompense desire my dog
again.

        Enter DUKE ORSINO, VIOLA, CURIO, *and Lords*

DUKE ORSINO

    Belong you to the Lady Olivia, friends?

CLOWN

    Ay, sir; we are some of her trappings.

DUKE ORSINO

    I know thee well; how dost thou, my good fellow?

CLOWN

Truly, sir, the better for my foes and the worse for my friends.

DUKE ORSINO

Just the contrary; the better for thy friends.

CLOWN

No, sir, the worse.

DUKE ORSINO

How can that be?

CLOWN

Marry, sir, they praise me and make an ass of me; now my foes tell me plainly I am an ass: so that by my foes, sir I profit in the knowledge of myself, and by my friends, I am abused: so that, conclusions to be as kisses, if your four negatives make your two affirmatives why then, the worse for my friends and the better for my foes.

DUKE ORSINO

Why, this is excellent.

CLOWN

By my troth, sir, no; though it please you to be one of my friends.

DUKE ORSINO

Thou shalt not be the worse for me: there's gold.

CLOWN

But that it would be double-dealing, sir, I would you could make it another.

DUKE ORSINO

O, you give me ill counsel.

CLOWN

Put your grace in your pocket, sir, for this once, and let your flesh and blood obey it.

DUKE ORSINO

Well, I will be so much a sinner, to be a double-dealer: there's another.

CLOWN

Primo, secundo, tertio, is a good play; and the old saying is, the third pays for all: the triplex, sir, is a good tripping measure; or the bells of Saint Bennet, sir, may put you in mind; one, two, three.

DUKE ORSINO

You can fool no more money out of me at this throw: if you will
let your lady know I am here to speak with her, and bring her
along with you, it may awake my bounty further.

CLOWN

Marry, sir, lullaby to your bounty till I come again. I go, sir; but
I would not have you to think that my desire of having is the sin
of covetousness: but, as you say, sir, let your bounty take a nap,
I will awake it anon.

Exit

VIOLA

Here comes the man, sir, that did rescue me.

Enter ANTONIO *and Officers*

DUKE ORSINO

That face of his I do remember well;
Yet, when I saw it last, it was besmear'd
As black as Vulcan in the smoke of war:
A bawbling vessel was he captain of,
For shallow draught and bulk unprizable;
With which such scathful grapple did he make
With the most noble bottom of our fleet,
That very envy and the tongue of loss
Cried fame and honour on him. What's the matter?

FIRST OFFICER

Orsino, this is that Antonio
That took the *Phoenix* and her fraught from Candy;
And this is he that did the *Tiger* board,
When your young nephew Titus lost his leg:
Here in the streets, desperate of shame and state,
In private brabble did we apprehend him.

VIOLA

He did me kindness, sir, drew on my side;
But in conclusion put strange speech upon me:
I know not what 'twas but distraction.

DUKE ORSINO

Notable pirate! Thou salt-water thief!
What foolish boldness brought thee to their mercies,

Whom thou, in terms so bloody and so dear,
Hast made thine enemies?

ANTONIO

Orsino, noble sir,
Be pleased that I shake off these names you give me:
Antonio never yet was thief or pirate,
Though I confess, on base and ground enough,
Orsino's enemy. A witchcraft drew me hither:
That most ingrateful boy there by your side,
From the rude sea's enraged and foamy mouth
Did I redeem; a wreck past hope he was:
His life I gave him and did thereto add
My love, without retention or restraint,
All his in dedication; for his sake
Did I expose myself, pure for his love,
Into the danger of this adverse town;
Drew to defend him when he was beset:
Where being apprehended, his false cunning,
Not meaning to partake with me in danger,
Taught him to face me out of his acquaintance,
And grew a twenty years removed thing
While one would wink; denied me mine own purse,
Which I had recommended to his use
Not half an hour before.

VIOLA

How can this be?

DUKE ORSINO

When came he to this town?

ANTONIO

To-day, my lord; and for three months before,
No interim, not a minute's vacancy,
Both day and night did we keep company.

Enter OLIVIA *and Attendants*

DUKE ORSINO

Here comes the countess: now heaven walks on earth.
But for thee, fellow; fellow, thy words are madness:

Three months this youth hath tended upon me;
But more of that anon. Take him aside.

OLIVIA

What would my lord, but that he may not have,
Wherein Olivia may seem serviceable?
Cesario, you do not keep promise with me.

VIOLA

Madam!

DUKE ORSINO

Gracious Olivia—

OLIVIA

What do you say, Cesario? Good my lord—

VIOLA

My lord would speak; my duty hushes me.

OLIVIA

If it be aught to the old tune, my lord,
It is as fat and fulsome to mine ear
As howling after music.

DUKE ORSINO

Still so cruel?

OLIVIA

Still so constant, lord.

DUKE ORSINO

What, to perverseness? You uncivil lady,
To whose ingrate and unauspicious altars
My soul the faithfull'st offerings hath breathed out
That e'er devotion tender'd! What shall I do?

OLIVIA

Even what it please my lord, that shall become him.

DUKE ORSINO

Why should I not, had I the heart to do it,
Like to the Egyptian thief at point of death,
Kill what I love?—a savage jealousy
That sometimes savours nobly. But hear me this:
Since you to non-regardance cast my faith,
And that I partly know the instrument

That screws me from my true place in your favour,
Live you the marble-breasted tyrant still;
But this your minion, whom I know you love,
And whom, by heaven I swear, I tender dearly,
Him will I tear out of that cruel eye,
Where he sits crowned in his master's spite.
Come, boy, with me; my thoughts are ripe in mischief:
I'll sacrifice the lamb that I do love,
To spite a raven's heart within a dove.

VIOLA

And I, most jocund, apt and willingly,
To do you rest, a thousand deaths would die.

OLIVIA

Where goes Cesario?

VIOLA

After him I love
More than I love these eyes, more than my life,
More, by all mores, than e'er I shall love wife.
If I do feign, you witnesses above
Punish my life for tainting of my love!

OLIVIA

Ay me, detested! How am I beguiled!

VIOLA

Who does beguile you? Who does do you wrong?

OLIVIA

Hast thou forgot thyself? Is it so long?
Call forth the holy father.

DUKE ORSINO

Come, away!

OLIVIA

Whither, my lord? Cesario, husband, stay.

DUKE ORSINO

Husband!

OLIVIA

Ay, husband: can he that deny?

DUKE ORSINO

Her husband, sirrah!

VIOLA

No, my lord, not I.

OLIVIA

Alas, it is the baseness of thy fear
That makes thee strangle thy propriety:
Fear not, Cesario; take thy fortunes up;
Be that thou know'st thou art, and then thou art
As great as that thou fear'st.

Enter Priest

O, welcome, father!
Father, I charge thee, by thy reverence,
Here to unfold, though lately we intended
To keep in darkness what occasion now
Reveals before 'tis ripe, what thou dost know
Hath newly pass'd between this youth and me.

PRIEST

A contract of eternal bond of love,
Confirm'd by mutual joinder of your hands,
Attested by the holy close of lips,
Strengthen'd by interchangement of your rings;
And all the ceremony of this compact
Seal'd in my function, by my testimony:
Since when, my watch hath told me, toward my grave
I have travell'd but two hours.

DUKE ORSINO

O thou dissembling cub! What wilt thou be
When time hath sow'd a grizzle on thy case?
Or will not else thy craft so quickly grow,
That thine own trip shall be thine overthrow?
Farewell, and take her; but direct thy feet
Where thou and I henceforth may never meet.

VIOLA

My lord, I do protest—

OLIVIA

O, do not swear!
Hold little faith, though thou hast too much fear.

Enter SIR ANDREW

SIR ANDREW

For the love of God, a surgeon! Send one presently to Sir Toby.

OLIVIA

What's the matter?

SIR ANDREW

He has broke my head across and has given Sir Toby a bloody coxcomb too: for the love of God, your help! I had rather than forty pound I were at home.

OLIVIA

Who has done this, Sir Andrew?

SIR ANDREW

The count's gentleman, one Cesario: we took him for a coward, but he's the very devil incardinate.

DUKE ORSINO

My gentleman, Cesario?

SIR ANDREW

'Od's lifelings, here he is! You broke my head for nothing; and that that I did, I was set on to do't by Sir Toby.

VIOLA

Why do you speak to me? I never hurt you:
You drew your sword upon me without cause;
But I bespoke you fair, and hurt you not.

SIR ANDREW

If a bloody coxcomb be a hurt, you have hurt me: I think you set nothing by a bloody coxcomb.

Enter SIR TOBY BELCH *and* CLOWN

Here comes Sir Toby halting; you shall hear more: but if he had not been in drink, he would have tickled you othergates than he did.

DUKE ORSINO

How now, gentleman! How is't with you?

SIR TOBY BELCH

That's all one: has hurt me, and there's the end on't. Sot, didst see Dick surgeon, sot?

CLOWN

O, he's drunk, Sir Toby, an hour agone; his eyes were set at eight i' the morning.

SIR TOBY BELCH

Then he's a rogue, and a passy measures panyn: I hate a drunken rogue.

OLIVIA

Away with him! Who hath made this havoc with them?

SIR ANDREW

I'll help you, Sir Toby, because we'll be dressed together.

SIR TOBY BELCH

Will you help? An ass-head and a coxcomb and a knave, a thin-faced knave, a gull!

OLIVIA

Get him to bed, and let his hurt be look'd to.

Exeunt CLOWN, FABIAN,
SIR TOBY BELCH, *and* SIR ANDREW
Enter SEBASTIAN

SEBASTIAN

I am sorry, madam, I have hurt your kinsman:
But, had it been the brother of my blood,
I must have done no less with wit and safety.
You throw a strange regard upon me, and by that
I do perceive it hath offended you:
Pardon me, sweet one, even for the vows
We made each other but so late ago.

DUKE ORSINO

One face, one voice, one habit, and two persons,
A natural perspective, that is and is not!

SEBASTIAN

Antonio, O my dear Antonio!
How have the hours rack'd and tortured me,
Since I have lost thee!

ANTONIO

Sebastian are you?

SEBASTIAN

Fear'st thou that, Antonio?

ANTONIO

How have you made division of yourself?

An apple, cleft in two, is not more twin
Than these two creatures. Which is Sebastian?

OLIVIA

Most wonderful!

SEBASTIAN

Do I stand there? I never had a brother;
Nor can there be that deity in my nature,
Of here and every where. I had a sister,
Whom the blind waves and surges have devour'd.
Of charity, what kin are you to me?
What countryman? What name? What parentage?

VIOLA

Of Messaline: Sebastian was my father;
Such a Sebastian was my brother too,
So went he suited to his watery tomb:
If spirits can assume both form and suit
You come to fright us.

SEBASTIAN

A spirit I am indeed;
But am in that dimension grossly clad
Which from the womb I did participate.
Were you a woman, as the rest goes even,
I should my tears let fall upon your cheek,
And say 'Thrice-welcome, drowned Viola!'

VIOLA

My father had a mole upon his brow.

SEBASTIAN

And so had mine.

VIOLA

And died that day when Viola from her birth
Had number'd thirteen years.

SEBASTIAN

O, that record is lively in my soul!
He finished indeed his mortal act
That day that made my sister thirteen years.

VIOLA

If nothing lets to make us happy both

But this my masculine usurp'd attire,
Do not embrace me till each circumstance
Of place, time, fortune, do cohere and jump
That I am Viola: which to confirm,
I'll bring you to a captain in this town,
Where lie my maiden weeds; by whose gentle help
I was preserved to serve this noble count.
All the occurrence of my fortune since
Hath been between this lady and this lord.

SEBASTIAN

[*To Olivia*] So comes it, lady, you have been mistook:
But nature to her bias drew in that.
You would have been contracted to a maid;
Nor are you therein, by my life, deceived,
You are betroth'd both to a maid and man.

DUKE ORSINO

Be not amazed; right noble is his blood.
If this be so, as yet the glass seems true,
I shall have share in this most happy wreck.
[*To Viola*] Boy, thou hast said to me a thousand times
Thou never shouldst love woman like to me.

VIOLA

And all those sayings will I overswear;
And those swearings keep as true in soul
As doth that orbed continent the fire
That severs day from night.

DUKE ORSINO

Give me thy hand;
And let me see thee in thy woman's weeds.

VIOLA

The captain that did bring me first on shore
Hath my maid's garments: he upon some action
Is now in durance, at Malvolio's suit,
A gentleman, and follower of my lady's.

OLIVIA

He shall enlarge him: fetch Malvolio hither:
And yet, alas, now I remember me,

They say, poor gentleman, he's much distract.
Re-enter CLOWN *with a letter, and* FABIAN
A most extracting frenzy of mine own
From my remembrance clearly banish'd his.
How does he, sirrah?

CLOWN

Truly, madam, he holds Belzebub at the staves's end as well as a man in his case may do: has here writ a letter to you; I should have given't you to-day morning, but as a madman's epistles are no gospels, so it skills not much when they are delivered.

OLIVIA

Open't, and read it.

CLOWN

Look then to be well edified when the fool delivers the madman. [*Reads*] 'By the Lord, madam,'——

OLIVIA

How now! Art thou mad?

CLOWN

No, madam, I do but read madness: an your ladyship will have it as it ought to be, you must allow *Vox.*

OLIVIA

Prithee, read i' thy right wits.

CLOWN

So I do, madonna; but to read his right wits is to read thus: therefore perpend, my princess, and give ear.

OLIVIA

[*To Fabian*] Read it you, sirrah.

FABIAN

[*Reads*] '*By the Lord, madam, you wrong me, and the world shall know it: though you have put me into darkness and given your drunken cousin rule over me, yet have I the benefit of my senses as well as your ladyship. I have your own letter that induced me to the semblance I put on; with the which I doubt not but to do myself much right, or you much shame. Think of me as you please. I leave my duty a little unthought of and speak out of my injury.*
The Madly-used Malvolio.'

OLIVIA

Did he write this?

CLOWN
    Ay, madam.
DUKE ORSINO
    This savours not much of distraction.
OLIVIA
    See him deliver'd, Fabian; bring him hither.

Exit FABIAN

    My lord so please you, these things furtherthought on,
    To think me as well a sister as a wife,
    One day shall crown the alliance on't, so please you,
    Here at my house and at my proper cost.
DUKE ORSINO
    Madam, I am most apt to embrace your offer.
    [*To Viola*] Your master quits you; and for your service done him,
    So much against the mettle of your sex,
    So far beneath your soft and tender breeding,
    And since you call'd me master for so long,
    Here is my hand: you shall from this time be
    Your master's mistress.
OLIVIA
    A sister! You are she.

Re-enter FABIAN, *with* MALVOLIO

DUKE ORSINO
    Is this the madman?
OLIVIA
    Ay, my lord, this same.
    How now, Malvolio!
MALVOLIO
    Madam, you have done me wrong,
    Notorious wrong.
OLIVIA
    Have I, Malvolio? No.
MALVOLIO
    Lady, you have. Pray you, peruse that letter.
    You must not now deny it is your hand:
    Write from it, if you can, in hand or phrase;
    Or say 'tis not your seal, nor your invention:

You can say none of this: well, grant it then
And tell me, in the modesty of honour,
Why you have given me such clear lights of favour,
Bade me come smiling and cross-garter'd to you,
To put on yellow stockings and to frown
Upon Sir Toby and the lighter people;
And, acting this in an obedient hope,
Why have you suffer'd me to be imprison'd,
Kept in a dark house, visited by the priest,
And made the most notorious geck and gull
That e'er invention play'd on? Tell me why.

OLIVIA

Alas, Malvolio, this is not my writing,
Though, I confess, much like the character
But out of question 'tis Maria's hand.
And now I do bethink me, it was she
First told me thou wast mad; then camest in smiling,
And in such forms which here were presupposed
Upon thee in the letter. Prithee, be content:
This practise hath most shrewdly pass'd upon thee;
But when we know the grounds and authors of it,
Thou shalt be both the plaintiff and the judge
Of thine own cause.

FABIAN

Good madam, hear me speak,
And let no quarrel nor no brawl to come
Taint the condition of this present hour,
Which I have wonder'd at. In hope it shall not,
Most freely I confess, myself and Toby
Set this device against Malvolio here,
Upon some stubborn and uncourteous parts
We had conceived against him: Maria writ
The letter at Sir Toby's great importance;
In recompense whereof he hath married her.
How with a sportful malice it was follow'd,
May rather pluck on laughter than revenge;

If that the injuries be justly weigh'd
That have on both sides pass'd.

OLIVIA

Alas, poor fool, how have they baffled thee!

CLOWN

Why, 'some are born great, some achieve greatness, and some have greatness thrown upon them.' I was one, sir, in this interlude; one Sir Topas, sir; but that's all one. 'By the Lord, fool, I am not mad.' But do you remember? 'Madam, why laugh you at such a barren rascal? An you smile not, he's gagged:' and thus the whirligig of time brings in his revenges.

MALVOLIO

I'll be revenged on the whole pack of you.

Exit

OLIVIA

He hath been most notoriously abused.

DUKE ORSINO

Pursue him and entreat him to a peace:
He hath not told us of the captain yet:
When that is known and golden time convents,
A solemn combination shall be made
Of our dear souls. Meantime, sweet sister,
We will not part from hence. Cesario, come;
For so you shall be, while you are a man;
But when in other habits you are seen,
Orsino's mistress and his fancy's queen.

Exeunt all, except CLOWN

CLOWN

[*Sings*] *When that I was and a little tiny boy,*
With hey, ho, the wind and the rain,
A foolish thing was but a toy,
For the rain it raineth every day.

But when I came to man's estate,
With hey, ho, & c.
'Gainst knaves and thieves men shut their gate,
For the rain, & c.

But when I came, alas! To wive,
With hey, ho, & c.
By swaggering could I never thrive,
For the rain, & c.

But when I came unto my beds,
With hey, ho, & c.
With toss-pots still had drunken heads,
For the rain, & c.
A great while ago the world begun,
With hey, ho, & c.
But that's all one, our play is done,
And we'll strive to please you every day.

Exit

As You Like It

"All the world's a stage,
And all the men and women merely players"

Characters of the Play

DUKE, living in exile
FREDERICK, his Brother, Usurper of his Dominions
AMIENS } Lords attending upon the
JAQUES } banished Duke
LE BEAU, a Courtier, attending upon Frederick
CHARLES, a Wrestler to Frederick
OLIVER }
JAQUES } Sons of Sir Rowland de Boys
ORLANDO }
ADAM }
DENNIS } Servants to Oliver
TOUCHSTONE, the court jester
SIR OLIVER MARTEXT, a Vicar
CORIN }
SILVIUS } Shepherds
WILLIAM, a Country Fellow, in love with Audrey
A person representing Hymen
ROSALIND, Daughter to the banished Duke
CELIA, Daughter to Frederick
PHEBE, a Shepherdess
AUDREY, a Country Wench
Lords, Pages, Foresters, and Attendants

SCENE:
OLIVER'S Orchard near his House;
the Usurper's Court; and the Forest of Arden

ACT

I

SCENE I.
ORCHARD OF OLIVER'S HOUSE.

Enter ORLANDO *and* ADAM

ORLANDO

As I remember, Adam, it was upon this fashion bequeathed me by will but poor a thousand crowns, and, as thou sayest, charged my brother, on his blessing, to breed me well; and there begins my sadness. My brother Jaques he keeps at school, and report speaks goldenly of his profit. For my part, he keeps me rustically at home, or, to speak more properly, stays me here at home unkept; for call you that keeping for a gentleman of my birth, that differs not from the stalling of an ox? His horses are bred better; for, besides that they are fair with their feeding, they are taught their manage, and to that end riders dearly hired; but I, his brother, gain nothing under him but growth; for the which his animals on his dunghills are as much bound to him as I. Besides this nothing that he so plentifully gives me, the something that nature gave me his countenance seems to take from me. He lets me feed with his hinds, bars me the place of a brother, and, as much as in him lies, mines my gentility with my education. This is it, Adam, that grieves me; and the spirit of my father, which I think is within me, begins to mutiny against this servitude. I will no longer endure it, though yet I know no wise remedy how to avoid it.

Enter OLIVER

ADAM

Yonder comes my master, your brother.

ORLANDO

Go apart, Adam, and thou shalt hear how he will shake me up.
[*ADAM retires*]

OLIVER

Now, sir! what make you here?

ORLANDO

Nothing; I am not taught to make any thing.

OLIVER

What mar you then, sir?

ORLANDO

Marry, sir, I am helping you to mar that which God made, a poor unworthy brother of yours, with idleness.

OLIVER

Marry, sir, be better employed, and be naught awhile.

ORLANDO

Shall I keep your hogs and eat husks with them? What prodigal portion have I spent, that I should come to such penury?

OLIVER

Know you where your are, sir?

ORLANDO

O, sir, very well; here in your orchard.

OLIVER

Know you before whom, sir?

ORLANDO

Ay, better than him I am before knows me. I know you are my eldest brother; and, in the gentle condition of blood, you should so know me. The courtesy of nations allows you my better, in that you are the first-born; but the same tradition takes not away my blood, were there twenty brothers betwixt us. I have as much of my father in me as you; albeit, I confess, your coming before me is nearer to his reverence.

OLIVER

What, boy! [*Strikes him*]

ORLANDO

Come, come, elder brother, you are too young in this.

OLIVER

Wilt thou lay hands on me, villain?

ORLANDO

I am no villain; I am the youngest son of Sir Rowland de Boys; he was my father, and he is thrice a villain that says such a father begot villains. Wert thou not my brother, I would not take this hand from thy throat till this other had pulled out thy tongue for saying so. Thou hast railed on thyself.

ADAM

Sweet masters, be patient; for your father's remembrance, be at accord.

OLIVER

Let me go, I say.

ORLANDO

I will not, till I please; you shall hear me. My father charged you in his will to give me good education: you have trained me like a peasant, obscuring and hiding from me all gentleman-like qualities. The spirit of my father grows strong in me, and I will no longer endure it; therefore allow me such exercises as may become a gentleman, or give me the poor allottery my father left me by testament; with that I will go buy my fortunes.

OLIVER

And what wilt thou do? Beg, when that is spent? Well, sir, get you in. I will not long be troubled with you; you shall have some part of your will. I pray you, leave me.

ORLANDO

I will no further offend you than becomes me for my good.

OLIVER

Get you with him, you old dog.

ADAM

Is 'old dog' my reward? Most true, I have lost my teeth in your service. God be with my old master! He would not have spoke such a word.

Exeunt ORLANDO *and* ADAM

OLIVER

Is it even so? Begin you to grow upon me? I will physic your rankness, and yet give no thousand crowns neither. Holla, Dennis!

Enter DENNIS

DENNIS

Calls your worship?

OLIVER

Was not Charles, the Duke's wrestler, here to speak with me?

DENNIS

So please you, he is here at the door and importunes access to you.

OLIVER

Call him in.

Exit DENNIS

'Twill be a good way; and to-morrow the wrestling is.

Enter CHARLES

CHARLES

Good morrow to your worship.

OLIVER

Good Monsieur Charles, what's the new news at the new court?

CHARLES

There's no news at the court, sir, but the old news; that is, the old Duke is banished by his younger brother the new Duke; and three or four loving lords have put themselves into voluntary exile with him, whose lands and revenues enrich the new Duke; therefore he gives them good leave to wander.

OLIVER

Can you tell if Rosalind, the Duke's daughter, be banished with her father?

CHARLES

O, no; for the Duke's daughter, her cousin, so loves her, being ever from their cradles bred together, that she would have followed her exile, or have died to stay behind her. She is at the court, and no less beloved of her uncle than his own daughter; and never two ladies loved as they do.

OLIVER

Where will the old Duke live?

CHARLES

They say he is already in the Forest of Arden, and a many merry men with him; and there they live like the old Robin Hood of England. They say many young gentlemen flock to him every day, and fleet the time carelessly, as they did in the golden world.

OLIVER

What, you wrestle to-morrow before the new Duke?

CHARLES

Marry, do I, sir; and I came to acquaint you with a matter. I am given, sir, secretly to understand that your younger brother Orlando hath a disposition to come in disguised against me to try a fall. To-morrow, sir, I wrestle for my credit; and he that escapes me without some broken limb shall acquit him well. Your brother is but young and tender; and, for your love, I would be loath to foil him, as I must, for my own honour, if he come in; therefore, out of my love to you, I came hither to acquaint you withal, that either you might stay him from his intendment or brook such disgrace well as he shall run into, in that it is a thing of his own search and altogether against my will.

OLIVER

Charles, I thank thee for thy love to me, which thou shalt find I will most kindly requite. I had myself notice of my brother's purpose herein and have by underhand means laboured to dissuade him from it, but he is resolute. I'll tell thee, Charles, it is the stubbornest young fellow of France, full of ambition, an envious emulator of every man's good parts, a secret and villainous contriver against me his natural brother. Therefore use thy discretion: I had as lief thou didst break his neck as his finger. And thou wert best look to't; for if thou dost him any slight disgrace or if he do not mightily grace himself on thee, he will practise against thee by poison, entrap thee by some treacherous device and never leave thee till he hath ta'en thy life by some indirect means or other; for, I assure thee, and almost with tears

I speak it, there is not one so young and so villainous this day living. I speak but brotherly of him; but should I anatomize him to thee as he is, I must blush and weep and thou must look pale and wonder.

CHARLES

I am heartily glad I came hither to you. If he come to-morrow, I'll give him his payment. If ever he go alone again, I'll never wrestle for prize more. And so God keep your worship!

OLIVER

Farewell, good Charles.

Exit CHARLES

Now will I stir this gamester. I hope I shall see an end of him; for my soul, yet I know not why, hates nothing more than he. Yet he's gentle, never schooled and yet learned, full of noble device, of all sorts enchantingly beloved, and indeed so much in the heart of the world, and especially of my own people, who best know him, that I am altogether misprised. But it shall not be so long; this wrestler shall clear all. Nothing remains but that I kindle the boy thither; which now I'll go about.

Exit

SCENE II.
LAWN BEFORE THE DUKE'S PALACE.

Enter CELIA *and* ROSALIND

CELIA

I pray thee, Rosalind, sweet my coz, be merry.

ROSALIND

Dear Celia, I show more mirth than I am mistress of; and would you yet I were merrier? Unless you could teach me to forget a banished father, you must not learn me how to remember any extraordinary pleasure.

CELIA

Herein I see thou lovest me not with the full weight that I love thee. If my uncle, thy banished father, had banished thy uncle, the Duke my father, so thou hadst been still with me, I could have taught my love to take thy father for mine; so wouldst thou, if the truth of thy love to me were so righteously tempered as mine is to thee.

ROSALIND

Well, I will forget the condition of my estate, to rejoice in yours.

CELIA

You know my father hath no child but I, nor none is like to have; and, truly, when he dies, thou shalt be his heir, for what he hath taken away from thy father perforce, I will render thee again in affection; by mine honour, I will; and when I break that oath, let me turn monster; therefore, my sweet Rose, my dear Rose, be merry.

ROSALIND

From henceforth I will, coz, and devise sports. Let me see; what think you of falling in love?

CELIA

Marry, I prithee, do, to make sport withal; but love no man in good earnest; nor no further in sport neither than with safety of a pure blush thou mayst in honour come off again.

ROSALIND

What shall be our sport, then?

CELIA

Let us sit and mock the good housewife Fortune from her wheel, that her gifts may henceforth be bestowed equally.

ROSALIND

I would we could do so, for her benefits are mightily misplaced, and the bountiful blind woman doth most mistake in her gifts to women.

CELIA

'Tis true; for those that she makes fair she scarce makes honest, and those that she makes honest she makes very ill-favouredly.

ROSALIND

Nay, now thou goest from Fortune's office to Nature's: Fortune reigns in gifts of the world, not in the lineaments of Nature.

Enter TOUCHSTONE

CELIA

No? When Nature hath made a fair creature, may she not by Fortune fall into the fire? Though Nature hath given us wit to flout at Fortune, hath not Fortune sent in this fool to cut off the argument?

ROSALIND

Indeed, there is Fortune too hard for Nature, when Fortune makes Nature's natural the cutter-off of Nature's wit.

CELIA

Peradventure this is not Fortune's work neither, but Nature's; who perceiveth our natural wits too dull to reason of such goddesses and hath sent this natural for our whetstone; for always the dullness of the fool is the whetstone of the wits. How now, wit! Whither wander you?

TOUCHSTONE

Mistress, you must come away to your father.

CELIA

Were you made the messenger?

TOUCHSTONE

No, by mine honour, but I was bid to come for you.

ROSALIND

Where learned you that oath, fool?

TOUCHSTONE

Of a certain knight that swore by his honour they were good pancakes and swore by his honour the mustard was naught. Now I'll stand to it, the pancakes were naught and the mustard was good, and yet was not the knight forsworn.

CELIA

How prove you that, in the great heap of your knowledge?

ROSALIND

Ay, marry, now unmuzzle your wisdom.

TOUCHSTONE

Stand you both forth now: stroke your chins, and swear by your beards that I am a knave.

CELIA

By our beards, if we had them, thou art.

TOUCHSTONE

By my knavery, if I had it, then I were; but if you swear by that that is not, you are not forsworn; no more was this knight swearing by his honour, for he never had any; or if he had, he had sworn it away before ever he saw those pancakes or that mustard.

CELIA

Prithee, who is't that thou meanest?

TOUCHSTONE

One that old Frederick, your father, loves.

CELIA

My father's love is enough to honour him. Enough! Speak no more of him; you'll be whipped for taxation one of these days.

TOUCHSTONE

The more pity, that fools may not speak wisely what wise men do foolishly.

CELIA

By my troth, thou sayest true; for since the little wit that fools have was silenced, the little foolery that wise men have makes a great show. Here comes Monsieur Le Beau.

ROSALIND

With his mouth full of news.

CELIA

Which he will put on us, as pigeons feed their young.

ROSALIND

Then shall we be news-crammed.

CELIA

All the better; we shall be the more marketable.

Enter LE BEAU

Bon jour, Monsieur Le Beau. What's the news?

LE BEAU

Fair princess, you have lost much good sport.

CELIA

Sport! of what colour?

LE BEAU

What colour, madam? How shall I answer you?

ROSALIND

As wit and fortune will.

TOUCHSTONE

Or as the Destinies decree.

CELIA

Well said; that was laid on with a trowel.

TOUCHSTONE

Nay, if I keep not my rank—

ROSALIND

Thou losest thy old smell.

LE BEAU

You amaze me, ladies. I would have told you of good wrestling, which you have lost the sight of.

ROSALIND

You tell us the manner of the wrestling.

LE BEAU

I will tell you the beginning; and, if it please your ladyships, you may see the end; for the best is yet to do; and here, where you are, they are coming to perform it.

CELIA

Well, the beginning, that is dead and buried.

LE BEAU

There comes an old man and his three sons—

CELIA

I could match this beginning with an old tale.

LE BEAU

Three proper young men, of excellent growth and presence.

ROSALIND

With bills on their necks, 'Be it known unto all men by these presents.'

LE BEAU

The eldest of the three wrestled with Charles, the Duke's wrestler; which Charles in a moment threw him and broke three of his ribs, that there is little hope of life in him. So he served the second, and so the third. Yonder they lie; the poor old man, their father, making such pitiful dole over them that all the beholders take his part with weeping.

ROSALIND

Alas!

TOUCHSTONE

But what is the sport, monsieur, that the ladies have lost?

LE BEAU

    Why, this that I speak of.

TOUCHSTONE

    Thus men may grow wiser every day. It is the first time that ever
    I heard breaking of ribs was sport for ladies.

CELIA

    Or I, I promise thee.

ROSALIND

    But is there any else longs to see this broken music in his sides?
    Is there yet another dotes upon rib-breaking? Shall we see this
    wrestling, cousin?

LE BEAU

    You must, if you stay here; for here is the place appointed for the
    wrestling, and they are ready to perform it.

CELIA

    Yonder, sure, they are coming. Let us now stay and see it.

          Flourish. Enter DUKE FREDERICK, *Lords,*
          ORLANDO, CHARLES, *and Attendants*

DUKE FREDERICK

    Come on; since the youth will not be entreated, his own peril on
    his forwardness.

ROSALIND

    Is yonder the man?

LE BEAU

    Even he, madam.

CELIA

    Alas, he is too young! yet he looks successfully.

DUKE FREDERICK

    How now, daughter and cousin! Are you crept hither to see the
    wrestling?

ROSALIND

    Ay, my liege, so please you give us leave.

DUKE FREDERICK

    You will take little delight in it, I can tell you; there is such
    odds in the man. In pity of the challenger's youth I would fain
    dissuade him, but he will not be entreated. Speak to him, ladies;
    see if you can move him.

CELIA

Call him hither, good Monsieur Le Beau.

DUKE FREDERICK

Do so; I'll not be by.

DUKE FREDERICK goes apart

LE BEAU

Monsieur the challenger, the princesses call for you.

ORLANDO

I attend them with all respect and duty.

ROSALIND

Young man, have you challenged Charles the wrestler?

ORLANDO

No, fair princess; he is the general challenger. I come but in, as others do, to try with him the strength of my youth.

CELIA

Young gentleman, your spirits are too bold for your years. You have seen cruel proof of this man's strength; if you saw yourself with your eyes or knew yourself with your judgment, the fear of your adventure would counsel you to a more equal enterprise. We pray you, for your own sake, to embrace your own safety and give over this attempt.

ROSALIND

Do, young sir; your reputation shall not therefore be misprised: we will make it our suit to the Duke that the wrestling might not go forward.

ORLANDO

I beseech you, punish me not with your hard thoughts; wherein I confess me much guilty, to deny so fair and excellent ladies any thing. But let your fair eyes and gentle wishes go with me to my trial; wherein if I be foiled, there is but one shamed that was never gracious; if killed, but one dead that is willing to be so. I shall do my friends no wrong, for I have none to lament me, the world no injury, for in it I have nothing; only in the world I fill up a place, which may be better supplied when I have made it empty.

ROSALIND

The little strength that I have, I would it were with you.

CELIA

And mine, to eke out hers.

ROSALIND

Fare you well. Pray heaven I be deceived in you!

CELIA

Your heart's desires be with you!

CHARLES

Come, where is this young gallant that is so desirous to lie with his mother earth?

ORLANDO

Ready, sir; but his will hath in it a more modest working.

DUKE FREDERICK

You shall try but one fall.

CHARLES

No, I warrant your grace, you shall not entreat him to a second, that have so mightily persuaded him from a first.

ORLANDO

An you mean to mock me after, you should not have mocked me before; but come your ways.

ROSALIND

Now Hercules be thy speed, young man!

CELIA

I would I were invisible, to catch the strong fellow by the leg.

They wrestle

ROSALIND

O excellent young man!

CELIA

If I had a thunderbolt in mine eye, I can tell who should down.

Shout. CHARLES is thrown

DUKE FREDERICK

No more, no more.

ORLANDO

Yes, I beseech your grace; I am not yet well breathed.

DUKE FREDERICK

How dost thou, Charles?

LE BEAU

He cannot speak, my lord.

DUKE FREDERICK

Bear him away. What is thy name, young man?

ORLANDO

Orlando, my liege; the youngest son of Sir Rowland de Boys.

DUKE FREDERICK

I would thou hadst been son to some man else.
The world esteem'd thy father honourable,
But I did find him still mine enemy.
Thou shouldst have better pleased me with this deed,
Hadst thou descended from another house.
But fare thee well; thou art a gallant youth;
I would thou hadst told me of another father.

Exeunt DUKE FREDERICK,
train, and LE BEAU

CELIA

Were I my father, coz, would I do this?

ORLANDO

I am more proud to be Sir Rowland's son,
His youngest son; and would not change that calling,
To be adopted heir to Frederick.

ROSALIND

My father loved Sir Rowland as his soul,
And all the world was of my father's mind;
Had I before known this young man his son,
I should have given him tears unto entreaties,
Ere he should thus have ventured.

CELIA

Gentle cousin,
Let us go thank him and encourage him;
My father's rough and envious disposition
Sticks me at heart. Sir, you have well deserved;
If you do keep your promises in love
But justly, as you have exceeded all promise,
Your mistress shall be happy.

ROSALIND

Gentleman,
Giving him a chain from her neck

Wear this for me, one out of suits with fortune,
That could give more, but that her hand lacks means.
Shall we go, coz?

CELIA

Ay. Fare you well, fair gentleman.

ORLANDO

Can I not say, I thank you? My better parts
Are all thrown down, and that which here stands up
Is but a quintain, a mere lifeless block.

ROSALIND

He calls us back. My pride fell with my fortunes;
I'll ask him what he would. Did you call, sir?
Sir, you have wrestled well and overthrown
More than your enemies.

CELIA

Will you go, coz?

ROSALIND

Have with you. Fare you well.

Exeunt ROSALIND *and* CELIA

ORLANDO

What passion hangs these weights upon my tongue?
I cannot speak to her, yet she urged conference.
O poor Orlando, thou art overthrown!
Or Charles or something weaker masters thee.

Re-enter LE BEAU

LE BEAU

Good sir, I do in friendship counsel you
To leave this place. Albeit you have deserved
High commendation, true applause and love,
Yet such is now the Duke's condition
That he misconstrues all that you have done.
The Duke is humorous; what he is indeed,
More suits you to conceive than I to speak of.

ORLANDO

I thank you, sir; and, pray you, tell me this:
Which of the two was daughter of the Duke
That here was at the wrestling?

LE BEAU
Neither his daughter, if we judge by manners;
But yet indeed the lesser is his daughter
The other is daughter to the banish'd Duke,
And here detain'd by her usurping uncle,
To keep his daughter company; whose loves
Are dearer than the natural bond of sisters.
But I can tell you that of late this Duke
Hath ta'en displeasure 'gainst his gentle niece,
Grounded upon no other argument
But that the people praise her for her virtues
And pity her for her good father's sake;
And, on my life, his malice 'gainst the lady
Will suddenly break forth. Sir, fare you well.
Hereafter, in a better world than this,
I shall desire more love and knowledge of you.
ORLANDO
I rest much bounden to you; fare you well.

Exit LE BEAU

Thus must I from the smoke into the smother;
From tyrant Duke unto a tyrant brother.
But heavenly Rosalind!

Exit

SCENE III.
A ROOM IN THE PALACE.

Enter CELIA *and* ROSALIND

CELIA
Why, cousin! why, Rosalind! Cupid have mercy! Not a word?
ROSALIND
Not one to throw at a dog.
CELIA
No, thy words are too precious to be cast away upon curs; throw
some of them at me; come, lame me with reasons.

ROSALIND

Then there were two cousins laid up; when the one should be lamed with reasons and the other mad without any.

CELIA

But is all this for your father?

ROSALIND

No, some of it is for my child's father. O, how full of briers is this working-day world!

CELIA

They are but burs, cousin, thrown upon thee in holiday foolery; if we walk not in the trodden paths our very petticoats will catch them.

ROSALIND

I could shake them off my coat: these burs are in my heart.

CELIA

Hem them away.

ROSALIND

I would try, if I could cry 'hem' and have him.

CELIA

Come, come, wrestle with thy affections.

ROSALIND

O, they take the part of a better wrestler than myself!

CELIA

O, a good wish upon you! you will try in time, in despite of a fall. But, turning these jests out of service, let us talk in good earnest. Is it possible, on such a sudden, you should fall into so strong a liking with old Sir Rowland's youngest son?

ROSALIND

The Duke my father loved his father dearly.

CELIA

Doth it therefore ensue that you should love his son dearly? By this kind of chase, I should hate him, for my father hated his father dearly; yet I hate not Orlando.

ROSALIND

No, faith, hate him not, for my sake.

CELIA

Why should I not? Doth he not deserve well?

ROSALIND

Let me love him for that, and do you love him because I do.
Look, here comes the Duke.

CELIA

With his eyes full of anger.

Enter DUKE FREDERICK, *with Lords*

DUKE FREDERICK

Mistress, dispatch you with your safest haste
And get you from our court.

ROSALIND

Me, uncle?

DUKE FREDERICK

You, cousin
Within these ten days if that thou be'st found
So near our public court as twenty miles,
Thou diest for it.

ROSALIND

I do beseech your grace,
Let me the knowledge of my fault bear with me.
If with myself I hold intelligence
Or have acquaintance with mine own desires,
If that I do not dream or be not frantic—
As I do trust I am not—then, dear uncle,
Never so much as in a thought unborn
Did I offend your highness.

DUKE FREDERICK

Thus do all traitors;
If their purgation did consist in words,
They are as innocent as grace itself.
Let it suffice thee that I trust thee not.

ROSALIND

Yet your mistrust cannot make me a traitor.
Tell me whereon the likelihood depends.

DUKE FREDERICK

Thou art thy father's daughter; there's enough.

ROSALIND

So was I when your highness took his dukedom;

So was I when your highness banish'd him.
Treason is not inherited, my lord;
Or, if we did derive it from our friends,
What's that to me? My father was no traitor.
Then, good my liege, mistake me not so much
To think my poverty is treacherous.

CELIA

Dear sovereign, hear me speak.

DUKE FREDERICK

Ay, Celia; we stay'd her for your sake,
Else had she with her father ranged along.

CELIA

I did not then entreat to have her stay;
It was your pleasure and your own remorse;
I was too young that time to value her;
But now I know her. If she be a traitor,
Why so am I; we still have slept together,
Rose at an instant, learn'd, play'd, eat together,
And wheresoever we went, like Juno's swans,
Still we went coupled and inseparable.

DUKE FREDERICK

She is too subtle for thee; and her smoothness,
Her very silence and her patience
Speak to the people, and they pity her.
Thou art a fool. She robs thee of thy name;
And thou wilt show more bright and seem more virtuous
When she is gone. Then open not thy lips.
Firm and irrevocable is my doom
Which I have pass'd upon her; she is banish'd.

CELIA

Pronounce that sentence then on me, my liege;
I cannot live out of her company.

DUKE FREDERICK

You are a fool. You, niece, provide yourself.
If you outstay the time, upon mine honour,
And in the greatness of my word, you die.

Exeunt DUKE FREDERICK *and Lords*

CELIA

 O my poor Rosalind, whither wilt thou go?
 Wilt thou change fathers? I will give thee mine.
 I charge thee, be not thou more grieved than I am.

ROSALIND

 I have more cause.

CELIA

 Thou hast not, cousin;
 Prithee be cheerful. Know'st thou not, the Duke
 Hath banish'd me, his daughter?

ROSALIND

 That he hath not.

CELIA

 No, hath not? Rosalind lacks then the love
 Which teacheth thee that thou and I am one.
 Shall we be sunder'd? Shall we part, sweet girl?
 No; let my father seek another heir.
 Therefore devise with me how we may fly,
 Whither to go and what to bear with us;
 And do not seek to take your change upon you,
 To bear your griefs yourself and leave me out;
 For, by this heaven, now at our sorrows pale,
 Say what thou canst, I'll go along with thee.

ROSALIND

 Why, whither shall we go?

CELIA

 To seek my uncle in the Forest of Arden.

ROSALIND

 Alas, what danger will it be to us,
 Maids as we are, to travel forth so far!
 Beauty provoketh thieves sooner than gold.

CELIA

 I'll put myself in poor and mean attire
 And with a kind of umber smirch my face;
 The like do you; so shall we pass along
 And never stir assailants.

ROSALIND

    Were it not better,
    Because that I am more than common tall,
    That I did suit me all points like a man?
    A gallant curtle-axe upon my thigh,
    A boar-spear in my hand; and—in my heart
    Lie there what hidden woman's fear there will—
    We'll have a swashing and a martial outside,
    As many other mannish cowards have
    That do outface it with their semblances.

CELIA

    What shall I call thee when thou art a man?

ROSALIND

    I'll have no worse a name than Jove's own page;
    And therefore look you call me Ganymede.
    But what will you be call'd?

CELIA

    Something that hath a reference to my state
    No longer Celia, but Aliena.

ROSALIND

    But, cousin, what if we assay'd to steal
    The clownish fool out of your father's court?
    Would he not be a comfort to our travel?

CELIA

    He'll go along o'er the wide world with me;
    Leave me alone to woo him. Let's away,
    And get our jewels and our wealth together,
    Devise the fittest time and safest way
    To hide us from pursuit that will be made
    After my flight. Now go we in content
    To liberty and not to banishment.

Exeunt

ACT

II

SCENE I.
THE FOREST OF ARDEN.

Enter Duke Senior, Amiens,
and two or three Lords, like foresters

Duke Senior

    Now, my co-mates and brothers in exile,
    Hath not old custom made this life more sweet
    Than that of painted pomp? Are not these woods
    More free from peril than the envious court?
    Here feel we but the penalty of Adam,
    The seasons' difference, as the icy fang
    And churlish chiding of the winter's wind,
    Which, when it bites and blows upon my body,
    Even till I shrink with cold, I smile and say
    'This is no flattery; these are counsellors
    That feelingly persuade me what I am.'
    Sweet are the uses of adversity,
    Which, like the toad, ugly and venomous,
    Wears yet a precious jewel in his head;
    And this our life exempt from public haunt

Finds tongues in trees, books in the running brooks,
Sermons in stones and good in every thing.
I would not change it.

AMIENS

Happy is your grace,
That can translate the stubbornness of fortune
Into so quiet and so sweet a style.

DUKE SENIOR

Come, shall we go and kill us venison?
And yet it irks me the poor dappled fools,
Being native burghers of this desert city,
Should in their own confines with forked heads
Have their round haunches gored.

FIRST LORD

Indeed, my lord,
The melancholy Jaques grieves at that,
And, in that kind, swears you do more usurp
Than doth your brother that hath banish'd you.
To-day my Lord of Amiens and myself
Did steal behind him as he lay along
Under an oak whose antique root peeps out
Upon the brook that brawls along this wood!
To the which place a poor sequester'd stag,
That from the hunter's aim had ta'en a hurt,
Did come to languish, and indeed, my lord,
The wretched animal heaved forth such groans
That their discharge did stretch his leathern coat
Almost to bursting, and the big round tears
Coursed one another down his innocent nose
In piteous chase; and thus the hairy fool
Much marked of the melancholy Jaques,
Stood on the extremest verge of the swift brook,
Augmenting it with tears.

DUKE SENIOR

But what said Jaques?
Did he not moralize this spectacle?

FIRST LORD
    O, yes, into a thousand similes.
    First, for his weeping into the needless stream;
    'Poor deer,' quoth he, 'thou makest a testament
    As worldlings do, giving thy sum of more
    To that which had too much'. Then, being there alone,
    Left and abandon'd of his velvet friends,
    ''Tis right'; quoth he; 'thus misery doth part
    The flux of company'. Anon a careless herd,
    Full of the pasture, jumps along by him
    And never stays to greet him; 'Ay' quoth Jaques,
    'Sweep on, you fat and greasy citizens;
    'Tis just the fashion. Wherefore do you look
    Upon that poor and broken bankrupt there?'
    Thus most invectively he pierceth through
    The body of the country, city, court,
    Yea, and of this our life, swearing that we
    Are mere usurpers, tyrants and what's worse,
    To fright the animals and to kill them up
    In their assign'd and native dwelling-place.

DUKE SENIOR
    And did you leave him in this contemplation?

SECOND LORD
    We did, my lord, weeping and commenting
    Upon the sobbing deer.

DUKE SENIOR
    Show me the place;
    I love to cope him in these sullen fits,
    For then he's full of matter.

FIRST LORD
    I'll bring you to him straight.

Exeunt

SCENE II.
A ROOM IN THE PALACE.

Enter DUKE FREDERICK, *with Lords*

DUKE FREDERICK

    Can it be possible that no man saw them?

    It cannot be; some villains of my court

    Are of consent and sufferance in this.

FIRST LORD

    I cannot hear of any that did see her.

    The ladies, her attendants of her chamber,

    Saw her abed, and in the morning early

    They found the bed untreasured of their mistress.

SECOND LORD

    My lord, the roynish clown, at whom so oft

    Your grace was wont to laugh, is also missing.

    Hisperia, the princess' gentlewoman,

    Confesses that she secretly o'erheard

    Your daughter and her cousin much commend

    The parts and graces of the wrestler

    That did but lately foil the sinewy Charles;

    And she believes, wherever they are gone,

    That youth is surely in their company.

DUKE FREDERICK

    Send to his brother; fetch that gallant hither;

    If he be absent, bring his brother to me;

    I'll make him find him. Do this suddenly,

    And let not search and inquisition quail

    To bring again these foolish runaways.

Exeunt

SCENE III.
BEFORE OLIVER'S HOUSE.

Enter ORLANDO *and* ADAM, *meeting*

ORLANDO

    Who's there?

ADAM

    What, my young master? O, my gentle master!
    O my sweet master! O you memory
    Of old Sir Rowland! why, what make you here?
    Why are you virtuous? Why do people love you?
    And wherefore are you gentle, strong and valiant?
    Why would you be so fond to overcome
    The bonny prizer of the humorous Duke?
    Your praise is come too swiftly home before you.
    Know you not, master, to some kind of men
    Their graces serve them but as enemies?
    No more do yours. Your virtues, gentle master,
    Are sanctified and holy traitors to you.
    O, what a world is this, when what is comely
    Envenoms him that bears it!

ORLANDO

    Why, what's the matter?

ADAM

    O unhappy youth!
    Come not within these doors; within this roof
    The enemy of all your graces lives.
    Your brother—no, no brother; yet the son—
    Yet not the son, I will not call him son
    Of him I was about to call his father—
    Hath heard your praises, and this night he means
    To burn the lodging where you use to lie
    And you within it. If he fail of that,
    He will have other means to cut you off.
    I overheard him and his practises.
    This is no place; this house is but a butchery;
    Abhor it, fear it, do not enter it.

ORLANDO
    Why, whither, Adam, wouldst thou have me go?
ADAM
    No matter whither, so you come not here.
ORLANDO
    What, wouldst thou have me go and beg my food?
    Or with a base and boisterous sword enforce
    A thievish living on the common road?
    This I must do, or know not what to do;
    Yet this I will not do, do how I can.
    I rather will subject me to the malice
    Of a diverted blood and bloody brother.
ADAM
    But do not so. I have five hundred crowns,
    The thrifty hire I saved under your father,
    Which I did store to be my foster-nurse
    When service should in my old limbs lie lame
    And unregarded age in corners thrown.
    Take that, and He that doth the ravens feed,
    Yea, providently caters for the sparrow,
    Be comfort to my age! Here is the gold;
    And all this I give you. Let me be your servant;
    Though I look old, yet I am strong and lusty;
    For in my youth I never did apply
    Hot and rebellious liquors in my blood,
    Nor did not with unbashful forehead woo
    The means of weakness and debility;
    Therefore my age is as a lusty winter,
    Frosty, but kindly. Let me go with you;
    I'll do the service of a younger man
    In all your business and necessities.
ORLANDO
    O good old man, how well in thee appears
    The constant service of the antique world,
    When service sweat for duty, not for meed!
    Thou art not for the fashion of these times,
    Where none will sweat but for promotion,

And having that, do choke their service up
Even with the having; it is not so with thee.
But, poor old man, thou prunest a rotten tree,
That cannot so much as a blossom yield
In lieu of all thy pains and husbandry
But come thy ways; well go along together,
And ere we have thy youthful wages spent,
We'll light upon some settled low content.

ADAM

Master, go on, and I will follow thee,
To the last gasp, with truth and loyalty.
From seventeen years till now almost fourscore
Here lived I, but now live here no more.
At seventeen years many their fortunes seek;
But at fourscore it is too late a week;
Yet fortune cannot recompense me better
Than to die well and not my master's debtor.

Exeunt

SCENE IV.
THE FOREST OF ARDEN.

Enter ROSALIND *for* GANYMEDE,
CELIA *for* ALIENA, *and* TOUCHSTONE

ROSALIND

O Jupiter, how weary are my spirits!

TOUCHSTONE

I care not for my spirits, if my legs were not weary.

ROSALIND

I could find in my heart to disgrace my man's apparel and to cry
like a woman; but I must comfort the weaker vessel, as doublet
and hose ought to show itself courageous to petticoat; therefore
courage, good Aliena!

CELIA

I pray you, bear with me; I cannot go no further.

TOUCHSTONE

For my part, I had rather bear with you than bear you; yet I

should bear no cross if I did bear you, for I think you have no
money in your purse.

ROSALIND

Well, this is the Forest of Arden.

TOUCHSTONE

Ay, now am I in Arden; the more fool I; when I was at home, I
was in a better place; but travellers must be content.

ROSALIND

Ay, be so, good Touchstone.

Enter CORIN *and* SILVIUS

Look you, who comes here; a young man and an old in solemn
talk.

CORIN

That is the way to make her scorn you still.

SILVIUS

O Corin, that thou knew'st how I do love her!

CORIN

I partly guess; for I have loved ere now.

SILVIUS

No, Corin, being old, thou canst not guess,
Though in thy youth thou wast as true a lover
As ever sigh'd upon a midnight pillow.
But if thy love were ever like to mine—
As sure I think did never man love so—
How many actions most ridiculous
Hast thou been drawn to by thy fantasy?

CORIN

Into a thousand that I have forgotten.

SILVIUS

O, thou didst then ne'er love so heartily!
If thou remember'st not the slightest folly
That ever love did make thee run into,
Thou hast not loved;
Or if thou hast not sat as I do now,
Wearying thy hearer in thy mistress' praise,
Thou hast not loved;
Or if thou hast not broke from company

Abruptly, as my passion now makes me,
Thou hast not loved.
O Phebe, Phebe, Phebe!

Exit SILVIUS

ROSALIND

Alas, poor shepherd! searching of thy wound,
I have by hard adventure found mine own.

TOUCHSTONE

And I mine. I remember, when I was in love I broke my sword
upon a stone and bid him take that for coming a-night to Jane
Smile; and I remember the kissing of her batlet and the cow's
dugs that her pretty chopt hands had milked; and I remember
the wooing of a peascod instead of her, from whom I took two
cods and, giving her them again, said with weeping tears 'Wear
these for my sake.' We that are true lovers run into strange
capers; but as all is mortal in nature, so is all nature in love
mortal in folly.

ROSALIND

Thou speakest wiser than thou art ware of.

TOUCHSTONE

Nay, I shall ne'er be ware of mine own wit till I break my shins
against it.

ROSALIND

Jove, Jove! this shepherd's passion
Is much upon my fashion.

TOUCHSTONE

And mine; but it grows something stale with me.

CELIA

I pray you, one of you question yond man
If he for gold will give us any food;
I faint almost to death.

TOUCHSTONE

Holla, you clown!

ROSALIND

Peace, fool; he's not thy kinsman.

CORIN

Who calls?

TOUCHSTONE

    Your betters, sir.

CORIN

    Else are they very wretched.

ROSALIND

    Peace, I say. Good even to you, friend.

CORIN

    And to you, gentle sir, and to you all.

ROSALIND

    I prithee, shepherd, if that love or gold

    Can in this desert place buy entertainment,

    Bring us where we may rest ourselves and feed.

    Here's a young maid with travel much oppress'd

    And faints for succor.

CORIN

    Fair sir, I pity her

    And wish, for her sake more than for mine own,

    My fortunes were more able to relieve her;

    But I am shepherd to another man

    And do not shear the fleeces that I graze.

    My master is of churlish disposition

    And little recks to find the way to heaven

    By doing deeds of hospitality.

    Besides, his cote, his flocks and bounds of feed

    Are now on sale, and at our sheepcote now,

    By reason of his absence, there is nothing

    That you will feed on; but what is, come see.

    And in my voice most welcome shall you be.

ROSALIND

    What is he that shall buy his flock and pasture?

CORIN

    That young swain that you saw here but erewhile,

    That little cares for buying any thing.

ROSALIND

    I pray thee, if it stand with honesty,

    Buy thou the cottage, pasture and the flock,

    And thou shalt have to pay for it of us.

CELIA

And we will mend thy wages. I like this place.
And willingly could waste my time in it.

CORIN

Assuredly the thing is to be sold.
Go with me; if you like upon report
The soil, the profit and this kind of life,
I will your very faithful feeder be
And buy it with your gold right suddenly.

Exeunt

SCENE V.
THE FOREST.

Enter AMIENS, JAQUES, *and others*
Song

AMIENS

Under the greenwood tree
Who loves to lie with me,
And turn his merry note
Unto the sweet bird's throat,
Come hither, come hither, come hither.
Here shall he see No enemy
But winter and rough weather.

JAQUES

More, more, I prithee, more.

AMIENS

It will make you melancholy, Monsieur Jaques.

JAQUES

I thank it. More, I prithee, more. I can suck melancholy out of a
song, as a weasel sucks eggs. More, I prithee, more.

AMIENS

My voice is ragged; I know I cannot please you.

JAQUES

I do not desire you to please me; I do desire you to sing. Come,
more; another stanzo. Call you 'em stanzos?

AMIENS

What you will, Monsieur Jaques.

JAQUES

Nay, I care not for their names; they owe me nothing. Will you sing?

AMIENS

More at your request than to please myself.

JAQUES

Well then, if ever I thank any man, I'll thank you; but that they call compliment is like the encounter of two dog-apes, and when a man thanks me heartily, methinks I have given him a penny and he renders me the beggarly thanks. Come, sing; and you that will not, hold your tongues.

AMIENS

Well, I'll end the song. Sirs, cover the while; the Duke will drink under this tree. He hath been all this day to look you.

JAQUES

And I have been all this day to avoid him. He is too disputable for my company. I think of as many matters as he, but I give heaven thanks and make no boast of them. Come, warble, come.

Song

All together here

Who doth ambition shun
And loves to live i' the sun,
Seeking the food he eats
And pleased with what he gets,
Come hither, come hither, come hither.
Here shall he see
No enemy
But winter and rough weather.

JAQUES

I'll give you a verse to this note that I made yesterday in despite of my invention.

AMIENS

And I'll sing it.

JAQUES

Thus it goes:—

If it do come to pass
That any man turn ass,
Leaving his wealth and ease,
A stubborn will to please,
Ducdame, ducdame, ducdame;
Here shall he see
Gross fools as he,
An if he will come to me.

AMIENS

What's that 'ducdame'?

JAQUES

'Tis a Greek invocation, to call fools into a circle. I'll go sleep,
if I can; if I cannot, I'll rail against all the first-born of Egypt.

AMIENS

And I'll go seek the Duke; his banquet is prepared.

Exeunt severally

SCENE VI.
THE FOREST.

Enter ORLANDO *and* ADAM

ADAM

Dear master, I can go no further. O, I die for food! Here lie I
down, and measure out my grave. Farewell, kind master.

ORLANDO

Why, how now, Adam! no greater heart in thee? Live a little;
comfort a little; cheer thyself a little. If this uncouth forest yield
any thing savage, I will either be food for it or bring it for food
to thee. Thy conceit is nearer death than thy powers. For my sake
be comfortable; hold death awhile at the arm's end. I will here be
with thee presently; and if I bring thee not something to eat, I
will give thee leave to die; but if thou diest before I come, thou
art a mocker of my labour. Well said! thou lookest cheerly, and
I'll be with thee quickly. Yet thou liest in the bleak air. Come, I
will bear thee to some shelter; and thou shalt not die for lack of a
dinner, if there live any thing in this desert. Cheerly, good Adam!

Exeunt

SCENE VII.
THE FOREST.

A table set out. Enter DUKE SENIOR,
AMIENS, *and Lords like outlaws*

DUKE SENIOR

I think he be transform'd into a beast;

For I can nowhere find him like a man.

FIRST LORD

My lord, he is but even now gone hence;

Here was he merry, hearing of a song.

DUKE SENIOR

If he, compact of jars, grow musical,

We shall have shortly discord in the spheres.

Go, seek him; tell him I would speak with him.

Enter JAQUES

FIRST LORD

He saves my labour by his own approach.

DUKE SENIOR

Why, how now, monsieur! what a life is this,

That your poor friends must woo your company?

What, you look merrily!

JAQUES

A fool, a fool! I met a fool i' the forest,

A motley fool; a miserable world!

As I do live by food, I met a fool

Who laid him down and bask'd him in the sun,

And rail'd on Lady Fortune in good terms,

In good set terms and yet a motley fool.

'Good morrow, fool,' quoth I. 'No, sir,' quoth he,

'Call me not fool till heaven hath sent me fortune.'

And then he drew a dial from his poke,

And, looking on it with lack-lustre eye,

Says very wisely, 'It is ten o'clock;

Thus we may see,' quoth he, 'how the world wags;

'Tis but an hour ago since it was nine,

And after one hour more 'twill be eleven;

And so, from hour to hour, we ripe and ripe,
And then, from hour to hour, we rot and rot;
And thereby hangs a tale.' When I did hear
The motley fool thus moral on the time,
My lungs began to crow like chanticleer,
That fools should be so deep-contemplative,
And I did laugh sans intermission
An hour by his dial. O noble fool!
A worthy fool! Motley's the only wear.

DUKE SENIOR
What fool is this?

JAQUES
O worthy fool! One that hath been a courtier,
And says, if ladies be but young and fair,
They have the gift to know it; and in his brain,
Which is as dry as the remainder biscuit
After a voyage, he hath strange places cramm'd
With observation, the which he vents
In mangled forms. O that I were a fool!
I am ambitious for a motley coat.

DUKE SENIOR
Thou shalt have one.

JAQUES
It is my only suit;
Provided that you weed your better judgments
Of all opinion that grows rank in them
That I am wise. I must have liberty
Withal, as large a charter as the wind,
To blow on whom I please; for so fools have;
And they that are most galled with my folly,
They most must laugh. And why, sir, must they so?
The 'why' is plain as way to parish church:
He that a fool doth very wisely hit
Doth very foolishly, although he smart,
Not to seem senseless of the bob; if not,
The wise man's folly is anatomized
Even by the squandering glances of the fool.

Invest me in my motley; give me leave
To speak my mind, and I will through and through
Cleanse the foul body of the infected world,
If they will patiently receive my medicine.

DUKE SENIOR

Fie on thee! I can tell what thou wouldst do.

JAQUES

What, for a counter, would I do but good?

DUKE SENIOR

Most mischievous foul sin, in chiding sin;
For thou thyself hast been a libertine,
As sensual as the brutish sting itself;
And all the embossed sores and headed evils,
That thou with licence of free foot hast caught,
Wouldst thou disgorge into the general world.

JAQUES

Why, who cries out on pride,
That can therein tax any private party?
Doth it not flow as hugely as the sea,
Till that the weary very means do ebb?
What woman in the city do I name,
When that I say the city-woman bears
The cost of princes on unworthy shoulders?
Who can come in and say that I mean her,
When such a one as she such is her neighbour?
Or what is he of basest function
That says his bravery is not of my cost,
Thinking that I mean him, but therein suits
His folly to the mettle of my speech?
There then; how then? what then? Let me see wherein
My tongue hath wrong'd him: if it do him right,
Then he hath wrong'd himself; if he be free,
Why then my taxing like a wild-goose flies,
Unclaim'd of any man. But who comes here?

            Enter ORLANDO, *with his sword drawn*

ORLANDO

Forbear, and eat no more.

JAQUES

Why, I have eat none yet.

ORLANDO

Nor shalt not, till necessity be served.

JAQUES

Of what kind should this cock come of?

DUKE SENIOR

Art thou thus bolden'd, man, by thy distress,
Or else a rude despiser of good manners,
That in civility thou seem'st so empty?

ORLANDO

You touch'd my vein at first: the thorny point
Of bare distress hath ta'en from me the show
Of smooth civility; yet am I inland bred
And know some nurture. But forbear, I say;
He dies that touches any of this fruit
Till I and my affairs are answered.

JAQUES

An you will not be answered with reason, I must die.

DUKE SENIOR

What would you have? Your gentleness shall force
More than your force move us to gentleness.

ORLANDO

I almost die for food; and let me have it.

DUKE SENIOR

Sit down and feed, and welcome to our table.

ORLANDO

Speak you so gently? Pardon me, I pray you;
I thought that all things had been savage here;
And therefore put I on the countenance
Of stern commandment. But whate'er you are
That in this desert inaccessible,
Under the shade of melancholy boughs,
Lose and neglect the creeping hours of time
If ever you have look'd on better days,
If ever been where bells have knoll'd to church,
If ever sat at any good man's feast,

If ever from your eyelids wiped a tear
And know what 'tis to pity and be pitied,
Let gentleness my strong enforcement be;
In the which hope I blush, and hide my sword.

DUKE SENIOR
True is it that we have seen better days,
And have with holy bell been knoll'd to church
And sat at good men's feasts and wiped our eyes
Of drops that sacred pity hath engender'd;
And therefore sit you down in gentleness
And take upon command what help we have
That to your wanting may be minister'd.

ORLANDO
Then but forbear your food a little while,
Whiles, like a doe, I go to find my fawn
And give it food. There is an old poor man,
Who after me hath many a weary step
Limp'd in pure love; till he be first sufficed,
Oppress'd with two weak evils, age and hunger,
I will not touch a bit.

DUKE SENIOR
Go find him out,
And we will nothing waste till you return.

ORLANDO
I thank ye; and be blest for your good comfort!

Exit

DUKE SENIOR
Thou seest we are not all alone unhappy:
This wide and universal theatre
Presents more woeful pageants than the scene
Wherein we play in.

JAQUES
All the world's a stage,
And all the men and women merely players;
They have their exits and their entrances;
And one man in his time plays many parts,
His acts being seven ages. At first the infant,

Mewling and puking in the nurse's arms.
And then the whining school-boy, with his satchel
And shining morning face, creeping like snail
Unwillingly to school. And then the lover,
Sighing like furnace, with a woeful ballad
Made to his mistress' eyebrow. Then a soldier,
Full of strange oaths and bearded like the pard,
Jealous in honour, sudden and quick in quarrel,
Seeking the bubble reputation
Even in the cannon's mouth. And then the justice,
In fair round belly with good capon lined,
With eyes severe and beard of formal cut,
Full of wise saws and modern instances;
And so he plays his part. The sixth age shifts
Into the lean and slipper'd pantaloon,
With spectacles on nose and pouch on side,
His youthful hose, well saved, a world too wide
For his shrunk shank; and his big manly voice,
Turning again toward childish treble, pipes
And whistles in his sound. Last scene of all,
That ends this strange eventful history,
Is second childishness and mere oblivion,
Sans teeth, sans eyes, sans taste, sans everything.

Re-enter ORLANDO, *with* ADAM

DUKE SENIOR
Welcome. Set down your venerable burthen,
And let him feed.

ORLANDO
I thank you most for him.

ADAM
So had you need;
I scarce can speak to thank you for myself.

DUKE SENIOR
Welcome; fall to. I will not trouble you
As yet, to question you about your fortunes.
Give us some music; and, good cousin, sing.

Song

Blow, blow, thou winter wind.
Thou art not so unkind
As man's ingratitude;
Thy tooth is not so keen,
Because thou art not seen,
Although thy breath be rude.
Heigh-ho! sing, heigh-ho! unto the green holly!
Most friendship is feigning, most loving mere folly.
Then, heigh-ho, the holly!
This life is most jolly.
Freeze, freeze, thou bitter sky,
That dost not bite so nigh
As benefits forgot;
Though thou the waters warp,
Thy sting is not so sharp
As friend remember'd not.
Heigh-ho! sing, etc.

DUKE SENIOR
If that you were the good Sir Rowland's son,
As you have whisper'd faithfully you were,
And as mine eye doth his effigies witness
Most truly limn'd and living in your face,
Be truly welcome hither. I am the Duke
That loved your father. The residue of your fortune,
Go to my cave and tell me. Good old man,
Thou art right welcome as thy master is.
Support him by the arm. Give me your hand,
And let me all your fortunes understand.

Exeunt

ACT

III

SCENE I.
A ROOM IN THE PALACE.

Enter DUKE FREDERICK, *Lords, and* OLIVER

DUKE FREDERICK
    Not see him since? Sir, sir, that cannot be.
    But were I not the better part made mercy,
    I should not seek an absent argument
    Of my revenge, thou present. But look to it:
    Find out thy brother, wheresoe'er he is;
    Seek him with candle; bring him dead or living
    Within this twelvemonth, or turn thou no more
    To seek a living in our territory.
    Thy lands and all things that thou dost call thine
    Worth seizure do we seize into our hands,
    Till thou canst quit thee by thy brothers mouth
    Of what we think against thee.

OLIVER
    O that your highness knew my heart in this!
    I never loved my brother in my life.

DUKE FREDERICK
    More villain thou. Well, push him out of doors;

And let my officers of such a nature
Make an extent upon his house and lands.
Do this expediently and turn him going.

Exeunt

SCENE II.
THE FOREST.

Enter ORLANDO, *with a paper*

ORLANDO

Hang there, my verse, in witness of my love;
And thou, thrice-crowned queen of night, survey
With thy chaste eye, from thy pale sphere above,
Thy huntress' name that my full life doth sway.
O Rosalind! these trees shall be my books
And in their barks my thoughts I'll character;
That every eye which in this forest looks
Shall see thy virtue witness'd every where.
Run, run, Orlando; carve on every tree
The fair, the chaste and unexpressive she.

Exit

Enter CORIN *and* TOUCHSTONE

CORIN

And how like you this shepherd's life, Master Touchstone?

TOUCHSTONE

Truly, shepherd, in respect of itself, it is a good life, but in respect
that it is a shepherd's life, it is naught. In respect that it is solitary,
I like it very well; but in respect that it is private, it is a very vile
life. Now, in respect it is in the fields, it pleaseth me well; but
in respect it is not in the court, it is tedious. As is it a spare life,
look you, it fits my humour well; but as there is no more plenty
in it, it goes much against my stomach. Hast any philosophy in
thee, shepherd?

CORIN

No more but that I know the more one sickens the worse at
ease he is; and that he that wants money, means and content is
without three good friends; that the property of rain is to wet

and fire to burn; that good pasture makes fat sheep, and that a great cause of the night is lack of the sun; that he that hath learned no wit by nature nor art may complain of good breeding or comes of a very dull kindred.

TOUCHSTONE

Such a one is a natural philosopher. Wast ever in court, shepherd?

CORIN

No, truly.

TOUCHSTONE

Then thou art damned.

CORIN

Nay, I hope.

TOUCHSTONE

Truly, thou art damned like an ill-roasted egg, all on one side.

CORIN

For not being at court? Your reason.

TOUCHSTONE

Why, if thou never wast at court, thou never sawest good manners; if thou never sawest good manners, then thy manners must be wicked; and wickedness is sin, and sin is damnation. Thou art in a parlous state, shepherd.

CORIN

Not a whit, Touchstone. Those that are good manners at the court are as ridiculous in the country as the behavior of the country is most mockable at the court. You told me you salute not at the court, but you kiss your hands; that courtesy would be uncleanly, if courtiers were shepherds.

TOUCHSTONE

Instance, briefly; come, instance.

CORIN

Why, we are still handling our ewes, and their fells, you know, are greasy.

TOUCHSTONE

Why, do not your courtier's hands sweat? And is not the grease of a mutton as wholesome as the sweat of a man? Shallow, shallow. A better instance, I say; come.

CORIN

Besides, our hands are hard.

TOUCHSTONE

Your lips will feel them the sooner. Shallow again. A more sounder instance, come.

CORIN

And they are often tarred over with the surgery of our sheep; and would you have us kiss tar? The courtier's hands are perfumed with civet.

TOUCHSTONE

Most shallow man! thou worms-meat, in respect of a good piece of flesh indeed! Learn of the wise, and perpend: civet is of a baser birth than tar, the very uncleanly flux of a cat. Mend the instance, shepherd.

CORIN

You have too courtly a wit for me; I'll rest.

TOUCHSTONE

Wilt thou rest damned? God help thee, shallow man! God make incision in thee! thou art raw.

CORIN

Sir, I am a true labourer: I earn that I eat, get that I wear, owe no man hate, envy no man's happiness, glad of other men's good, content with my harm, and the greatest of my pride is to see my ewes graze and my lambs suck.

TOUCHSTONE

That is another simple sin in you, to bring the ewes and the rams together and to offer to get your living by the copulation of cattle; to be bawd to a bell-wether, and to betray a she-lamb of a twelvemonth to a crooked-pated, old, cuckoldly ram, out of all reasonable match. If thou beest not damned for this, the devil himself will have no shepherds; I cannot see else how thou shouldst scape.

CORIN

Here comes young Master Ganymede, my new mistress's brother.

Enter ROSALIND, *with a paper, reading*

ROSALIND

From the east to western Ind,

No jewel is like Rosalind.
Her worth, being mounted on the wind,
Through all the world bears Rosalind.
All the pictures fairest lined
Are but black to Rosalind.
Let no fair be kept in mind
But the fair of Rosalind.

TOUCHSTONE

I'll rhyme you so eight years together, dinners and suppers and sleeping-hours excepted. It is the right butter-women's rank to market.

ROSALIND

Out, fool!

TOUCHSTONE

For a taste:
If a hart do lack a hind,
Let him seek out Rosalind.
If the cat will after kind,
So be sure will Rosalind.
Winter garments must be lined,
So must slender Rosalind.
They that reap must sheaf and bind;
Then to cart with Rosalind.
Sweetest nut hath sourest rind,
Such a nut is Rosalind.
He that sweetest rose will find
Must find love's prick and Rosalind.
This is the very false gallop of verses; why do you infect yourself with them?

ROSALIND

Peace, you dull fool! I found them on a tree.

TOUCHSTONE

Truly, the tree yields bad fruit.

ROSALIND

I'll graff it with you, and then I shall graff it with a medlar. Then it will be the earliest fruit i' the country; for you'll be rotten ere you be half ripe, and that's the right virtue of the medlar.

TOUCHSTONE
    You have said; but whether wisely or no, let the forest judge.
                Enter CELIA, *with a writing*
ROSALIND
    Peace! Here comes my sister, reading; stand aside.
CELIA
    [*Reads*]
    'Why should this a desert be?
    For it is unpeopled? No;
    Tongues I'll hang on every tree,
    That shall civil sayings show.
    Some, how brief the life of man
    Runs his erring pilgrimage,
    That the stretching of a span
    Buckles in his sum of age;
    Some, of violated vows
    'Twixt the souls of friend and friend;
    But upon the fairest boughs,
    Or at every sentence end,
    Will I Rosalinda write,
    Teaching all that read to know
    The quintessence of every sprite
    Heaven would in little show.
    Therefore Heaven Nature charged
    That one body should be fill'd
    With all graces wide-enlarged.
    Nature presently distill'd
    Helen's cheek, but not her heart,
    Cleopatra's majesty,
    Atalanta's better part,
    Sad Lucretia's modesty.
    Thus Rosalind of many parts
    By heavenly synod was devised,
    Of many faces, eyes and hearts,
    To have the touches dearest prized.
    Heaven would that she these gifts should have,
    And I to live and die her slave.'

ROSALIND

O most gentle pulpiter! What tedious homily of love have you
wearied your parishioners withal, and never cried 'Have patience,
good people!'

CELIA

How now! back, friends! Shepherd, go off a little.
Go with him, sirrah.

TOUCHSTONE

Come, shepherd, let us make an honourable retreat; though not
with bag and baggage, yet with scrip and scrippage.

Exeunt CORIN *and* TOUCHSTONE

CELIA

Didst thou hear these verses?

ROSALIND

O, yes, I heard them all, and more too; for some of them had in
them more feet than the verses would bear.

CELIA

That's no matter; the feet might bear the verses.

ROSALIND

Ay, but the feet were lame and could not bear themselves without
the verse and therefore stood lamely in the verse.

CELIA

But didst thou hear without wondering how thy name should be
hanged and carved upon these trees?

ROSALIND

I was seven of the nine days out of the wonder before you came;
for look here what I found on a palm-tree. I was never so be-
rhymed since Pythagoras' time, that I was an Irish rat, which I
can hardly remember.

CELIA

Trow you who hath done this?

ROSALIND

Is it a man?

CELIA

And a chain, that you once wore, about his neck.
Change you colour?

ROSALIND

I prithee, who?

CELIA

O Lord, Lord! it is a hard matter for friends to meet; but mountains may be removed with earthquakes and so encounter.

ROSALIND

Nay, but who is it?

CELIA

Is it possible?

ROSALIND

Nay, I prithee now with most petitionary vehemence, tell me who it is.

CELIA

O wonderful, wonderful, and most wonderful wonderful! and yet again wonderful, and after that, out of all hooping!

ROSALIND

Good my complexion! dost thou think, though I am caparisoned like a man, I have a doublet and hose in my disposition? One inch of delay more is a South-sea of discovery; I prithee, tell me who is it quickly, and speak apace. I would thou couldst stammer, that thou mightst pour this concealed man out of thy mouth, as wine comes out of a narrow-mouthed bottle, either too much at once, or none at all. I prithee, take the cork out of thy mouth that may drink thy tidings.

CELIA

So you may put a man in your belly.

ROSALIND

Is he of God's making? What manner of man? Is his head worth a hat, or his chin worth a beard?

CELIA

Nay, he hath but a little beard.

ROSALIND

Why, God will send more, if the man will be thankful. Let me stay the growth of his beard, if thou delay me not the knowledge of his chin.

CELIA

It is young Orlando, that tripped up the wrestler's heels and your heart both in an instant.

ROSALIND

Nay, but the devil take mocking!

Speak, sad brow and true maid.

CELIA

I' faith, coz, 'tis he.

ROSALIND

Orlando?

CELIA

Orlando.

ROSALIND

Alas the day! what shall I do with my doublet and hose? What did he when thou sawest him? What said he? How looked he? Wherein went he? What makes him here? Did he ask for me? Where remains he? How parted he with thee? and when shalt thou see him again? Answer me in one word.

CELIA

You must borrow me Gargantua's mouth first; 'tis a word too great for any mouth of this age's size. To say ay and no to these particulars is more than to answer in a catechism.

ROSALIND

But doth he know that I am in this forest and in man's apparel? Looks he as freshly as he did the day he wrestled?

CELIA

It is as easy to count atomies as to resolve the propositions of a lover; but take a taste of my finding him, and relish it with good observance. I found him under a tree, like a dropped acorn.

ROSALIND

It may well be called Jove's tree, when it drops forth such fruit.

CELIA

Give me audience, good madam.

ROSALIND

Proceed.

CELIA

There lay he, stretched along, like a wounded knight.

ROSALIND

Though it be pity to see such a sight, it well becomes the ground.

CELIA

Cry 'holla' to thy tongue, I prithee; it curvets unseasonably. He was furnished like a hunter.

ROSALIND

O, ominous! he comes to kill my heart.

CELIA

I would sing my song without a burden; thou bringest me out of tune.

ROSALIND

Do you not know I am a woman?

When I think, I must speak. Sweet, say on.

CELIA

You bring me out. Soft! comes he not here?

Enter ORLANDO *and* JAQUES

ROSALIND

'Tis he; slink by, and note him.

JAQUES

I thank you for your company; but, good faith, I had as lief have been myself alone.

ORLANDO

And so had I; but yet, for fashion sake, I thank you too for your society.

JAQUES

God be wi' you; let's meet as little as we can.

ORLANDO

I do desire we may be better strangers.

JAQUES

I pray you, mar no more trees with writing love-songs in their barks.

ORLANDO

I pray you, mar no more of my verses with reading them ill-favouredly.

JAQUES

Rosalind is your love's name?

ORLANDO

Yes, just.

JAQUES

I do not like her name.

ORLANDO

There was no thought of pleasing you when she was christened.

JAQUES

What stature is she of?

ORLANDO

Just as high as my heart.

JAQUES

You are full of pretty answers. Have you not been acquainted
with goldsmiths' wives, and conned them out of rings?

ORLANDO

Not so; but I answer you right painted cloth, from whence you
have studied your questions.

JAQUES

You have a nimble wit; I think 'twas made of Atalanta's heels.
Will you sit down with me? and we two will rail against our
mistress the world and all our misery.

ORLANDO

I will chide no breather in the world but myself, against whom
I know most faults.

JAQUES

The worst fault you have is to be in love.

ORLANDO

'Tis a fault I will not change for your best virtue. I am weary of
you.

JAQUES

By my troth, I was seeking for a fool when I found you.

ORLANDO

He is drowned in the brook; look but in, and you shall see him.

JAQUES

There I shall see mine own figure.

ORLANDO

Which I take to be either a fool or a cipher.

JAQUES

I'll tarry no longer with you; farewell, good Signior Love.

ORLANDO

I am glad of your departure; adieu, good Monsieur Melancholy.

Exit JAQUES

ROSALIND

[*Aside to* CELIA] I will speak to him, like a saucy lackey and under that habit play the knave with him. Do you hear, forester?

ORLANDO

Very well; what would you?

ROSALIND

I pray you, what is't o'clock?

ORLANDO

You should ask me what time o' day; there's no clock in the forest.

ROSALIND

Then there is no true lover in the forest; else sighing every minute and groaning every hour would detect the lazy foot of Time as well as a clock.

ORLANDO

And why not the swift foot of Time? Had not that been as proper?

ROSALIND

By no means, sir. Time travels in divers paces with divers persons. I'll tell you who Time ambles withal, who Time trots withal, who Time gallops withal and who he stands still withal.

ORLANDO

I prithee, who doth he trot withal?

ROSALIND

Marry, he trots hard with a young maid between the contract of her marriage and the day it is solemnized; if the interim be but a se'nnight, Time's pace is so hard that it seems the length of seven year.

ORLANDO

Who ambles Time withal?

ROSALIND

With a priest that lacks Latin and a rich man that hath not the gout, for the one sleeps easily because he cannot study, and the other lives merrily because he feels no pain, the one lacking the burden of lean and wasteful learning, the other knowing no burden of heavy tedious penury; these Time ambles withal.

ORLANDO

Who doth he gallop withal?

ROSALIND

With a thief to the gallows, for though he go as softly as foot can fall, he thinks himself too soon there.

ORLANDO

Who stays it still withal?

ROSALIND

With lawyers in the vacation, for they sleep between term and term and then they perceive not how Time moves.

ORLANDO

Where dwell you, pretty youth?

ROSALIND

With this shepherdess, my sister; here in the skirts of the forest, like fringe upon a petticoat.

ORLANDO

Are you native of this place?

ROSALIND

As the cony that you see dwell where she is kindled.

ORLANDO

Your accent is something finer than you could purchase in so removed a dwelling.

ROSALIND

I have been told so of many; but indeed an old religious uncle of mine taught me to speak, who was in his youth an inland man; one that knew courtship too well, for there he fell in love. I have heard him read many lectures against it, and I thank God I am not a woman, to be touched with so many giddy offences as he hath generally taxed their whole sex withal.

ORLANDO

Can you remember any of the principal evils that he laid to the charge of women?

ROSALIND

There were none principal; they were all like one another as half-pence are, every one fault seeming monstrous till his fellow fault came to match it.

ORLANDO

I prithee, recount some of them.

ROSALIND

No, I will not cast away my physic but on those that are sick. There is a man haunts the forest, that abuses our young plants with carving 'Rosalind' on their barks; hangs odes upon hawthorns and elegies on brambles, all, forsooth, deifying the name of Rosalind. If I could meet that fancy-monger I would give him some good counsel, for he seems to have the quotidian of love upon him.

ORLANDO

I am he that is so love-shaked; I pray you tell me your remedy.

ROSALIND

There is none of my uncle's marks upon you; he taught me how to know a man in love; in which cage of rushes I am sure you are not prisoner.

ORLANDO

What were his marks?

ROSALIND

A lean cheek, which you have not, a blue eye and sunken, which you have not, an unquestionable spirit, which you have not, a beard neglected, which you have not; but I pardon you for that, for simply your having in beard is a younger brother's revenue. Then your hose should be ungartered, your bonnet unbanded, your sleeve unbuttoned, your shoe untied and every thing about you demonstrating a careless desolation; but you are no such man; you are rather point-device in your accoutrements as loving yourself than seeming the lover of any other.

ORLANDO

Fair youth, I would I could make thee believe I love.

ROSALIND

Me believe it! you may as soon make her that you love believe it; which, I warrant, she is apter to do than to confess she does.

That is one of the points in the which women still give the lie to their consciences. But, in good sooth, are you he that hangs the verses on the trees, wherein Rosalind is so admired?

ORLANDO

I swear to thee, youth, by the white hand of Rosalind, I am that he, that unfortunate he.

ROSALIND

But are you so much in love as your rhymes speak?

ORLANDO

Neither rhyme nor reason can express how much.

ROSALIND

Love is merely a madness, and, I tell you, deserves as well a dark house and a whip as madmen do; and the reason why they are not so punished and cured is, that the lunacy is so ordinary that the whippers are in love too. Yet I profess curing it by counsel.

ORLANDO

Did you ever cure any so?

ROSALIND

Yes, one, and in this manner. He was to imagine me his love, his mistress; and I set him every day to woo me; at which time would I, being but a moonish youth, grieve, be effeminate, changeable, longing and liking, proud, fantastical, apish, shallow, inconstant, full of tears, full of smiles, for every passion something and for no passion truly any thing, as boys and women are for the most part cattle of this colour; would now like him, now loathe him; then entertain him, then forswear him; now weep for him, then spit at him; that I drave my suitor from his mad humour of love to a living humour of madness; which was, to forswear the full stream of the world, and to live in a nook merely monastic. And thus I cured him; and this way will I take upon me to wash your liver as clean as a sound sheep's heart, that there shall not be one spot of love in't.

ORLANDO

I would not be cured, youth.

ROSALIND

I would cure you, if you would but call me Rosalind and come every day to my cote and woo me.

ORLANDO

Now, by the faith of my love, I will. Tell me where it is.

ROSALIND

Go with me to it and I'll show it you and by the way you shall tell me where in the forest you live. Will you go?

ORLANDO

With all my heart, good youth.

ROSALIND

Nay you must call me Rosalind. Come, sister, will you go?

Exeunt

SCENE III.
THE FOREST.

Enter TOUCHSTONE *and* AUDREY; JAQUES *behind*

TOUCHSTONE

Come apace, good Audrey; I will fetch up your goats, Audrey. And how, Audrey, am I the man yet? Doth my simple feature content you?

AUDREY

Your features! Lord warrant us! what features!

TOUCHSTONE

I am here with thee and thy goats, as the most capricious poet, honest Ovid, was among the Goths.

JAQUES

[*Aside*] O knowledge ill-inhabited, worse than Jove in a thatched house!

TOUCHSTONE

When a man's verses cannot be understood, nor a man's good wit seconded with the forward child Understanding, it strikes a man more dead than a great reckoning in a little room. Truly, I would the gods had made thee poetical.

AUDREY

I do not know what 'poetical' is. Is it honest in deed and word? Is it a true thing?

TOUCHSTONE

No, truly; for the truest poetry is the most feigning; and lovers are given to poetry, and what they swear in poetry may be said as lovers they do feign.

AUDREY

Do you wish then that the gods had made me poetical?

TOUCHSTONE

I do, truly; for thou swearest to me thou art honest; now, if thou wert a poet, I might have some hope thou didst feign.

AUDREY

Would you not have me honest?

TOUCHSTONE

No, truly, unless thou wert hard-favoured; for honesty coupled to beauty is to have honey a sauce to sugar.

JAQUES

[*Aside*] A material fool!

AUDREY

Well, I am not fair; and therefore I pray the gods make me honest.

TOUCHSTONE

Truly, and to cast away honesty upon a foul slut were to put good meat into an unclean dish.

AUDREY

I am not a slut, though I thank the gods I am foul.

TOUCHSTONE

Well, praised be the gods for thy foulness; sluttishness may come hereafter. But be it as it may be, I will marry thee, and to that end I have been with Sir Oliver Martext, the vicar of the next village, who hath promised to meet me in this place of the forest and to couple us.

JAQUES

[*Aside*] I would fain see this meeting.

AUDREY

Well, the gods give us joy!

TOUCHSTONE

Amen. A man may, if he were of a fearful heart, stagger in this attempt; for here we have no temple but the wood, no assembly but horn-beasts. But what though? Courage! As horns are odious, they are necessary. It is said, 'many a man knows no end of his goods'. Right! many a man has good horns, and knows no end of them. Well, that is the dowry of his wife; 'tis none of his own getting. Horns? Even so. Poor men alone? No, no; the noblest deer hath them as huge as the rascal. Is the single man therefore blessed? No; as a walled town is more worthier than a village, so is the forehead of a married man more honourable than the bare brow of a bachelor; and by how much defence is better than no skill, by so much is a horn more precious than to want. Here comes Sir Oliver.

Enter SIR OLIVER MARTEXT

Sir Oliver Martext, you are well met. Will you dispatch us here under this tree, or shall we go with you to your chapel?

SIR OLIVER MARTEXT

Is there none here to give the woman?

TOUCHSTONE

I will not take her on gift of any man.

SIR OLIVER MARTEXT

Truly, she must be given, or the marriage is not lawful.

JAQUES

[*Advancing*] Proceed, proceed I'll give her.

TOUCHSTONE

Good even, good Master What-ye-call't; how do you, sir? You are very well met. God 'ild you for your last company. I am very glad to see you. Even a toy in hand here, sir. Nay, pray be covered.

JAQUES

Will you be married, motley?

TOUCHSTONE

As the ox hath his bow, sir, the horse his curb and the falcon her bells, so man hath his desires; and as pigeons bill, so wedlock would be nibbling.

JAQUES

And will you, being a man of your breeding, be married under a bush like a beggar? Get you to church, and have a good priest that can tell you what marriage is; this fellow will but join you together as they join wainscot; then one of you will prove a shrunk panel and, like green timber, warp, warp.

TOUCHSTONE

[*Aside*] I am not in the mind but I were better to be married of him than of another; for he is not like to marry me well; and not being well married, it will be a good excuse for me hereafter to leave my wife.

JAQUES

Go thou with me, and let me counsel thee.

TOUCHSTONE

'Come, sweet Audrey;
We must be married, or we must live in bawdry.
Farewell, good Master Oliver. Not—
O sweet Oliver,
O brave Oliver,
Leave me not behind thee. But—
Wind away,
Begone, I say,
I will not to wedding with thee.

Exeunt JAQUES, TOUCHSTONE
and AUDREY

SIR OLIVER MARTEXT

'Tis no matter; ne'er a fantastical knave of them all shall flout me out of my calling.

Exit

SCENE IV.
THE FOREST.

Enter ROSALIND *and* CELIA

ROSALIND

Never talk to me; I will weep.

CELIA

Do, I prithee; but yet have the grace to consider that tears do not become a man.

ROSALIND

But have I not cause to weep?

CELIA

As good cause as one would desire; therefore weep.

ROSALIND

His very hair is of the dissembling colour.

CELIA

Something browner than Judas's marry, his kisses are Judas's own children.

ROSALIND

I' faith, his hair is of a good colour.

CELIA

An excellent colour: your chestnut was ever the only colour.

ROSALIND

And his kissing is as full of sanctity as the touch of holy bread.

CELIA

He hath bought a pair of cast lips of Diana. A nun of winter's sisterhood kisses not more religiously; the very ice of chastity is in them.

ROSALIND

But why did he swear he would come this morning, and comes not?

CELIA

Nay, certainly, there is no truth in him.

ROSALIND

Do you think so?

CELIA

Yes; I think he is not a pick-purse nor a horse-stealer, but for his verity in love, I do think him as concave as a covered goblet or a worm-eaten nut.

ROSALIND

Not true in love?

CELIA

Yes, when he is in; but I think he is not in.

ROSALIND

You have heard him swear downright he was.

CELIA

'Was' is not 'is'; besides, the oath of a lover is no stronger than the word of a tapster; they are both the confirmer of false reckonings. He attends here in the forest on the Duke your father.

ROSALIND

I met the Duke yesterday and had much question with him. He asked me of what parentage I was; I told him, of as good as he; so he laughed and let me go. But what talk we of fathers, when there is such a man as Orlando?

CELIA

O, that's a brave man! he writes brave verses, speaks brave words, swears brave oaths and breaks them bravely, quite traverse, athwart the heart of his lover; as a puisny tilter, that spurs his horse but on one side, breaks his staff like a noble goose. But all's brave that youth mounts and folly guides. Who comes here?

Enter CORIN

CORIN

Mistress and master, you have oft inquired
After the shepherd that complain'd of love,
Who you saw sitting by me on the turf,
Praising the proud disdainful shepherdess
That was his mistress.

CELIA

Well, and what of him?

CORIN

If you will see a pageant truly play'd,
Between the pale complexion of true love
And the red glow of scorn and proud disdain,
Go hence a little and I shall conduct you,
If you will mark it.

ROSALIND

O, come, let us remove!
The sight of lovers feedeth those in love.
Bring us to this sight, and you shall say
I'll prove a busy actor in their play.

Exeunt

SCENE V.
ANOTHER PART OF THE FOREST.

Enter SILVIUS *and* PHEBE

SILVIUS

    Sweet Phebe, do not scorn me; do not, Phebe;
    Say that you love me not, but say not so
    In bitterness. The common executioner,
    Whose heart the accustom'd sight of death makes hard,
    Falls not the axe upon the humbled neck
    But first begs pardon. Will you sterner be
    Than he that dies and lives by bloody drops?

Enter ROSALIND, CELIA, *and* CORIN, *behind*

PHEBE

    I would not be thy executioner;
    I fly thee, for I would not injure thee.
    Thou tell'st me there is murder in mine eye.
    'Tis pretty, sure, and very probable,
    That eyes, that are the frail'st and softest things,
    Who shut their coward gates on atomies,
    Should be call'd tyrants, butchers, murderers!
    Now I do frown on thee with all my heart;
    And if mine eyes can wound, now let them kill thee.
    Now counterfeit to swoon; why now fall down;
    Or if thou canst not, O, for shame, for shame,
    Lie not, to say mine eyes are murderers!
    Now show the wound mine eye hath made in thee.
    Scratch thee but with a pin, and there remains
    Some scar of it; lean but upon a rush,
    The cicatrice and capable impressure
    Thy palm some moment keeps; but now mine eyes,
    Which I have darted at thee, hurt thee not,
    Nor, I am sure, there is no force in eyes
    That can do hurt.

SILVIUS

    O dear Phebe,
    If ever, as that ever may be near,

You meet in some fresh cheek the power of fancy,
Then shall you know the wounds invisible
That love's keen arrows make.

PHEBE
But till that time
Come not thou near me; and when that time comes,
Afflict me with thy mocks, pity me not;
As till that time I shall not pity thee.

ROSALIND
[*Advancing*] And why, I pray you?
Who might be your mother,
That you insult, exult, and all at once,
Over the wretched? What though you have no beauty—
As, by my faith, I see no more in you
Than without candle may go dark to bed—
Must you be therefore proud and pitiless?
Why, what means this? Why do you look on me?
I see no more in you than in the ordinary
Of nature's sale-work. 'Od's my little life,
I think she means to tangle my eyes too!
No, faith, proud mistress, hope not after it;
'Tis not your inky brows, your black silk hair,
Your bugle eyeballs, nor your cheek of cream,
That can entame my spirits to your worship.
You foolish shepherd, wherefore do you follow her,
Like foggy south puffing with wind and rain?
You are a thousand times a properer man
Than she a woman. 'Tis such fools as you
That makes the world full of ill-favour'd children.
'Tis not her glass, but you, that flatters her;
And out of you she sees herself more proper
Than any of her lineaments can show her.
But, mistress, know yourself. Down on your knees,
And thank heaven, fasting, for a good man's love;
For I must tell you friendly in your ear,
Sell when you can; you are not for all markets.
Cry the man mercy; love him; take his offer;

Foul is most foul, being foul to be a scoffer.
So take her to thee, shepherd. Fare you well.

PHEBE

Sweet youth, I pray you, chide a year together;
I had rather hear you chide than this man woo.

ROSALIND

He's fallen in love with your foulness and she'll fall in love with
my anger. If it be so, as fast as she answers thee with frowning
looks, I'll sauce her with bitter words. Why look you so upon
me?

PHEBE

For no ill will I bear you.

ROSALIND

I pray you, do not fall in love with me,
For I am falser than vows made in wine;
Besides, I like you not. If you will know my house,
'Tis at the tuft of olives here hard by.
Will you go, sister? Shepherd, ply her hard.
Come, sister. Shepherdess, look on him better,
And be not proud; though all the world could see,
None could be so abused in sight as he.
Come, to our flock.

Exeunt ROSALIND, CELIA *and* CORIN

PHEBE

Dead Shepherd, now I find thy saw of might,
'Who ever loved that loved not at first sight?'

SILVIUS

Sweet Phebe—

PHEBE

Ha, what say'st thou, Silvius?

SILVIUS

Sweet Phebe, pity me.

PHEBE

Why, I am sorry for thee, gentle Silvius.

SILVIUS

Wherever sorrow is, relief would be.
If you do sorrow at my grief in love,

By giving love your sorrow and my grief
Were both extermined.

PHEBE

Thou hast my love; is not that neighbourly?

SILVIUS

I would have you.

PHEBE

Why, that were covetousness.
Silvius, the time was that I hated thee,
And yet it is not that I bear thee love;
But since that thou canst talk of love so well,
Thy company, which erst was irksome to me,
I will endure, and I'll employ thee too.
But do not look for further recompense
Than thine own gladness that thou art employ'd.

SILVIUS

So holy and so perfect is my love,
And I in such a poverty of grace,
That I shall think it a most plenteous crop
To glean the broken ears after the man
That the main harvest reaps; loose now and then
A scatter'd smile, and that I'll live upon.

PHEBE

Know'st now the youth that spoke to me erewhile?

SILVIUS

Not very well, but I have met him oft;
And he hath bought the cottage and the bounds
That the old carlot once was master of.

PHEBE

Think not I love him, though I ask for him;
'Tis but a peevish boy; yet he talks well;
But what care I for words? Yet words do well
When he that speaks them pleases those that hear.
It is a pretty youth—not very pretty;
But, sure, he's proud, and yet his pride becomes him,
He'll make a proper man. The best thing in him
Is his complexion; and faster than his tongue

Did make offence his eye did heal it up.
He is not very tall; yet for his years he's tall;
His leg is but so-so; and yet 'tis well.
There was a pretty redness in his lip,
A little riper and more lusty red
Than that mix'd in his cheek; 'twas just the difference
Between the constant red and mingled damask.
There be some women, Silvius, had they mark'd him
In parcels as I did, would have gone near
To fall in love with him; but, for my part,
I love him not nor hate him not; and yet
I have more cause to hate him than to love him;
For what had he to do to chide at me?
He said mine eyes were black and my hair black,
And, now I am remember'd, scorn'd at me.
I marvel why I answer'd not again;
But that's all one; omittance is no quittance.
I'll write to him a very taunting letter,
And thou shalt bear it; wilt thou, Silvius?

SILVIUS

Phebe, with all my heart.

PHEBE

I'll write it straight;
The matter's in my head and in my heart;
I will be bitter with him and passing short.
Go with me, Silvius.

Exeunt

ACT

IV

SCENE I.
THE FOREST.

Enter ROSALIND, CELIA, *and* JAQUES

JAQUES

I prithee, pretty youth, let me be better acquainted with thee.

ROSALIND

They say you are a melancholy fellow.

JAQUES

I am so; I do love it better than laughing.

ROSALIND

Those that are in extremity of either are abominable fellows and betray themselves to every modern censure worse than drunkards.

JAQUES

Why, 'tis good to be sad and say nothing.

ROSALIND

Why then, 'tis good to be a post.

JAQUES

I have neither the scholar's melancholy, which is emulation, nor the musician's, which is fantastical, nor the courtier's, which is proud, nor the soldier's, which is ambitious, nor the lawyer's, which is politic, nor the lady's, which is nice, nor the lover's, which is all these; but it is a melancholy of mine own, compounded of many simples, extracted from many objects, and indeed the sundry's contemplation of my travels, in which my often rumination wraps me m a most humorous sadness.

ROSALIND

A traveller! By my faith, you have great reason to be sad. I fear you have sold your own lands to see other men's; then, to have seen much and to have nothing, is to have rich eyes and poor hands.

JAQUES

Yes, I have gained my experience.

ROSALIND

And your experience makes you sad. I had rather have a fool to make me merry than experience to make me sad; and to travel for it too!

Enter ORLANDO

ORLANDO

Good day and happiness, dear Rosalind!

JAQUES

Nay, then, God be wi' you, an you talk in blank verse.

Exit

ROSALIND

Farewell, Monsieur Traveller; look you lisp and wear strange suits, disable all the benefits of your own country, be out of love with your nativity and almost chide God for making you that countenance you are, or I will scarce think you have swam in a gondola. Why, how now, Orlando! where have you been all this while? You a lover! An you serve me such another trick, never come in my sight more.

ORLANDO

My fair Rosalind, I come within an hour of my promise.

ROSALIND

Break an hour's promise in love! He that will divide a minute into a thousand parts and break but a part of the thousandth part of a minute in the affairs of love, it may be said of him that Cupid hath clapped him o' the shoulder, but I'll warrant him heart-whole.

ORLANDO

Pardon me, dear Rosalind.

ROSALIND

Nay, an you be so tardy, come no more in my sight. I had as lief be wooed of a snail.

ORLANDO

Of a snail?

ROSALIND

Ay, of a snail; for though he comes slowly, he carries his house on his head; a better jointure, I think, than you make a woman; besides he brings his destiny with him.

ORLANDO

What's that?

ROSALIND

Why, horns, which such as you are fain to be beholding to your wives for; but he comes armed in his fortune and prevents the slander of his wife.

ORLANDO

Virtue is no horn-maker; and my Rosalind is virtuous.

ROSALIND

And I am your Rosalind.

CELIA

It pleases him to call you so; but he hath a Rosalind of a better leer than you.

ROSALIND

Come, woo me, woo me, for now I am in a holiday humour and like enough to consent. What would you say to me now, an I were your very very Rosalind?

ORLANDO

I would kiss before I spoke.

ROSALIND

Nay, you were better speak first, and when you were gravelled for lack of matter, you might take occasion to kiss. Very good orators, when they are out, they will spit; and for lovers lacking— God warn us!—matter, the cleanliest shift is to kiss.

ORLANDO

How if the kiss be denied?

• 456 •

ROSALIND

Then she puts you to entreaty, and there begins new matter.

ORLANDO

Who could be out, being before his beloved mistress?

ROSALIND

Marry, that should you, if I were your mistress, or I should think my honesty ranker than my wit.

ORLANDO

What, of my suit?

ROSALIND

Not out of your apparel, and yet out of your suit.

Am not I your Rosalind?

ORLANDO

I take some joy to say you are, because I would be talking of her.

ROSALIND

Well in her person I say I will not have you.

ORLANDO

Then in mine own person I die.

ROSALIND

No, faith, die by attorney. The poor world is almost six thousand years old, and in all this time there was not any man died in his own person, videlicet, in a love-cause. Troilus had his brains dashed out with a Grecian club; yet he did what he could to die before, and he is one of the patterns of love. Leander, he would have lived many a fair year, though Hero had turned nun, if it had not been for a hot midsummer night; for, good youth, he went but forth to wash him in the Hellespont and being taken with the cramp was drowned and the foolish coroners of that age found it was 'Hero of Sestos.' But these are all lies: men have died from time to time and worms have eaten them, but not for love.

ORLANDO

I would not have my right Rosalind of this mind, for, I protest, her frown might kill me.

ROSALIND

By this hand, it will not kill a fly. But come, now I will be your Rosalind in a more coming-on disposition, and ask me what you will. I will grant it.

ORLANDO

Then love me, Rosalind.

ROSALIND

Yes, faith, will I, Fridays and Saturdays and all.

ORLANDO

And wilt thou have me?

ROSALIND

Ay, and twenty such.

ORLANDO

What sayest thou?

ROSALIND

Are you not good?

ORLANDO

I hope so.

ROSALIND

Why then, can one desire too much of a good thing?
Come, sister, you shall be the priest and marry us.
Give me your hand, Orlando. What do you say, sister?

ORLANDO

Pray thee, marry us.

CELIA

I cannot say the words.

ROSALIND

You must begin, 'Will you, Orlando—'
CELIA Go to. Will you, Orlando, have to wife this Rosalind?

ORLANDO

I will.

ROSALIND

Ay, but when?

ORLANDO

Why now; as fast as she can marry us.

ROSALIND

Then you must say 'I take thee, Rosalind, for wife.'

ORLANDO

I take thee, Rosalind, for wife.

ROSALIND

I might ask you for your commission; but I do take thee,

Orlando, for my husband. There's a girl goes before the priest; and certainly a woman's thought runs before her actions.

ORLANDO

So do all thoughts; they are winged.

ROSALIND

Now tell me how long you would have her after you have possessed her.

ORLANDO

For ever and a day.

ROSALIND

Say 'a day,' without the 'ever.' No, no, Orlando; men are April when they woo, December when they wed: maids are May when they are maids, but the sky changes when they are wives. I will be more jealous of thee than a Barbary cock-pigeon over his hen, more clamorous than a parrot against rain, more new-fangled than an ape, more giddy in my desires than a monkey. I will weep for nothing, like Diana in the fountain, and I will do that when you are disposed to be merry; I will laugh like a hyen, and that when thou art inclined to sleep.

ORLANDO

But will my Rosalind do so?

ROSALIND

By my life, she will do as I do.

ORLANDO

O, but she is wise.

ROSALIND

Or else she could not have the wit to do this. The wiser, the waywarder. Make the doors upon a woman's wit and it will out at the casement; shut that and 'twill out at the key-hole; stop that, 'twill fly with the smoke out at the chimney.

ORLANDO

A man that had a wife with such a wit, he might say 'Wit, whither wilt?'

ROSALIND

Nay, you might keep that cheque for it till you met your wife's wit going to your neighbour's bed.

ORLANDO

And what wit could wit have to excuse that?

ROSALIND

Marry, to say she came to seek you there. You shall never take her without her answer, unless you take her without her tongue. O, that woman that cannot make her fault her husband's occasion, let her never nurse her child herself, for she will breed it like a fool!

ORLANDO

For these two hours, Rosalind, I will leave thee.

ROSALIND

Alas! dear love, I cannot lack thee two hours.

ORLANDO

I must attend the Duke at dinner; by two o'clock I will be with thee again.

ROSALIND

Ay, go your ways, go your ways; I knew what you would prove; my friends told me as much, and I thought no less. That flattering tongue of yours won me. 'Tis but one cast away, and so, come, death! Two o'clock is your hour?

ORLANDO

Ay, sweet Rosalind.

ROSALIND

By my troth, and in good earnest, and so God mend me, and by all pretty oaths that are not dangerous, if you break one jot of your promise or come one minute behind your hour, I will think you the most pathetical break-promise and the most hollow lover and the most unworthy of her you call Rosalind that may be chosen out of the gross band of the unfaithful. therefore beware my censure and keep your promise.

ORLANDO

With no less religion than if thou wert indeed my Rosalind; so adieu.

ROSALIND

Well, Time is the old justice that examines all such offenders, and let Time try. Adieu.

Exit ORLANDO

CELIA

You have simply misused our sex in your love-prate. We must have your doublet and hose plucked over your head, and show the world what the bird hath done to her own nest.

ROSALIND

O coz, coz, coz, my pretty little coz, that thou didst know how many fathom deep I am in love! But it cannot be sounded; my affection hath an unknown bottom, like the bay of Portugal.

CELIA

Or rather, bottomless, that as fast as you pour affection in, it runs out.

ROSALIND

No, that same wicked bastard of Venus that was begot of thought, conceived of spleen and born of madness, that blind rascally boy that abuses every one's eyes because his own are out, let him be judge how deep I am in love. I'll tell thee, Aliena, I cannot be out of the sight of Orlando. I'll go find a shadow and sigh till he come.

CELIA

And I'll sleep.

Exeunt

SCENE II.
THE FOREST.

Enter JAQUES, *Lords, and Foresters*

JAQUES

Which is he that killed the deer?

LORD

Sir, it was I.

JAQUES

Let's present him to the Duke, like a Roman conqueror; and it would do well to set the deer's horns upon his head, for a branch of victory. Have you no song, forester, for this purpose?

LORD

Yes, sir.

JAQUES

Sing it; 'tis no matter how it be in tune, so it make noise enough.

SONG

What shall he have that kill'd the deer?
His leather skin and horns to wear.
Then sing him home;
The rest shall bear this burden
Take thou no scorn to wear the horn;
It was a crest ere thou wast born.
Thy father's father wore it,
And thy father bore it.
The horn, the horn, the lusty horn
Is not a thing to laugh to scorn.

Exeunt

SCENE III.
THE FOREST.

Enter ROSALIND *and* CELIA

ROSALIND

How say you now? Is it not past two o'clock? And here much
Orlando!

CELIA

I warrant you, with pure love and troubled brain, he hath ta'en
his bow and arrows and is gone forth to sleep. Look, who comes
here.

Enter SILVIUS

SILVIUS

My errand is to you, fair youth;
My gentle Phebe bid me give you this.
I know not the contents; but, as I guess
By the stern brow and waspish action
Which she did use as she was writing of it,
It bears an angry tenor. Pardon me,
I am but as a guiltless messenger.

ROSALIND

Patience herself would startle at this letter
And play the swaggerer; bear this, bear all.
She says I am not fair, that I lack manners;

She calls me proud, and that she could not love me,
Were man as rare as phoenix. 'Od's my will!
Her love is not the hare that I do hunt;
Why writes she so to me? Well, shepherd, well,
This is a letter of your own device.

SILVIUS

No, I protest, I know not the contents; Phebe did write it.

ROSALIND

Come, come, you are a fool
And turn'd into the extremity of love.
I saw her hand; she has a leathern hand.
A freestone-colour'd hand; I verily did think
That her old gloves were on, but 'twas her hands;
She has a huswife's hand; but that's no matter.
I say she never did invent this letter;
This is a man's invention and his hand.

SILVIUS

Sure, it is hers.

ROSALIND

Why, 'tis a boisterous and a cruel style.
A style for-challengers; why, she defies me,
Like Turk to Christian. Women's gentle brain
Could not drop forth such giant-rude invention
Such Ethiope words, blacker in their effect
Than in their countenance. Will you hear the letter?

SILVIUS

So please you, for I never heard it yet;
Yet heard too much of Phebe's cruelty.

ROSALIND

She Phebes me: mark how the tyrant writes.
[Reads]
Art thou god to shepherd turn'd,
That a maiden's heart hath burn'd?
Can a woman rail thus?

SILVIUS

Call you this railing?

ROSALIND
[*Reads*]
'Why, thy godhead laid apart,
Warr'st thou with a woman's heart?'
Did you ever hear such railing?
'Whiles the eye of man did woo me,
That could do no vengeance to me.'
Meaning me a beast.
'If the scorn of your bright eyne
Have power to raise such love in mine,
Alack, in me what strange effect
Would they work in mild aspect!
Whiles you chid me, I did love;
How then might your prayers move!
He that brings this love to thee
Little knows this love in me;
And by him seal up thy mind;
Whether that thy youth and kind
Will the faithful offer take
Of me and all that I can make;
Or else by him my love deny,
And then I'll study how to die.'

SILVIUS
Call you this chiding?

CELIA
Alas, poor shepherd!

ROSALIND
Do you pity him? No, he deserves no pity. Wilt thou love such a woman? What, to make thee an instrument and play false strains upon thee! Not to be endured! Well, go your way to her, for I see love hath made thee a tame snake, and say this to her: that if she love me, I charge her to love thee; if she will not, I will never have her unless thou entreat for her. If you be a true lover, hence, and not a word; for here comes more company.

Exit SILVIUS

Enter OLIVER

OLIVER

    Good morrow, fair ones; pray you, if you know,
    Where in the purlieus of this forest stands
    A sheep-cote fenced about with olive trees?

CELIA

    West of this place, down in the neighbour bottom.
    The rank of osiers by the murmuring stream
    Left on your right hand brings you to the place.
    But at this hour the house doth keep itself;
    There's none within.

OLIVER

    If that an eye may profit by a tongue,
    Then should I know you by description;
    Such garments and such years: 'The boy is fair,
    Of female favour, and bestows himself
    Like a ripe sister; the woman low
    And browner than her brother.' Are not you
    The owner of the house I did inquire for?

CELIA

    It is no boast, being ask'd, to say we are.

OLIVER

    Orlando doth commend him to you both,
    And to that youth he calls his Rosalind
    He sends this bloody napkin. Are you he?

ROSALIND

    I am. What must we understand by this?

OLIVER

    Some of my shame; if you will know of me
    What man I am, and how, and why, and where
    This handkercher was stain'd.

CELIA

    I pray you, tell it.

OLIVER

    When last the young Orlando parted from you
    He left a promise to return again
    Within an hour, and pacing through the forest,

Chewing the food of sweet and bitter fancy,
Lo, what befell! he threw his eye aside,
And mark what object did present itself.
Under an oak, whose boughs were moss'd with age
And high top bald with dry antiquity,
A wretched ragged man, o'ergrown with hair,
Lay sleeping on his back. About his neck
A green and gilded snake had wreathed itself,
Who with her head nimble in threats approach'd
The opening of his mouth; but suddenly,
Seeing Orlando, it unlink'd itself,
And with indented glides did slip away
Into a bush; under which bush's shade
A lioness, with udders all drawn dry,
Lay couching, head on ground, with catlike watch,
When that the sleeping man should stir; for 'tis
The royal disposition of that beast
To prey on nothing that doth seem as dead.
This seen, Orlando did approach the man
And found it was his brother, his elder brother.

CELIA
O, I have heard him speak of that same brother;
And he did render him the most unnatural
That lived amongst men.

OLIVER
And well he might so do,
For well I know he was unnatural.

ROSALIND
But, to Orlando: did he leave him there,
Food to the suck'd and hungry lioness?

OLIVER
Twice did he turn his back and purposed so;
But kindness, nobler ever than revenge,
And nature, stronger than his just occasion,
Made him give battle to the lioness,
Who quickly fell before him; in which hurtling
From miserable slumber I awaked.

CELIA
    Are you his brother?
ROSALIND
    Wast you he rescued?
CELIA
    Was't you that did so oft contrive to kill him?
OLIVER
    'Twas I; but 'tis not I. I do not shame
    To tell you what I was, since my conversion
    So sweetly tastes, being the thing I am.
ROSALIND
    But, for the bloody napkin?
OLIVER
    By and by.
    When from the first to last betwixt us two
    Tears our recountments had most kindly bathed,
    As how I came into that desert place—
    In brief, he led me to the gentle Duke,
    Who gave me fresh array and entertainment,
    Committing me unto my brother's love;
    Who led me instantly unto his cave,
    There stripp'd himself, and here upon his arm
    The lioness had torn some flesh away,
    Which all this while had bled; and now he fainted
    And cried, in fainting, upon Rosalind.
    Brief, I recover'd him, bound up his wound;
    And, after some small space, being strong at heart,
    He sent me hither, stranger as I am,
    To tell this story, that you might excuse
    His broken promise, and to give this napkin
    Dyed in his blood unto the shepherd youth
    That he in sport doth call his Rosalind.
                                    ROSALIND swoons
CELIA
    Why, how now, Ganymede! sweet Ganymede!
OLIVER
    Many will swoon when they do look on blood.

CELIA

There is more in it. Cousin Ganymede!

OLIVER

Look, he recovers.

ROSALIND

I would I were at home.

CELIA

We'll lead you thither.

I pray you, will you take him by the arm?

OLIVER

Be of good cheer, youth. You a man!

You lack a man's heart.

ROSALIND

I do so, I confess it. Ah, sirrah, a body would think this was well counterfeited! I pray you, tell your brother how well I counterfeited. Heigh-ho!

OLIVER

This was not counterfeit; there is too great testimony in your complexion that it was a passion of earnest.

ROSALIND

Counterfeit, I assure you.

OLIVER

Well then, take a good heart and counterfeit to be a man.

ROSALIND

So I do; but, i' faith, I should have been a woman by right.

CELIA

Come, you look paler and paler; pray you, draw homewards. Good sir, go with us.

OLIVER

That will I, for I must bear answer back

How you excuse my brother, Rosalind.

ROSALIND

I shall devise something; but, I pray you, commend my counterfeiting to him. Will you go?

Exeunt

ACT

V

SCENE I.
THE FOREST.

Enter TOUCHSTONE *and* AUDREY

TOUCHSTONE
We shall find a time, Audrey; patience, gentle Audrey.

AUDREY
Faith, the priest was good enough, for all the old gentleman's saying.

TOUCHSTONE
A most wicked Sir Oliver, Audrey, a most vile Martext. But, Audrey, there is a youth here in the forest lays claim to you.

AUDREY
Ay, I know who 'tis; he hath no interest in me in the world; here comes the man you mean.

TOUCHSTONE
It is meat and drink to me to see a clown. By my troth, we that have good wits have much to answer for; we shall be flouting; we cannot hold.

Enter WILLIAM

WILLIAM

Good even, Audrey.

AUDREY

God ye good even, William.

WILLIAM

And good even to you, sir.

TOUCHSTONE

Good even, gentle friend. Cover thy head, cover thy head; nay, prithee, be covered. How old are you, friend?

WILLIAM

Five and twenty, sir.

TOUCHSTONE

A ripe age. Is thy name William?

WILLIAM

William, sir.

TOUCHSTONE

A fair name. Wast born i' the forest here?

WILLIAM

Ay, sir, I thank God.

TOUCHSTONE

'Thank God;' a good answer. Art rich?

WILLIAM

Faith, sir, so so.

TOUCHSTONE

'So so' is good, very good, very excellent good; and yet it is not; it is but so so. Art thou wise?

WILLIAM

Ay, sir, I have a pretty wit.

TOUCHSTONE

Why, thou sayest well. I do now remember a saying, 'The fool doth think he is wise, but the wise man knows himself to be a fool.' The heathen philosopher, when he had a desire to eat a grape, would open his lips when he put it into his mouth; meaning thereby that grapes were made to eat and lips to open. You do love this maid?

WILLIAM

I do, sir.

TOUCHSTONE

Give me your hand. Art thou learned?

WILLIAM

No, sir.

TOUCHSTONE

Then learn this of me: to have, is to have; for it is a figure in rhetoric that drink, being poured out of a cup into a glass, by filling the one doth empty the other; for all your writers do consent that ipse is he; now, you are not ipse, for I am he.

WILLIAM

Which he, sir?

TOUCHSTONE

He, sir, that must marry this woman. Therefore, you clown, abandon—which is in the vulgar leave—the society—which in the boorish is company—of this female—which in the common is woman—which together is: abandon the society of this female; or, clown, thou perishest; or, to thy better understanding, diest; or, to wit I kill thee, make thee away, translate thy life into death, thy liberty into bondage. I will deal in poison with thee, or in bastinado, or in steel; I will bandy with thee in faction; I will o'errun thee with policy; I will kill thee a hundred and fifty ways; therefore tremble and depart.

AUDREY

Do, good William.

WILLIAM

God rest you merry, sir.

Exit

Enter CORIN

CORIN

Our master and mistress seeks you; come, away, away!

TOUCHSTONE

Trip, Audrey! trip, Audrey! I attend, I attend.

Exeunt

SCENE II.
THE FOREST.

Enter ORLANDO *and* OLIVER

ORLANDO

Is't possible that on so little acquaintance you should like her? that but seeing you should love her? and loving woo? and, wooing, she should grant? and will you persever to enjoy her?

OLIVER

Neither call the giddiness of it in question, the poverty of her, the small acquaintance, my sudden wooing, nor her sudden consenting; but say with me, I love Aliena; say with her that she loves me; consent with both that we may enjoy each other. It shall be to your good; for my father's house and all the revenue that was old Sir Rowland's will I estate upon you, and here live and die a shepherd.

ORLANDO

You have my consent. Let your wedding be to-morrow. Thither will I invite the Duke and all's contented followers. Go you and prepare Aliena; for look you, here comes my Rosalind.

Enter ROSALIND

ROSALIND

God save you, brother.

OLIVER

And you, fair sister.

Exit

ROSALIND

O, my dear Orlando, how it grieves me to see thee wear thy heart in a scarf!

ORLANDO

It is my arm.

ROSALIND

I thought thy heart had been wounded with the claws of a lion.

ORLANDO

Wounded it is, but with the eyes of a lady.

ROSALIND

Did your brother tell you how I counterfeited to swoon when he showed me your handkerchief?

ORLANDO

Ay, and greater wonders than that.

ROSALIND

O, I know where you are. Nay, 'tis true. There was never any thing so sudden but the fight of two rams and Caesar's thrasonical brag of 'I came, saw, and overcame'. For your brother and my sister no sooner met but they looked, no sooner looked but they loved, no sooner loved but they sighed, no sooner sighed but they asked one another the reason, no sooner knew the reason but they sought the remedy; and in these degrees have they made a pair of stairs to marriage which they will climb incontinent, or else be incontinent before marriage. They are in the very wrath of love and they will together; clubs cannot part them.

ORLANDO

They shall be married to-morrow, and I will bid the Duke to the nuptial. But, O, how bitter a thing it is to look into happiness through another man's eyes! By so much the more shall I to-morrow be at the height of heart-heaviness, by how much I shall think my brother happy in having what he wishes for.

ROSALIND

Why then, to-morrow I cannot serve your turn for Rosalind?

ORLANDO

I can live no longer by thinking.

ROSALIND

I will weary you then no longer with idle talking. Know of me then, for now I speak to some purpose, that I know you are a gentleman of good conceit. I speak not this that you should bear a good opinion of my knowledge, insomuch I say I know you are; neither do I labour for a greater esteem than may in some little measure draw a belief from you, to do yourself good and not to grace me. Believe then, if you please, that I can do strange things. I have, since I was three year old, conversed with a magician, most profound in his art and yet not damnable. If you do love Rosalind so near the heart as your gesture cries it out, when your brother marries Aliena, shall you marry her. I know into what straits of fortune she is driven; and it is not impossible to me, if it appear not inconvenient to you, to set her before your eyes to-morrow human as she is and without any danger.

ORLANDO

Speakest thou in sober meanings?

ROSALIND

By my life, I do; which I tender dearly, though I say I am a magician. Therefore, put you in your best array, bid your friends; for if you will be married to-morrow, you shall, and to Rosalind, if you will.

Enter SILVIUS *and* PHEBE

Look, here comes a lover of mine and a lover of hers.

PHEBE

Youth, you have done me much ungentleness,
To show the letter that I writ to you.

ROSALIND

I care not if I have. It is my study
To seem despiteful and ungentle to you.
You are there followed by a faithful shepherd;
Look upon him, love him; he worships you.

PHEBE

Good shepherd, tell this youth what 'tis to love.

SILVIUS

It is to be all made of sighs and tears;
And so am I for Phebe.

PHEBE

And I for Ganymede.

ORLANDO

And I for Rosalind.

ROSALIND

And I for no woman.

SILVIUS

It is to be all made of faith and service;
And so am I for Phebe.

PHEBE
> And I for Ganymede.

ORLANDO
> And I for Rosalind.

ROSALIND
> And I for no woman.

SILVIUS
> It is to be all made of fantasy,
> All made of passion and all made of wishes,
> All adoration, duty, and observance,
> All humbleness, all patience and impatience,
> All purity, all trial, all observance;
> And so am I for Phebe.

PHEBE
> And so am I for Ganymede.

ORLANDO
> And so am I for Rosalind.

ROSALIND
> And so am I for no woman.

PHEBE
> If this be so, why blame you me to love you?

SILVIUS
> If this be so, why blame you me to love you?

ORLANDO
> If this be so, why blame you me to love you?

ROSALIND
> Who do you speak to, 'Why blame you me to love you?'

ORLANDO
> To her that is not here, nor doth not hear.

ROSALIND
> Pray you, no more of this; 'tis like the howling of Irish wolves
> against the moon.
> [To SILVIUS]
> I will help you, if I can.
> [To PHEBE]
> I would love you, if I could. To-morrow meet me all together.

[To PHEBE]

I will marry you, if ever I marry woman, and I'll be married to-morrow.

[To ORLANDO]

I will satisfy you, if ever I satisfied man, and you shall be married to-morrow.

[To SILVIUS]

I will content you, if what pleases you contents you, and you shall be married to-morrow.

[To ORLANDO]

As you love Rosalind, meet.

[To SILVIUS]

As you love Phebe, meet; and as I love no woman, I'll meet. So fare you well; I have left you commands.

SILVIUS

I'll not fail, if I live.

PHEBE

Nor I.

ORLANDO

Nor I.

Exeunt

SCENE III.
THE FOREST.

Enter TOUCHSTONE *and* AUDREY

TOUCHSTONE

To-morrow is the joyful day, Audrey; to-morrow will we be married.

AUDREY

I do desire it with all my heart; and I hope it is no dishonest desire to desire to be a woman of the world. Here comes two of the banished Duke's pages.

Enter two Pages

FIRST PAGE

Well met, honest gentleman.

TOUCHSTONE

By my troth, well met. Come, sit, sit, and a song.

SECOND PAGE

We are for you; sit i' the middle.

FIRST PAGE

Shall we clap into't roundly, without hawking or spitting or saying we are hoarse, which are the only prologues to a bad voice?

SECOND PAGE

I'faith, i'faith; and both in a tune, like two gipsies on a horse.

SONG

It was a lover and his lass,
   With a hey, and a ho, and a hey nonino,
That o'er the green corn-field did pass
   In the spring time, the only pretty ring time,
When birds do sing, hey ding a ding, ding.
Sweet lovers love the spring.
Between the acres of the rye,
   With a hey, and a ho, and a hey nonino
These pretty country folks would lie,
   In spring time, etc.
This carol they began that hour,
   With a hey, and a ho, and a hey nonino,
How that a life was but a flower
   In spring time, etc.

And therefore take the present time,
   With a hey, and a ho, and a hey nonino;
For love is crowned with the prime
   In spring time, etc.

TOUCHSTONE

Truly, young gentlemen, though there was no great matter in the ditty, yet the note was very untuneable.

FIRST PAGE

You are deceived, sir; we kept time, we lost not our time.

TOUCHSTONE

By my troth, yes; I count it but time lost to hear such a foolish
song. God be wi' you; and God mend your voices! Come, Audrey.

Exeunt

SCENE IV.
THE FOREST.

Enter DUKE SENIOR, AMIENS, JAQUES,
ORLANDO, OLIVER, *and* CELIA

DUKE SENIOR

Dost thou believe, Orlando, that the boy
Can do all this that he hath promised?

ORLANDO

I sometimes do believe, and sometimes do not;
As those that fear they hope, and know they fear.

Enter ROSALIND, SILVIUS, *and* PHEBE

ROSALIND

Patience once more, whiles our compact is urged:
You say, if I bring in your Rosalind,
You will bestow her on Orlando here?

DUKE SENIOR

That would I, had I kingdoms to give with her.

ROSALIND

And you say, you will have her, when I bring her?

ORLANDO

That would I, were I of all kingdoms king.

ROSALIND

You say, you'll marry me, if I be willing?

PHEBE

That will I, should I die the hour after.

ROSALIND

But if you do refuse to marry me,
You'll give yourself to this most faithful shepherd?

PHEBE

So is the bargain.

ROSALIND

You say, that you'll have Phebe, if she will?

SILVIUS

Though to have her and death were both one thing.

ROSALIND

I have promised to make all this matter even.
Keep you your word, O Duke, to give your daughter;
You yours, Orlando, to receive his daughter;
Keep your word, Phebe, that you'll marry me,
Or else refusing me, to wed this shepherd;
Keep your word, Silvius, that you'll marry her.
If she refuse me; and from hence I go,
To make these doubts all even.

Exeunt ROSALIND *and* CELIA

DUKE SENIOR

I do remember in this shepherd boy
Some lively touches of my daughter's favour.

ORLANDO

My lord, the first time that I ever saw him
Methought he was a brother to your daughter.
But, my good lord, this boy is forest-born,
And hath been tutor'd in the rudiments
Of many desperate studies by his uncle,
Whom he reports to be a great magician,
Obscured in the circle of this forest.

Enter TOUCHSTONE *and* AUDREY

JAQUES

There is, sure, another flood toward, and these couples are coming to the ark. Here comes a pair of very strange beasts, which in all tongues are called fools.

TOUCHSTONE

Salutation and greeting to you all!

JAQUES

Good my lord, bid him welcome. This is the motley-minded gentleman that I have so often met in the forest. He hath been a courtier, he swears.

TOUCHSTONE

If any man doubt that, let him put me to my purgation. I have
trod a measure; I have flattered a lady; I have been politic with
my friend, smooth with mine enemy; I have undone three tailors;
I have had four quarrels, and like to have fought one.

JAQUES

And how was that ta'en up?

TOUCHSTONE

Faith, we met, and found the quarrel was upon the seventh
cause.

JAQUES

How seventh cause? Good my lord, like this fellow.

DUKE SENIOR

I like him very well.

TOUCHSTONE

God 'ild you, sir; I desire you of the like. I press in here, sir,
amongst the rest of the country copulatives, to swear and to
forswear, according as marriage binds and blood breaks. A
poor virgin, sir, an ill-favoured thing, sir, but mine own; a poor
humour of mine, sir, to take that that no man else will. Rich
honesty dwells like a miser, sir, in a poor house; as your pearl in
your foul oyster.

DUKE SENIOR

By my faith, he is very swift and sententious.

TOUCHSTONE

According to the fool's bolt, sir, and such dulcet diseases.

JAQUES

But, for the seventh cause; how did you find the quarrel on the
seventh cause?

TOUCHSTONE

Upon a lie seven times removed—bear your body more seeming,
Audrey—as thus, sir. I did dislike the cut of a certain courtier's
beard; he sent me word, if I said his beard was not cut well, he
was in the mind it was. This is called the Retort Courteous. If
I sent him word again 'it was not well cut,' he would send me
word, he cut it to please himself. This is called the Quip Modest.
If again 'it was not well cut,' he disabled my judgment. This is

called the Reply Churlish. If again 'it was not well cut,' he would answer, I spake not true. This is called the Reproof Valiant. If again 'it was not well cut,' he would say I lied. This is called the Countercheque Quarrelsome. And so to the Lie Circumstantial and the Lie Direct.

JAQUES

And how oft did you say his beard was not well cut?

TOUCHSTONE

I durst go no further than the Lie Circumstantial, nor he durst not give me the Lie Direct; and so we measured swords and parted.

JAQUES

Can you nominate in order now the degrees of the lie?

TOUCHSTONE

O sir, we quarrel in print, by the book; as you have books for good manners. I will name you the degrees. The first, the Retort Courteous; the second, the Quip Modest; the third, the Reply Churlish; the fourth, the Reproof Valiant; the fifth, the Countercheque Quarrelsome; the sixth, the Lie with Circumstance; the seventh, the Lie Direct. All these you may avoid but the Lie Direct; and you may avoid that too, with an If. I knew when seven justices could not take up a quarrel, but when the parties were met themselves, one of them thought but of an If, as, 'If you said so, then I said so;' and they shook hands and swore brothers. Your If is the only peacemaker; much virtue in If.

JAQUES

Is not this a rare fellow, my lord? He's as good at any thing and yet a fool.

DUKE SENIOR

He uses his folly like a stalking horse and under the presentation of that he shoots his wit.

Enter HYMEN, ROSALIND, *and* CELIA

Still Music

HYMEN

Then is there mirth in heaven,
When earthly things made even

Atone together.
Good Duke, receive thy daughter
Hymen from heaven brought her,
Yea, brought her hither,
That thou mightst join her hand with his
Whose heart within his bosom is.

ROSALIND

[*To* DUKE SENIOR] To you I give myself, for I am yours.
[*To* ORLANDO]
To you I give myself, for I am yours.

DUKE SENIOR

If there be truth in sight, you are my daughter.

ORLANDO

If there be truth in sight, you are my Rosalind.

PHEBE

If sight and shape be true,
Why then, my love adieu!

ROSALIND

I'll have no father, if you be not he;
I'll have no husband, if you be not he;
Nor ne'er wed woman, if you be not she.

HYMEN

Peace, ho! I bar confusion;
'Tis I must make conclusion
Of these most strange events.
Here's eight that must take hands
To join in Hymen's bands,
If truth holds true contents.
You and you no cross shall part;
You and you are heart in heart
You to his love must accord,
Or have a woman to your lord;
You and you are sure together,
As the winter to foul weather.
Whiles a wedlock-hymn we sing,
Feed yourselves with questioning;

That reason wonder may diminish,
How thus we met, and these things finish.

SONG

>Wedding is great Juno's crown;
>O blessed bond of board and bed!
>'Tis Hymen peoples every town;
>High wedlock then be honoured.
>Honour, high honour and renown,
>To Hymen, god of every town!

DUKE SENIOR

O my dear niece, welcome thou art to me!
Even daughter, welcome, in no less degree.

PHEBE

I will not eat my word, now thou art mine;
Thy faith my fancy to thee doth combine.

Enter JAQUES DE BOYS

JAQUES DE BOYS

Let me have audience for a word or two.
I am the second son of old Sir Rowland,
That bring these tidings to this fair assembly.
Duke Frederick, hearing how that every day
Men of great worth resorted to this forest,
Address'd a mighty power; which were on foot,
In his own conduct, purposely to take
His brother here and put him to the sword;
And to the skirts of this wild wood he came;
Where meeting with an old religious man,
After some question with him, was converted
Both from his enterprise and from the world,
His crown bequeathing to his banish'd brother,
And all their lands restored to them again
That were with him exiled. This to be true,
I do engage my life.

DUKE SENIOR

Welcome, young man;
Thou offer'st fairly to thy brothers' wedding:

To one his lands withheld, and to the other
A land itself at large, a potent dukedom.
First, in this forest, let us do those ends
That here were well begun and well begot;
And after, every of this happy number
That have endured shrewd days and nights with us
Shall share the good of our returned fortune,
According to the measure of their states.
Meantime, forget this new-fall'n dignity
And fall into our rustic revelry.
Play, music! And you, brides and bridegrooms all,
With measure heap'd in joy, to the measures fall.

JAQUES

Sir, by your patience. If I heard you rightly,
The Duke hath put on a religious life
And thrown into neglect the pompous court?

JAQUES DE BOYS

He hath.

JAQUES

To him will I. Out of these convertites
There is much matter to be heard and learn'd.
[*To* DUKE SENIOR]
You to your former honour I bequeath;
Your patience and your virtue well deserves it.
[*To* ORLANDO]
You to a love that your true faith doth merit;
[*To* OLIVER]
You to your land and love and great allies;
[*To* SILVIUS]
You to a long and well-deserved bed;
[*To* TOUCHSTONE]
And you to wrangling; for thy loving voyage
Is but for two months victuall'd. So, to your pleasures;
I am for other than for dancing measures.

DUKE SENIOR

Stay, Jaques, stay.

JAQUES
    To see no pastime I what you would have
    I'll stay to know at your abandon'd cave.

                                  Exit

DUKE SENIOR
    Proceed, proceed. We will begin these rites,
    As we do trust they'll end, in true delights.

                   A dance

                             Exeunt

EPILOGUE

ROSALIND

It is not the fashion to see the lady the epilogue; but it is no more unhandsome than to see the lord the prologue. If it be true that good wine needs no bush, 'tis true that a good play needs no epilogue; yet to good wine they do use good bushes, and good plays prove the better by the help of good epilogues. What a case am I in then, that am neither a good epilogue nor cannot insinuate with you in the behalf of a good play! I am not furnished like a beggar, therefore to beg will not become me. My way is to conjure you; and I'll begin with the women. I charge you, O women, for the love you bear to men, to like as much of this play as please you; and I charge you, O men, for the love you bear to women—as I perceive by your simpering, none of you hates them—that between you and the women the play may please. If I were a woman I would kiss as many of you as had beards that pleased me, complexions that liked me and breaths that I defied not; and, I am sure, as many as have good beards or good faces or sweet breaths will, for my kind offer, when I make curtsy, bid me farewell.

Exeunt